PUBLIC SERVICES YEARBOOK 1997-98

Edited by

Peter M. Jackson and

Michaela Lavender

CIPFA
PUBLIC FINANCE FOUNDATION

London · Hong Kong · Johannesburg · Melbourne · Singapore · Washington DC

The Public Finance Foundation is the independent research arm of CIPFA—the Chartered Institute of Public Finance and Accountancy.

The Foundation provides an impartial forum for debate and the exchange of ideas on public expenditure and related aspects of public finance, and on the management and administration of public services. It aims to promote objective and authoritative analysis and comment on these issues, drawing both on the work of the academic research community and on the practical knowledge and experience of senior and general managers from across the public sector.

In pursuing this aim, the Foundation:

- undertakes or commissions original research;
- disseminates the results of its own or others' research through:
  - a range of publications, research reports, working papers and bulletins; and
  - the Foundation's quarterly journal, *Public Money & Management*;
- organizes conferences, seminars and lectures to promote discussion of topical issues and developments.

The Foundation can be contacted at 3 Robert Street, London WC2N 6BH. Tel. 0171 543 5600.

PITMAN PUBLISHING
128 Long Acre, London WC2E 9AN
Tel: +44 (0)171 447 2000
Fax: +44 (0)171 240 5771

A Division of Pearson Professional Limited

First published in Great Britain in 1997

ISBN 0 273 62766 X

British Library Cataloguing in Publication Data
A CIP catalogue record for this book can be obtained from the British Library.

10 9 8 7 6 5 4 3 2 1

Printed and bound in Great Britain by Bell and Bain Ltd, Glasgow.

The Publishers' policy is to use paper manufactured from sustainable forests.

Contents

Introduction

Peter M. Jackson
University of Leicester

The Public Services Yearbook is aimed at public sector managers and students of public policy who wish to be kept up to date with the many changes that take place in the public sector during the course of one year. The Yearbook provides a comprehensive review of the most recent developments that have taken place within the public services. At the same time, it places these developments within a wider context by examining social, economic and political trends. A strength of the Yearbook is that it presents public sector change in an objective and balanced manner. No author writes to any particular political agenda.

Each of the authors is an authority in his/her field and the editors wish to thank them for preparing their chapters to a tight specification and a rigid deadline.

The demographic profile of Britain is changing—it is becoming older and more and more women are in employment. By the year 2006, it is expected that 46% of the work force will be women. The number of children of school age is likely to fall—by the year 2034 there will be 15% fewer people in the age group 0–16 years compared to 1994. By the year 2016, the number who are over 65 years will exceed those under 16 years. Expected changes in the UK's dependency ratio are for it to fall from 64 dependants per 100 people of working age in 1994 to 58 by 2020. It is then expected to rise to 72 by 2040.

There are an additional 1.4 million people expected to be in the work force by 2006; about 1 million of whom will be women.

The rise in the number of single person households is set to continue. In 1971, these households accounted for 18% of the total. By 1994 it was 28% and is expected rise to 35% by 2011. Such households are not confined to single parents but also include pensioners and divorcees—categories which are increasing over time. The impact of these changes are to increase the demand for smaller houses.

Education

A recent OECD report, *Education at a Glance* (1996), reveals that growing student numbers in the face of slow growing, and in some cases stagnant, education budgets means that the volume of resources devoted to each student will fall. In 1975, the OECD average for GDP spent on education was 5.8%. By 1993, it had remained at 5.8%.

If the resources allocated to each primary education pupil is standardized at 100 units, then Britain spent 250 units on each tertiary-level student. This is close to the OECD average of 253. The USA spent 266 and Australia 303. When countries are compared in terms of how much direct public spending is allocated to higher education, Britain is found to spend 0.7% of GDP. This is the lowest in Europe (Germany and France spent 0.9%). In Britain, 8% of 22 to 25 year olds are in full time education compared to the OECD average of 15%. Britain's university degree courses are of a shorter duration than those elsewhere in Europe. There is also a faster turnout of graduates from British universities. Britain has a relatively high proportion of science graduates amongst the 25 to 34 year old age cohort of the work force, but a much lower proportion of mathematics and computer science graduates.

As a result of the Education Bill, schools will be granted powers to refuse to admit pupils whose parents do not agree to sign documents accepting rules on behaviour and attendance. The Bill also extends the powers of schools to select pupils. Grant-maintained schools will be allowed to select up to 50% of their intake on the basis of academic ability. New powers will be introduced that will allow grant-maintained schools to introduce sixth forms, nurseries and to become boarding schools.

The estimated shortfall in education funding is £1 billion. This is the amount required to prevent further cuts in services. Local authorities are already spending £668M above government estimates. A survey by the Association of Teachers and Lecturers suggests that one in 10 schools is threatening to sack teachers because of spending cuts. This would mean 4,000 teachers losing their jobs. In primary schools, there is an increase in the number of teachers working part time, which is producing a casualization of the teaching work force.

Teachers are working up to two hours a week longer than they were two years ago, but many are spending less time teaching. A survey by the School Teachers' Review Body found that teachers carry out more than 25% of their work at weekends and in the evenings. Primary heads work 55.7 hours a week; their deputies 54.5 hours; and classroom teachers 50.8 hours. Secondary heads work 61.7 hours; deputies 56.5 hours; department heads 53; and classroom teachers 50.3. One in ten primary heads are working up to 70 hours a week, as are one in five secondary heads.

Housing

The number of new houses started by housing associations was 30% down in 1996 on the previous year. Increasingly housing associations have had to rely on private finance. This has pushed up rents and slowed down the rate of new building. The Housing Act (1996) makes provision for using private finance for social housing. Local housing companies can now be formed and will include local authority representatives. These companies will be independent and will be free to borrow money for repairs and to match government grants to build new houses. In July 1996, several local authorities were awarded grants from central government to transfer a substantial proportion of their housing stock to LHCs (Local Housing Corporations).

The Government announced targets for social housing of between 60,999 and 100,000 homes per annum. These figures were, however, challenged by the National Federation of Housing Associations, which estimated that current levels of funding will only finance 55,600 houses in 1997.

A report prepared by the Joseph Rowntree Foundation for the Housing Forum concludes that homeless people suffer significantly worse health than the rest of the population—especially with chest problems, digestive disorders and mental illness. Those in poor housing are badly affected by poor heating, indoor pollutants and crime. There are 1.65 million homes in England and Wales that are unfit for human habitation and a further 65,000 in Scotland are below tolerable standards. Poor housing, plus poverty and growing homelessness, result in the creation of unstable communities and greater health and crime problems.

Health

The health of the nation appears to be improving—individuals are living longer. Death rates for those under 65 years are falling. There has been significant a decline in male deaths from coronary heart disease; from 148 per 100,000 in 1972 to 76 per 100,000 in 1995. Life expectancy for 1994 was 79 years for women and 74 for men and is rising by about two years every 10 years. However, while individuals are living longer, they are experiencing chronic sickness.

Welfare

Those in the top 20% of the distribution of incomes obviously pay much more in taxation than those in the bottom 20%. However, those in the top 20% receive about £4,000 p.a. in services from the NHS, education, pensions and child benefits. They also received £139 per capita in rail, underground and travel subsidies.

The top 20% of the population's income in 1994-95 was about £40,000, which was £28,840 net after taxes etc. The bottom 20% had an income of £2,040. This rose to a net of £7,720 after benefits, subsidies etc. The proportion of people whose incomes were below the average increased from 8% in 1982 to 20% in 1990.

Crime

Over 5.1 million crimes were recorded by the police in the year to June 1996. This represents an increase of 0.4% over the previous year and brings to an end the decline in the crime rate over the previous three years. Violent crime, which accounts for 6.0% of the offences experienced its largest increase for eight years, rising by 10% to 331,000. Rapes increased by 14% and robberies by 15%—largely due to an increase in street muggings.

The British Crime Survey (BCS) is carried out every two years. The figures are compiled by asking individuals if they have been the victims of crime. This survey provides a very comprehensive set of statistics and reveals that between 1993 and 1995 crime rose by 2%, a period over which the Home Secretary was claiming that there had been the largest fall in crime for 40 years. Experts regard the BCS data to be more accurate than the recorded crime figures, which depend upon individuals' willingness to report crimes to the police. The BCS figures do, however, show that the increase in crime has been the smallest rise since 1981. Why is this? One hypothesis is that the fall in unemployment would be associated with a fall in crime and that the number of male teenagers, who are the majority of criminals, is declining.

World Trade

The most recent World Trade Organization (WTO) ministerial conference was held in Singapore in December 1996. Meetings of this kind enable trade ministers to address issues relating to tariff reductions and non-tariff barriers to trade. Wider issues, such as trade and the environment and trade and competition policy, are also discussed at this forum.

Economic development in Europe in the foreseeable future is gloomy. The brakes on European growth are a welfare state with unfunded pension liabilities and a Bundesbank that is intent upon fighting inflation wars that have long since disappeared. The consequence is most likely to be rising unemployment in Europe.

The European picture is in sharp contrast to that of the US which has enjoyed much higher levels of employment for many years. The spectre of inflation is looming on the American horizon, but these will likely to be very moderate rates of inflation which are unlikely to give cause for much concern.

Japanese growth will result from monetary and fiscal expansions. The yen has almost depreciated by 50% against sterling during calendar year 1996. Japan is working at about 4% below capacity and has experienced very low rates of economic growth for the past five years. The expansionary Japanese policies will give a boost that is much needed by Japan and the economies of South East Asia. Economies within the region have enjoyed growth rates of over 8% p.a. for many years. What has been the cause and can it be sustained? Malaysia provides an interesting case study with growth rates of around 7% p.a. for the past 10 years.

Malaysia's growth is explained by the importation of labour from Indonesia and Bangladesh. Very high rates of investment have resulted in the capital stock growing at 10% p.a. Similar results are found in Singapore and Korea.

What does, however, seem clear is that while such growth rates are observed in the earlier phase of development they cannot be sustained. Appreciating exchange rates, plus differences in the attitudes and expectations of new generations compared to the old, will tend to moderate the growth rates of Asian Tigers and their cubs. Given the potential for the growth of emerging economies such as those of Indonesia and Vietnam these will provide markets for the Tigers and will keep economies in the region buoyant at rates of growth closer to 5% p.a., compared to the recent historical 8% p.a.

Territorial Public Spending

Public expenditure varies regionally and locally throughout the UK. Whether or not these differences are justified or if they reflect variations in service quality remains a matter of debate. A study, commissioned by the Scottish Office and conducted by Coopers/Pieda, shows that Scottish local authorities spent £184.20 per head more compared to England in 1994-95. This figure takes into consideration structural factors such as the fact that there are more grant maintained schools in England and that Scottish local authorities have higher debt charges because they have higher levels of accumulated debt.

Scottish local authority expenditure is determined by the Secretary of State for Scotland who funds it from the Scottish block grant. Changes in this grant are based upon the Barnett formula, which takes into account changes in comparable English spending programmes. If there is a difference between Scottish and English local authority expenditures per capita, then it is due to a decision taken by the Sottish Secretary of State: but what factors influence and inform that decision?

Scottish local authorities' expenditures were 16.5% and 18.5% higher than English authorities' expenditures for 1993-94 and 1994-95 respectively. The corresponding figures for the Scottish/Welsh comparison were +8.2% and +9.0%. Of the difference between the Scottish and the English figures 80% is accounted for by higher expenditures on education; roads; transport; social work and leisure and recreation. In 1994-95, Scottish local authorities spent £80.30 per person (23.16%) more than English authorities on education. Once differences in responsibilities are taken into account, plus the fact that a greater proportion of Scottish children attend local authority schools is recognized, then the difference falls to £29 per person (8.7%). There are more children in grant maintained schools in England. Higher pupil/teacher ratios due to contractual agreements and the greater proportion of Scottish children who go on to the colleges of further education will contribute to an explanation of any residual differences.

Expenditures on Scottish roads was 42% higher in 1994-95 compared to England, and 47% higher compared to Wales. These differences are in part explained by the greater sparsity of the population in Scotland.

Variations in personal social services spending is accounted for by the level of residential care provided for the elderly, which is greater in Scotland. The number of children in residential care is higher in Scotland than in England.

The figures in the report reveal that variations within England are greater than between Scotland and England. More work remains to be carried out explaining rather than simply accounting for the variations.

The Social Chapter

Attitudes towards the European Social Chapter divide the political parties. Prime Minister John Major has referred to it as a 'Trojan Horse'. On the other hand, the Labour Party regards it as a means of establishing minimum standards in the labour market, but it does not accept any European regulation of the UK labour market. The main issue which divides opinion is the likely impact of the Social Chapter upon job security and job creation. Will its adoption, as the Prime Minister suggests, destroy a million jobs, or will it add to employers' labour costs?

The 'Social Chapter' refers to the Protocol and Agreement on Social Policy annexed to the (Maastricht) Treaty on European Union. It contains a statement of principles relating to social policy. While 14 EU member states have agreed on these principles the UK has not, on the grounds that they are interventionist and counter to the free market principles advocated by the British Conservative Government. The Labour Party regards the spirit of the Social Chapter to be 'good treatment of employees' and that this is compatible with efficient labour markets.

The essential features of the Social Chapter are set out in figures 1 and 2. A recent report by the Employment Policy Institute (1996) summarizes the academic research that has examined the impact which the Social Chapter might have on labour markets. There is little strong empirical support for the proposition that payroll costs (especially from a payroll tax increase) will result in job losses, although this conclusion probably needs to be moderated

Figure 1. What is covered by the Social Chapter?

Areas subject to qualified majority vote of EU member states:
•Improvement in working environment to protect workers' health and safety.
•Working conditions.
•Information and consultation of workers.
•Equality between men and women.
•Integration of persons excluded from the labour market.

Areas subject to unanimous vote of EU member states:
•Social security and social protection.
•Protection of workers where their employment contract is terminated.
•Representation and collective defence of the interests of workers and employers.
•Financial contribution for promotion of employment and job creation.

Areas excluded:
•Pay.
•Right of association.
•Right to strike.
•Right to impose lock outs.

Source: Treaty on European Union, Annexed Agreement on Social Policy, Article 2.

for low-paid low-skill jobs. Since the Social Chapter does not advocate the harmonization of wages or social policies across Europe, it is not clear why the UK should not sign and thereby signal a commitment to assuming a future of high wages, low unemployment and improved working conditions.

Pensions

A report published recently by the IMF (Chand and Jaeger, 1996) demonstrates that the generosity of pensions varies considerably between countries and that the costs of pensions to the exchequer depends more upon their generosity rather than upon demographics—this is not, however, to deny the importance of the number of pensions within the population.

Pensions as a proportion of GDP varies considerably within Europe. State

Figure 2. EU legislation adopted or considered under the Social Chapter.

Adopted (date of adoption in bracket):

- European Works Council Directive (1994). Requires companies with more than 1,000 employees to establish works councils. Directive applies to UK companies with at least 150 employees in at least two member states.
- Parental and Family Leave Directive (1996). Requires companies to provide three months' unpaid leave (part or full-time) to employees on the birth or adoption of a child. Leave must be taken before a child's eighth birthday. The Directive also covers the rights of employees to take time off for urgent family reasons in the event of an accident or sickness. Based on framework agreement made by the ETUC, UNICE and CEEP.

EU legislation under consideration:

- Shifting the burden of proof onto employers in sex discrimination cases.
- Extending part-time and temporary workers' terms and conditions to match those on offer to full-timers.
- Requiring companies with 50 or more employees to establish works councils at national level.
- Requiring employers to provide full sick pay and holiday pay.
- Requiring employers to implement policy statements about sexual harassment and designating sexual harassment officers.

pensions in Britain are well below those in other European countries—see table 1. A recent survey carried out by Mintel concludes that 17 million people face financial hardship in Britain when they retire. That is, they receive a pension which is less than 40% of average earnings.

The IMF report asks the question—suppose that a country stabilizes its public debt to GDP ratio and, therefore, does not build up pension debt, then by how much would contribution rates have to increase? The answer for the UK is that virtually nothing needs to happen—it will not be necessary to divert resources into public pensions up to the year 2050. The growth in real GDP will be sufficient to fund public pensions. In other countries, such as Italy, Germany and France, a much greater amount of GDP will need to be allocated to the funding of public pensions.

Table 1. State pensions as a percentage of GDP (1995).

Britain	4.2
France	12.1
Germany	10.3
Italy	16.0
USA	4.7
Canada	3.8
Japan	3.9
Major industrial countries	6.5

Sources: Eurolink Age; OECD.

In continental Europe, the contributions to pensions as a proportion of the wage bill is much higher than that for the UK. This will present problems for these countries' labour markets in the future.

Private Welfare Insurance

In the general debate about the future of the welfare state, it is often suggested that private insurance should be used to replace many activities undertaken by the state in the provision of welfare. The workability of this has been explored by Jackson (1996) and is the focus of a major report produced for the Rowntree Foundation by Burchardt and Hills (1997). They conclude that even for people on average earnings and who face average risks the costs of private welfare insurance will be substantial. A married man on average earnings would need to pay £900 per annum to cover:

- Mortgage payment protection.
- Sickness or accident and permanent health insurance.
- Long-term care, nursing homes etc.

The situation with state welfare is that mortgage protection is severely limited and applies only to new mortgages and is withdrawn after the first nine months of unemployment. Incapacity benefit (which used to be called invalidity benefit) has fallen considerably in value in relation to earnings.

Hills and Burchardt present a case study of a married man aged 45 with average earnings (about £400 per week in April 1996). He takes out private insurance to cover mortgage payment protection against unemployment for payments of £250 per month, to pay out £200 per week in income replacement during long-term incapacity and long term care insurance to pay £1,250 per month. The premiums for these insurances are respectively £121 p.a.; £295 p.a.; £506 p.a. (i.e. £900 p.a.). They then compare this with a one penny increase in income tax. This would cost the same man £150 p.a. Note that it is only three risks that are being covered. There are many more which are significant.

Another feature is that state insurance payments are progressive—they rise with income, whereas those for private insurance are flat rate, they are regressive. The private insurance option is not only socially unjust it is also expensive.

Private insurance is not always available on a universal basis. For example, people who have not been continuously employed for six months prior to taking out a policy are ineligible. Also, those who face a higher risk of unemployment are charged higher premiums which they might not be able to afford.

Minimum Wage and Low Pay

The issue of the minimum wage and the level at which it should be set continued to be a political debating point during 1996. A survey of senior managers conducted by the Employment Policy Institute (1996) found that a national minimum wage of £3.50 per hour would not lead to a net loss of jobs. It was, however, found that the industries which would be most affected are catering, textiles, cleaning and hairdressing. In these industries workers are predominantly female and earn less than any likely minimum wage.

A consequence of the introduction of a minimum wage would be to upset existing wage relativities within industries. This could set off a general escalation of wage increases which would then show up as wage inflation. This reaction would leave the relative position of low paid workers unchanged.

The starting wage rates in many jobs have been declining and have not kept pace with inflation. The number earning less than £2.40 per hour increased by 20% between 1994 and 1995.

Home workers are no better off than they were 90 years ago. Currently there are about 1.2 million people who work from their own home performing tasks such as sewing, packaging, and toy making. The number of home workers has increased by 50% over the past 10 years. Case studies reveal that home workers earn on average £1.28 per hour. Real rates of pay are even lower when off set against home workers' other costs, for example buying equipment. About one third of home workers do not refuse extra work because they fear that if they were to do so that they would lose their job.

The Wages Council system, which was set up by Winston Churchill, was abolished in 1993. The Wages Councils set minimum wage rates and other conditions for the working poor, including home workers.

A recent report published by Kempson (1996) analysed 31 qualitative research studies commissioned by the Joseph Rowntree Foundation . These studies reveal that the poor are not an 'under class' but are instead people who have ordinary ambitions of having a good job, home and adequate income. An extra £15 per week would make a tremendous difference to them. Many families who rely upon social security would have that extra £15 per week if the link between benefits and average earnings had not been broken in 1980. ■

References

Burchardt, T. and Hills, J. (1997), *Private Welfare Insurance and Social Security: Pushing the Boundaries* (York Publishing Services, York).

Chand, S. K. and Jaeger, A. (1996), *Aging Populations and Public Pension Schemes,* Occasional Paper 147 (IMF, Washington, D.C.).

Employment Policy Institute (1996), *Employers and a National Minimum Wage.*

Jackson, P. M. (1996), A qualified defence. In Seldon, A. (Ed), *Re-Privatizing Welfare: After The Lost Century* (Institute of Economic Affairs, London).

Kempson, E. (1996), *Life on a Low Income* (Joseph Rowntree Foundation, York).

1 Economic Performance

Peter M. Jackson
University of Leicester

Gross domestic product has been growing at an average rate of 2.4% p.a. Unemployment has fallen to the two million mark with prospects of a further reduction during 1997. Inflation has averaged 2.7% and real incomes have grown 1% above inflation. The remarkable strengthening of sterling in the second half the of 1996 threatened output growth and employment.

The boom which began four years ago is not as strong as that of the late 1980s, which ended up in high rates of inflation. Indeed, the performance of the economy over the past few years is the best for almost 30 years. Growth in output, very low rates of inflation and falling levels of unemployment are all favourable indicators and should give the Chancellor of the Exchequer no real cause for concern during the build up to the general election.

Recent research carried out by the Economic Group of Lloyds Bank reveals that the UK economy is the most unstable amongst the 14 largest industrial countries. The UK's inflation rate has been three times as unstable as the best performing country and its unemployment rate has been four and a half times as unstable. Interest rates, short or long term, have been twice as volatile as the best performer.

Economic instability is bad for the long-term economic health of an economy. It creates uncertainty which has adverse effects upon savings and investment. Delays to investment (a coping strategy in the face of uncertainty) reduce long-run economic growth.

Output

Since mid-1995, the rate of growth of output has been increasing. This has been promoted mainly by the growth in consumer spending brought about by healthy increases in real disposable incomes.

The annualized rate of growth in GDP for 1996 was 2.4%; consumer spending increased by 3.2% over the year; and real personal disposable income grew by 4.6%. These growth rates are slightly above trend.

Industrial production, which accounts for less than 30% of the whole economy, was 2.3% higher than a year previously. This represents the fastest rate of growth since 1994. Output in the engineering industry was up by 2.8%; chemicals by 2.0%; and textile and clothing by 0.5%. In contrast, food, drink and tobacco declined by 0.8% and building materials by 0.9%.

The strength of sterling during the last few months of 1996 places a question-mark over the rate of economic growth during 1997. Forecasters had been expecting improvements in the rate of economic growth to about 3.3%. These forecasts for 1997 have now been reduced to 2.5%, indicating little expected improvement.

The CBI Regional Survey indicates that producers in the north of England expect their biggest fall in output since 1994. Producers elsewhere expect order books to increase, but at a greatly reduced rate. The strength of sterling has badly hit companies' exports in the south east, east Midlands, Scotland and the north. Companies have been revising down their export expectations since October 1996.

Inflation

The UK economy finished the year 1996 with a headline rate of inflation of 2.7% p.a. The retail price index was 3.3%, which was above the Government's target of 2.5% by mid-1997.

Those items, which make up the index, showing rates of price increase in excess of 2.7% were tobacco (6.9%); motoring costs (6.8%); catering (4.0%); leisure services (3.6%); food (3.3%). The increase in motoring costs was due mainly to an increase in petrol prices.

The appreciation in sterling, coupled with the improvement in producer factory gate prices, will contribute to a reduction in the rate of increase in the retail price index to about the Government's target of 2.5%.

The outlook for inflation for 1997-98 is that there is a danger the rate of increase in prices will increase. There is a fear that as economic growth picks up the economy will start to overheat. This will be due to a shortage of capacity plus rising consumer confidence, increases in the money supply (M0 and M4), and increases in house prices.

By how much is inflation likely to increase by mid-1998? The answer to this question depends upon what is happening in many other parts of the economy. Assuming that base rates increase to about 7.25%, then inflation by mid-1998 will be in the region of 3.5%.

Producer prices remained stable during 1996. Output prices, excluding excise duties, rose by 2.0% p.a. Producer input prices fell by 5.5% during 1996. The main reason for the decline in producer input prices was the appreciation in sterling. This increase in sterling will eventually feed through into moderations in the rate of retail price inflation and is the main factor which will enable the Government to hit its inflation target in mid-1997.

House prices, as reflected in the Halifax house price index, increased by 7.0% during 1996. The Nationwide index suggests an even greater increase at 8.8%. The number of transactions in the housing market increased by 24% during 1996 and mortgage lending was 4.0% up on 1995.

This activity in the housing market is due to a number of factors:

- Growth in real incomes.
- Improvements in consumer confidence.
- Mortgage interest rates at their lowest level for 30 years.

It is expected that house price inflation will continue into 1997-98.

Investment

Despite an improvement in the volume of manufacturing investment in the third quarter of 1995, it was 14% below the 1995 figure and 25% below the peak level in 1989. The volume of investment in the private services sector is only 2% below the 1989 peak. Public sector investment is 25% down on the first quarter 1994; see table 1 for details.

Foreign direct investment by the advanced industrial nations of the OECD increased by 25% in 1995. This investment flows between

OECD countries, however, the share which goes to third world countries has been increasing. Britain is the second largest foreign direct investor (FDI). The merger of British Telecom with the US company MCI (costing £12 billion) is an example of foreign direct investment. The OECD figures, however, tend to understate the volume of foreign direct investment, since they do not include FDI from profits made abroad. This is important in the cases of Japan and France, whose FDI from overseas profits is greater than capital transferred abroad; see table 2 for details.

Taxation

In the financial year 1978-79 the total yield of taxes was 34.25% of GDP. This had increased to 36% by 1995-96. The contribution of income tax to total tax revenue fell significantly from 34.4% in 1978 to 26.8% in 1995. The share of VAT increased by almost 10% from 9.6% in 1978 to 19.3% in 1995—total indirect taxes increased from 25.2% to 34%.

Does it matter how the tax revenues are raised; does it matter which taxes are used? The straight answer is *yes it does*. Indirect taxes, such as VAT, fall more heavily upon those on lower incomes—they are

Table 1. Capital expenditure (£M), 1990 prices.

	Manufacturing	*Services**	*Total*
1989	14,980	31,730	111,460
1990	14,230	30,170	107,580
1991	12,800	28,270	97,400
1992	11,830	26,310	96,000
1993	11,230	24,760	96,590
1994	12,000	27,870	99,420
1995	12,530	30,170	99,190
1996:			
Q1	3,010	7,480	25,180
Q2	2,780	7,730	25,700
Q3	2,810	7,780	25,140

*Excluding the public sector, water and air transport.
Source: Office for National Statistics.

Table 2. Direct investment flows in OECD countries (£ billion).

	Outflows		*Inflows*	
	1994	*1995*	*1994*	*1995*
US	32.3	63.4	29.4	18.9
UK	18.4	25.5	6.8	20.5
Germany	9.5	22.0	-2.0	5.7
France*	7.1	6.1	7.2	7.7
Netherlands	7.5	5.0	3.5	3.7
Japan*	11.7	14.1	0.6	-
Sweden	4.3	6.6	4.1	8.6
Total (OECD)	122.9	153.8	90.7	120.7

*Re-invested profits are excluded.
Source: OECD Observer (October-November 1996).

Table 3. Selected taxes as a percentage of central government current revenue.

	1978 (£M)	*% total*	*1995 (£M)*	*% total*
Income tax	18,767	34.4	67,448	26.8
NI contributions*	4,009	7.4	20,045	8.0
Total direct taxes	22,776	41.8	87,493	34.8
Corporation tax	3,586	6.7	22,404	8.9
VAT	5,239	9.6	48,413	19.3
Excise duties	9,570	15.6	36,94	14.7
Total indirect taxes	14,809	25.2	85,354	34.0
Total current revenue	54,518	100.0	250,942	100.0

*National insurance contributions paid by employees and self-employed persons.
Source: National Income Blue Book (1996), table 7.2.

regressive. In 1994-95, VAT took 11% of the incomes of the bottom 20% of non-retired households, compared to 6.7% of the top 20%. Total indirect taxes took 30.6% from the incomes of the bottom 20%, compared with 14.8% from the top 20%; see table 3 for details.

Public Spending

Total social spending by central and local government as a proportion of GDP increased from 24.37% in 1979 to 27.39% in 1995—the definition of social spending is given in table 4.

The greatest increase in social spending has taken place in the area of social security—up from 10.6% of GDP in 1979 to 14.4% in 1995. This has happened while the real value of benefits has greatly declined. The increases in the social security budget can be traced to increases in the number of pensioners and the unemployed, plus an increase in poverty. The number of pensioners and poverty have also placed pressures upon personal social services.

The dramatic decline in public sector housing expenditure reflects the Government's attempts to contain public spending by cutting back on capital spending. This policy has had a massive impact upon the construction industry which has been in recession since the mid-1980s.

Education spending has increased but not as a share of GDP despite

Table 4. Social expenditure 1979-95 as a percentage of GDP (market prices).

	1979 (%)	*1995 (%)*	*1995 (£M)*
Education	5.20	5.40	38,330
Health	4.58	5.75	40,842
Personal Social Services	0.86	1.17	8,376
Housing	3.13	0.65	4,607
Social Security	10.60	14.42	102,483
Total	24.37	27.39	190,069
Defence	4.53	3.26	23,154

Source: National Income Blue Book (1996), table 9.4.

the general view that education spending will increase more than in proportion to real income increases. The NHS share of GDP increased from 4.58% in 1979 to 5.7% in 1995. While this seems to be an impressive increase it should be remembered that the rising costs of medical equipment and drugs, plus the increase in the number of elderly people (especially those over 75 years) needing treatment, has put considerable pressures on health care budgets.

Combining expenditure on public sector and private sector health care the UK spends around 7.0% of GDP. This compares with a range between 8% and 9.5% for other major OECD countries, such as France, Germany, Australia and Canada. Also, as in the case of education, it is generally thought that health care spending increases more than in proportion to real income increases. Since 1979, real GDP has increased by about 33%, however, education spending per pupil or health spending per patient have increased by much less than 33%.

Public expenditure continues to be tightly squeezed. Real public spending increased by 0.1% in the financial year 1996-97, and is planned to grow by 0.4% in 1997-98. If the Government manages to maintain its tight control over public spending programmes, then given the projected increases in GDP (about 2.5%–3.0%), public expenditure as a proportion of GDP could fall below 40% by the end of the millennium.

International Tax Comparisons

Britain is now regarded as a low tax country. This is demonstrated in table 5, which shows that few countries now take less out of GDP in taxation than the UK.

The Public Finances

Government receipts have been increasing faster than that projected in the budget for 1996-97. It is, therefore, expected that the public sector borrowing requirement (PSBR) will undershoot the budget forecast by around £2.5 billion for 1996-97. The PSBR is expected to fall to £26.4 billion in 1996-97 and to £19.2 billion for 1997-98. This puts the PSBR at around 3.5% of GDP. The general government financial deficit will be about 3.0% of GDP, which is important in terms of the Maastricht requirements. There is, however, little prospect of the Government

Table 5. Taxes and social security contributions as a percentage of GDP (1995).

Denmark	51.6
Sweden	51.0
Belgium	46.6
Finland	47.3
France	44.1
Netherlands	45.9
Luxembourg	45.0
Austria	42.8
Italy	41.7
Norway	41.2
Germany	39.3
Ireland	37.3
Spain	35.8
UK	34.1
Switzerland	33.9
Portugal	33.0
Iceland	30.0

Source: Economic Trends (November 1996).

realizing its objective of making a massive repayment of public debt over the next few years.

During January 1997, a debt repayment of almost £6 billion was made. This was possible because of the substantial increase in revenues from the corporate sector, i.e. increases in revenues from VAT and corporation tax. The corporation tax take was £7.65 billion and was greatly above anything that had been expected. VAT receipts of £5.22 billion for December 1996 were 60% up on the December 1995 figure. These increases flow from the growth in the economy and resulted in a downward revision to the PSBR figure. Borrowing for the first 10 months of the financial year 1996-97 was £10.3 billion, compared to £19.3 billion for the same period in the previous year. Excluding privatization proceeds, the PSBR to December 1996 was £14.5 billion, compared to £20.2 billion a year ago. The improvements in tax revenue receipts, plus the sale of the Housing Corporation loans book to the private sector, puts the PSBR on target for 1996-97.

Monetary Policy

Throughout 1996 there has been a tension between the Treasury and the Bank of England regarding the appropriateness of interest rate policy. The Chancellor, with an eye on the state of the real economy, has been keen to keep interest rates as low as possible. Fears of overheating of the economy and increasing rates of inflation have caused the Governor of the Bank of England to advocate increases in interest rates.

Base rates were raised from 5.75% to 6.00% on 30 October 1996. Given that the leading indicators of house prices, labour market conditions and money supply growth are all pointing to an increase in rates of inflation during 1997 it is most likely that base rates will be increased to almost 7% by end 1997.

The money supply, as measured by M4, grew by 10.8% in 1996. This was the fastest annual rate since 1991. The M0 measure increased by 7.5% in 1996. Both M0 and M4 grew substantially above their monitoring ranges (4% for M0 and 9% for M4). This gives strength to the fears that inflationary pressures are building up and a demand for increases in base rates.

Personal Finance

Consumption levels in the personal sector are influenced by real personal disposable incomes and real personal wealth. The largest element of personal incomes is derived from income from employment (60% in 1995). Receipts from government, for example social security payments, were 15% of personal incomes. The remainder comes from self-employment and investment income (dividends and interest payments). Non-wage sources of income have been growing at about 17% a year in 1996, compared to 4% for wages and salaries. The increase in non-wage income has come mainly from dividend payments and payments made when companies merge or demerge, for example the $1 billion payment made by the regional electricity companies. This was not an insignificant amount given that in 1995 personal incomes grew by £36 billion. Dividend payments, however, tend to be less liquid because the majority are paid into life assurance and pension funds.

The ratio of personal financial assets to liabilities rose to its highest peak in 1995: 3.58% in 1995 compared with 2.65% in 1990. The personal sector's financial assets are held mainly in life assurance and pension funds (over 50%), about 23% are held in bank, building society and national savings accounts, and 21% in stocks and unit trusts. What accounts for the rise in the ratio of personal financial assets to liabilities? The main reason is the increase in the value of pension and life assurance funds. Because these are relatively illiquid forms of wealth, changes in their value are not likely to have a great impact upon consumer expenditures.

The ratio of personal sector debt to incomes has fallen from 116% in 1990 to 106% in 1996. This is mainly due to the slow down in mortgages. Consumer credit has been growing by about 12% per annum.

Measuring personal savings is full of problems. The conventional method simply looks at savings in the form of the accumulation of financial assets. Savings on this measure is about 10% for 1996. Financial transactions, however, exclude many important factors that influence the wealth of the personal sector. To capture these other factors, flow-of-funds analysis is used to measure the gross savings ratio which gives a more accurate picture of the rate of asset accumulation by the personal sector. The long-term average for the gross savings ratio is 20%. Savings in financial assets is about half of gross savings.

The financial position of the personal sector is favourable. This is due to growth in income from dividends and interest payments and special windfall factors such as the 'de-mutualization' of building societies and financial gains from privatizations. Improvements in the financial position of the personal sector is likely to continue for the next few years.

International Trade

The deficit in traded goods (i.e. visible trade) was almost unchanged between 1995 and 1996 at £12 billion. The growth in imports remains strong due to consumer demand but this might be moderated by companies' attempts to reduce stocks of imported goods. Export growth has been buoyant due to the growth in world economic activity. This has, however, been dampened by the loss of competitiveness arising from the appreciation in sterling. Given this background, forecasters are expecting non-oil imports to grow in the region of 6% in 1997 and exports by 4%. These relative rates of growth would lead to a widening of the trade deficit to about £18 billion by the end of 1997.

The current account of the balance-of-payments was close to equilibrium in 1996 (£1 billion—0.1% GDP—deficit). This is likely to rise to a £7 billion (1% GDP) deficit in 1997.

Sterling

Sterling has appreciated during 1996 due in part to the strength of economic activity in the UK economy relative to that in other countries and to the expectations of increases in short-term interest rates. During the last three months of 1996, sterling moved close to either side of DM 2.50. If those forces remained in place, then sterling could increase to DM 2.6 or £/$1.68 by mid-1997.

There are, however, reasons to believe that such increases in sterling will be checked. As the balance-of-payments deteriorates in 1997, then sterling will begin to fall back.

Labour Market

How many people in Britain are unemployed? This is an awkward political question. There are so many different numbers that can be run. Some measures have greater insights than others.

Britain's official measure of unemployment is the *claimant count,* i.e. the number of people in receipt of unemployment benefit. On this basis there were 1.8 million unemployed as at December 1996. There definition, however, leaves many people out of the picture and is very sensitive to changes in eligibility for benefits and, moreover, has been criticised by the Royal Statistical Society and by the House of Commons Employment Committee. A more meaningful definition used by the International Labour Organization in Geneva classifies someone as unemployed if they are available for work and have been actively searching for work over the previous six weeks. Using this definition, there are about four million people unemployed in the UK.

The number of households who have no-one earning a wage is now 20% of the total. This number has increased significantly over the past 20 years. In 1995, the number of 'workless households' increased by

250,000.

While unemployment has been falling during 1996, the work force in employment is 1.1 million below the 1990 level. There is, however, a strong indication that people have been dropping out of the labour market.

A feature of life in modern Britain is that the majority of jobs that are being created are part time rather than permanent. The number of people on temporary contacts is about 1.5 million or 7% of the work force (this compares with 5% in 1986). Many of these temporary contracts only last for up to six months. While in the past it was generally women who took on part-time and temporary contracts, a recent feature is that this is an emerging characteristic of male jobs. Since 1993, the number of male part-time employees has increased by 40%.

Over the past 20 years, the number of jobs someone can expect to have in a life time has increased from seven to 11. The concept of a 'job for life' has disappeared for all but a diminishing core of employees.

Finally, the real earnings of those in low-paid jobs failed to increase significantly over the past 20 years. This traps some individuals and households into dependency on state benefits because they are better off out of work rather than accepting low-paid work.

Unemployment, as at January 1997, was 1.8 million or 6.5% of the work force. This is 391,000 below the level 18 months ago. There has been a fall in unemployment for 11 consecutive months. The labour market statistics for the period October 1996 to January 1997 must, however, be treated with caution. While they show a fall in unemployment of 255,000, this overstates the true position. About 137,000 of the reduction in unemployment is due to administrative changes. First, the introduction of the Job Seeker's Allowance in October 1996 resulted in a delay in processing applications for unemployment benefits. This means that the recorded claimants count has been reduced. The effect of this change has been to take 10,000 people off the register per month since October 1996. In addition, about 3,000 people per month have been discouraged from signing on because of the Job Seeker's tougher rules. Another group who are no long signing on are those who have been cheating the system by, for example, having two jobs.

Manufacturing employment fell to 3.9 million in December 1996. This was 38,000 down on December 1995. Despite the fall in the number of people employed in the manufacturing sector, the manufacturing industry faces a shortage of qualified engineers. There has been a failure to fill apprenticeships. Some apprenticeships are now going to adults—those in their late twenties or early thirties.

Europe

Europe has turned out to be a political minefield for the British Government. Deep divisions in attitudes towards European Union have shown up as internal divisions within the major political parties and the emergence of Sir James Goldsmith's Referendum Party is aimed at forcing open political debate in those constituencies where the standing MP opposes a referendum on Europe.

There are many dimensions to the European debate. One central issue is that of the Economic Monetary Union (EMU) and the role of fiscal policy. The creation of a European Economic and Monetary Union (EMU) was set out in the Treaty on European Union and agreed by the European Council in Maastricht in December 1991. The Treaty became effective on 1 November 1993. The Maastricht Treaty is a set of additions and amendments to the Treaty of Rome, which established the European Economic Community in 1958 and covers political and economic reforms.

Within the Maastricht Treaty, there is a set of convergence criteria which form the basis of deciding whether a country can move to the final stage of joining the EMU. The four convergence criteria are:

- Average consumer price inflation should be sustainable and, in the past year prior to examination, should not be more than 1.5% percentage points above that of, at most, the three best performing countries.
- The country should not have an excessive deficit—a government's budget deficit should not exceed 3% of GDP and its debt should not be more than 60% of GDP.
- Average nominal long-term interest rates, in the year prior to examination, should not exceed by more than two percentage points the long-term interest rates of, at most, the three best performing

Member States in terms of price stability.

- A Member State should respect the normal fluctuation margins provided for by the ERM without severe tensions for at least two years, in particular without initiating a devaluation of its currency's bilateral central rate.

It is not clear that Germany will be in a position to meet these criteria in 2002. The planned time table is set out in figure 1.

Figure 1. Planned timetable for the introduction of the euro.

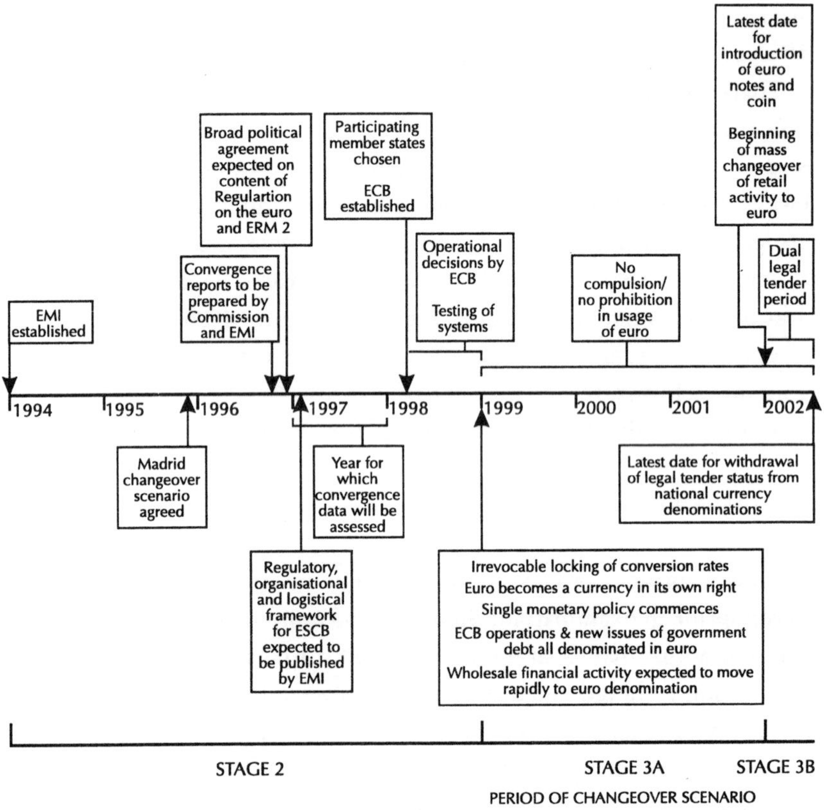

The Maastricht fiscal convergence criteria are aimed at ensuring that members of the EMU restrain their fiscal policies. This raises a number of challenging technical questions regarding the role of fiscal policy when nominal exchange rates are fixed and the monetary policies of the different members are harmonized. Does this mean that the scope and freedom to use fiscal policy as a means of short run stabilization is now severely constrained? What form might fiscal policy take?

The Maastricht Treaty set out the convergence criteria that placed limits of 3% for government deficits and 60% for government debt. Most countries, including France and Germany, might not be in a position to meet these criteria. The recession in Europe and the payment of social security has meant that deficits lie above the 3% criterion. For example, the UK's public sector financial balance was 4.8% in deficit in 1996. Corresponding figures for other European countries were Germany (4.1%); France (4.3%); Italy (6.3%) and Spain (5.2%). If the convergence criteria are to be met, then it will be necessary for severe tightening of public expenditures. The Waigel Plan has advocated that the criteria should be more stringent, and this has been accepted by the IMF and the OECD, who favour greater fiscal restraint.

The Maastricht rules contain no technical logic. They are the outcome of political bargaining. The convergence criteria do, however, have a high price tag attached to them. As countries adjust their fiscal policies to meet the criteria, they are likely to exacerbate further the recession in Europe. Maastricht will do nothing for European unemployment.

Conclusion

While the economic indicators of the UK economy are pointing in a favourable direction, there is not a widespread feel-good factor on the run up to the general election. Many individuals are anxious about their employment prospects over the medium term and are uncertain about the availability of pensions and other social services which were once taken for granted.

The real earnings of those with low-paid jobs have not increased over the past 20 years. This traps many individuals and households into dependency on state benefits because they are better out of work rather than accepting low-paid work. The answer to this problem is not to cut back on state benefits. Rather, it is to create better paid low-paid jobs.

For many, the feel-good factor is an illusion. Being in a workless household with only the prospects of a low-paid or part-time job, or fearing that a responsible well-paid job might be the objective of a downsizing cost-cutting exercise, hardly promotes a feeling of well being. For an increasing number of people the current boom and the favourable economic indicators have simply passed them by. ■

2 The Budget, 1997-2000

Alan Gillie

The Open University

Kenneth Clarke could not have known in 1996—as he set draconian government spending targets for the years after 1997, forecast a UK government deficit below that required by the Maastricht Treaty, and cut the basic rate of income tax to 23%—that Gordon Brown would pledge the Labour Party to adopt the same spending targets until 2000 and a rule for borrowing compatible with the EMU stability pact, and would undertake not to increase income tax rates in the next Parliament if a Labour government were elected. Mr Clarke's incredulity may have been reinforced by independent observers' queries about the credibility of his own budget statement.

The final budget of the 1992-97 Conservative Government, announced in November 1996 for the three years up to 1999-2000, was, as the last budget before the 1997 general election, examined for signs of a partisan or even reckless pursuit of electoral popularity. Since the Government's long-standing unpopularity suggested that it would be defeated in the election, the budget seemed likely to be the last of the unbroken series of 19 budgets presented by Conservative Chancellors since 1979, and, therefore, to be of special interest as an apparently valedictory statement of successive Conservative Governments' plans for public expenditure and taxation. In January 1997, however, interest in the budget intensified when the Labour Party's 'Shadow Chancellor', Gordon Brown, announced that if a Labour government were elected in 1997 it would adopt prominent and controversial features of the Conservative Government's plans. His announcement startled many people, for different reasons. It is considered below, after an outline of the November 1996 budget's principal features.

Here is how Kenneth Clarke summarized them, in the introduction to his budget statement:

This budget reduces public spending plans further, while providing more money for priority services. It makes responsible progress on our tax cutting agenda, while getting borrowing down faster. This is not a reckless Budget on either tax or spending.

Not surprisingly, these claims require careful interpretation. A helpful way to put them into context is to examine the development of the public finances shown in table 1, looking first at the public sector borrowing requirement.

Table 1. The public finances (£ billion).

	1996-97				
	1995 budget	*Latest forecast*	*Forecast/projection 97-98*	*98-99*	*99-00*
General government expenditure	308.3	308.5	319.0	327	336
General government receipts	284.8	280.9	299.4	315	333
General government borrowing requirement	23.5	27.7	19.6	12	4
Public corporations MOB*	-1.1	-1.3	-0.4	0	0
PSBR	**22.4**	**26.4**	**19.2**	**12**	**3**
PSBR path in 1995 Budget		*22.4*	*15*	*5*	*-2*
PSBR path in 1994 Budget		*13*	*5*	*-1*	*-9*
GDP (£ billion)	754	745.7	786.9	826	864
Percentage of GDP:					
GGE	40.9	41.4	40.5	39.6	38.9
GGR	37.8	37.7	38.1	38.1	38.5
of which, total taxes and NICs	35.6	35.6	35.8	36.5	37
GGBR	3.1	3.7	2.5	1.4	0.5
PSBR	3.0	3.5	2.4	1.5	0.4

*Market and overseas borrowing. *Note*: Totals may not sum because of rounding.
Source: HM Treasury (1996), tables 1.5, 5A.1.

Borrowing

The PSBR for 1996-97 is now expected to be higher than forecast in the November 1995 budget, and to be more than double what was forecast in the budget before that. The projected figures for subsequent years show, in fact, that borrowing is coming down not faster, but more slowly than had been suggested at the time of the 1994 and 1995 budgets. However, the PSBR in the Treasury's July 1996 Summer Economic Forecast was (at £27 billion for 1996-97, and £23 billion for 1997-98) higher than the average forecasts of the Chancellor's panel of independent forecasters, published at the same time, and higher than the forecasts in the subsequent November 1996 budget statement. And so it is true that the budget was 'getting borrowing down faster' than forecast only four months earlier! Table 1 also shows why borrowing in 1996-97 was higher than forecast in the 1995 budget. General government expenditure (GGE) was higher than planned. More importantly, gross domestic product (GDP) and tax revenues were lower than forecast. As noted in this *Yearbook* last year, most independent forecasters thought that the Government's 3% GDP growth forecast for 1996 was implausibly high, and 'if growth is less than forecast, as it was in 1995-96, then the same problems of lower revenues and higher borrowing will recur'.

These problems were stressed in the annual report on the UK by the International Monetary Fund (IMF). In a break from previous years' practice, Mr Clarke published its concluding statement, and highlighted the IMF's view that 'recent economic performance has been enviable'. Since the long recession of the early 1990s (following the unsustainable high growth in the late 1980s, an inflation rate over 10%, and the forced exit from the EU's Exchange Rate Mechanism in 1992) economic performance has undoubtedly improved: in the recovery phase of the economic cycle, the existence of spare capacity enables the economy to grow above its long-run trend rate, and unemployment to fall, without an increase in inflation. But the IMF found that the recent generally positive picture was marred by the increasing slippage in the public finances, and recommended that the budget 'should put the PSBR back on the medium-term track foreseen in last year's budget, with about half of the most recent slippage being made up in 1997-98'. And, noting that recent reductions in planned expenditure had fallen disproportionately on public investment, the IMF proposed reductions in the Government's planned current expenditure instead, saw 'no scope for tax cuts', and noted that 'bolstering the revenue-generating capability of the tax system is a priority...exemptions and preferences have tended to proliferate and have turned out much more expensive than anticipated'. The IMF also noted that returning to the 1995 budget's PSBR track would be credibility-enhancing, and help establish eligibility for European Monetary Union (EMU).

One of the Maastricht Treaty's convergence criteria for EMU, determining eligibility for participation in a single currency in 1999, is that gross general government debt should be less than 60% of GDP in 1997. In the UK, higher than forecast borrowing has increased this debt, but it is still projected to peak at less than 56% in 1997-98 and, with lower levels of borrowing, to fall thereafter. The other criterion is that the general government financial deficit, GGFD, should not exceed 3% of GDP in 1997. (The GGDF is greater than the GGBR by the amount of privatization proceeds and some other accounting adjustments.) It is forecast to fall from 4% of GDP in 1996-97, to 2.6% in 1997-98, and to continue falling in the four following years (HM Treasury, 1996, tables 4.2 and 4.3). If the forecast turns out to be correct, then the UK will meet the Maastricht criteria, although it is not committed to join a single currency. Countries joining the single currency will be bound by a more demanding 'stability pact', and are expected to have deficits no greater than 3% of GDP, even in recessions. This means that they should probably aim for a deficit of about 1% when the economy is not operating below its trend capacity, to leave room for the usual increase in borrowing at times of recession.

The UK Government's deficit target is usually expressed in terms of the PSBR, although it is not very clearly specified. One formulation is that the budget should balance over the economic cycle, which suggests debt repayments at high points (as in the late 1980s) and a zero PSBR target when the economy is at a cycle's mid-point. Another formulation is the 'golden rule': that borrowing should not be undertaken to finance current expenditure but should be enough to finance public net capital expenditure. In the UK, this rule would put the PSBR target at an average of about 1% of GDP, corresponding to the target suggested by the EMU 'stability pact'.

Are the tax and spending plans announced in the 1996 budget consistent with a PSBR target of 1%? The fall in the projected PSBR in table 1 depends upon the assumption that there is still, after the recession and after some growth in productivity, sufficient spare capacity (often described as 'the output gap') to allow GDP to grow more rapidly than its long-run trend rate of growth, currently put at 2½%. Therefore, in the Government's projections, GDP growth is forecast to grow at 3½% in 1997-98 and 3% in 1998-99 (and 2½% in the following years) without hitting short-run capacity constraints and increasing the rate of inflation. But if the output gap is smaller than assumed in these projections, the increasing demand in the economy will result in prices rising more quickly. This would conflict with the Government's stated intention to reduce the rate of inflation (as measured by the retail price index excluding mortgage interest payments, RPIX) to 2½% from 1997; and so the Government's inflation target would require an increase in interest rates, to reduce demand to the level that can be supplied with a continuing fall in inflation to its target rate. Reducing the growth in demand will result in GDP growth below the above-trend levels currently projected; but this will reduce tax revenues too (as it did in 1995-96). In short, if the output gap is not sufficiently large to allow the projected above-trend growth, then the PSBR target will not be met, and fiscal policy will need to be tightened further, by reducing expenditure or by increasing tax revenues by more than was envisaged in the 1996 budget.

In his budget statement the Chancellor said: 'The reason why I am tightening fiscal policy now is to reduce the risk of having to tighten monetary policy excessively as I set policy to hit my inflation target' (HCDeb., 26 November 1996, c. 147). However, two weeks later, the Governor of the Bank of England advised the Chancellor to raise interest rates. The rapid growth in the economy was being led by consumer demand, and in a speech in January 1997 the Governor said there was 'a need to anticipate what was to come and begin to moderate the pace of the upswing before the evidence of imbalance comes through into the statistics' (*Financial Times*, 21 January 1997). The Chancellor was not persuaded to increase interest rates.

Some observers think that the Governor and his advisers are over-cautious. Others disagree because they think the Chancellor has not tightened fiscal policy sufficiently. In the budget debate an Opposition MP argued that the Chancellor's strategy was 'to introduce a budget that would stoke up a consumer-led boom, while posturing as a responsible Chancellor who was giving us a virtuous budget...the Budget...will fuel a boom that will last until the election, after which a Labour Chancellor will have to pick up the pieces' (HCDeb., 3 December 1997, c. 875).

The reduction in public spending plans referred to by the Chancellor in his summary of the budget measures is not shown in table 1, but the plan to increase public spending more slowly than the increase in GDP is shown, with GGE falling as a percentage of GDP. As for the Chancellor's 'tax cutting agenda', note that taxes and national insurance contributions (NICs) are projected to rise each year, as a percentage of GDP.

Expenditure

Table 2 provides an aggregate view of the new spending plans. Since 1992 the reserve for the following year has been gradually reduced from £4 billion to £2.5 billion, with correspondingly lower reserves for the two following years than used to be the case. This reduces the Government's margin for manoeuvre, and its ability to respond to unexpected demands for expenditure within the control total; and, of course, it also reduces the total of planned expenditure in future years. When questioned in 1995 about this tactic to cut planned spending, the Chancellor argued that the Government had previously been 'putting in figures for the contingency reserve that were far too big. We did not need a reserve of that size' (Treasury Committee, 1996, Q. 651). By the following year, however, it was clear that the Government's new contingency reserve was too small, although the reserve for 1997-98 has again been set at £2.5 billion. This sum was insufficient to finance unplanned extra expenditure in 1996-97. After allocating the reserve, the control total, which excludes expenditure which varies with the economic cycle and expenditure financed by the lottery, is expected to be about £½ billion more than planned in the 1995 budget (in cash terms).

In real terms, the control total for 1996-97 is expected to be £1.9 billion more than planned in 1995. The main reason for this is that inflation (measured by the GDP deflator) was, again, less than forecast. A lower than expected level of prices should make it easier not to exceed spending limits set in cash terms (in the expectation of higher prices). Nevertheless, all departments spent more than planned in cash terms. (The largest increase, by the Ministry of Agriculture, Fisheries and Food, was due to expenditure of £1.54 billion associated with BSE. Payments to the European Communities were £0.9 billion less than expected, part of which may be linked to a reduction in payments related to BSE.) The control total was planned to be 0.9% less in real terms than in 1995-96; the outturn was 0.3% lower.

The Government's preferred measure of government expenditure is GGE(X). Compared to last year's plans, GGE(X) took a higher proportion of GDP, was higher in cash terms, and higher by almost £3 billion in real terms. It was also higher than in 1995-96, although it was planned to be about 1% lower. These outturns, shown in table 3, suggest that the spending plans were unrealistically tight. Nevertheless, the Chancellor claimed that his 1996 budget 'reduces public spending plans further'. Table 3 shows that this is true only in cash terms. Compared to cash plans announced in 1995, the planned control totals and GGE(X) for 1997-98 and the following year are cut by £3.6 billion and £2.6 billion, but because price levels are now expected to be lower than forecast in 1995, these cash cuts are equivalent to real increases of £2.1 billion and £3.9 billion. And GGE(X) will be higher as a proportion of GDP than forecast in 1995.

New Ways of Cutting Expenditure Programmes

The only real reduction in spending plans shown in table 3 is for cyclical social

Table 2. The new public spending plans (£ billion).

	1996-97				
	1995 Budget	*Estimated outturn*	*New plans 97-98*	*98-99*	*99-00*
Departmental expenditure*	257.6	260.6	264.0	268.7	273.4
Reserve	2.5	2.5	5.0	7.5	
Control Total	**260.1**	**260.6**	**266.5**	**273.7**	**280.9**
Cyclical social security	13.9	14.3	14.1	14.3	14.7
Central government net debt interest	22.3	22.2	24.8	24.4	24.0
Accounting adjustments	9.7	10.3	9.2	9.8	11.0
GGE(X)	**306.1**	**307.4**	**314.7**	**322.2**	**330.6**
Privatization proceeds	-4.0	-4.5	-2.0	-1.5	-1.0
Lottery-financed spending and interest and dividend receipts	6.2	5.6	6.3	6.5	6.6
GGE	**308.3**	**308.5**	**319.0**	**327.2**	**336.3**

*Excluding cyclical social security. *Note*: Totals may not sum because of rounding.
Source: Based on HM Treasury (1996), table 5.3

security (job seeker's allowance, plus income support to non-pensioners) and this cut accompanies an abrupt change in the long-standing convention in the public expenditure plans, of not publishing forecasts of unemployment. In 1995, the Government's Chief Economic Adviser explained the reasoning supporting that convention: 'The main reason, in fact most of the entire reason, for not publishing these forecasts, is because of the extreme difficulty of producing accurate forecasts of unemployment. So our view is that they

Table 3. Changes to 1995's expenditure plans and real spending growth.

	96-97	*97-98*	*98-99*	*99-00*
GGE(X) as % GDP				
(95 FSBR)	40.6	39.7	38.8	
(96 FSBR)	41.2	40	39	
GDP deflator (95-96 = 100)	102.5	104.6	106.7	
Changes in planned spending				
GGE(X):				
Cash (£M)	1,300	-800	-1,800	
Real (£M 95-96)	2,900	2,000	1,900	
Cyclical social security:				
Cash (£M)	400	0	-400	
Real (£M 95-96)	500	100	-200	
Control total:				
Cash (£M)	500	-1,700	-1,900	
Real (£M 95-96)	1,900	800	1,300	
Total local authority:				
Cash (£M)	1,200	900	400	
Real (£M 95-96)	1,600	1,500	1,200	
*Annual real growth in 1996 FSBR**				
GGE(X)	0.1%	0.3%	0.4%	0.6%
Cyclical social security	-3.5%	-3.4%	-0.6%	0.5%
Control total	-0.3%	0.2%	0.7%	0.6%
Total local authority	-1.4%	-1.7%	-0.8%	-0.8%

**Financial Statement and Budget Report*

Sources: HM Treasury (1995, 1996), and Treasury Committee (1997), pp. 102-103.

are simply not useful and it is better to produce this conventional assumption...that unemployment stays at the level it has just reached and that is the basis on which the public expenditure figures are based...So rather than attempt the impossible we make it quite clear, and always have done, that we assume that unemployment is unchanged' (Treasury and Civil Service Committee, 1995, Q. 180).

The Government has now attempted 'the impossible'. The 1995 budget had assumed that there would be 2.1M unemployed claimants in each of the three years beginning in 1996-97. Since unemployment was really expected to fall over that period, the social security costs of supporting the unemployed were overestimated and savings were easy to achieve in the following years when the unemployed were fewer than projected. Abandoning the convention, the 1996 budget forecast a fall from 1.98M unemployed in 1996-97 to 1.8M, 1.7M and 1.6M in the three following years (HM Treasury, 1996, p. 72). The effect of this is to reduce planned DSS (excluding Northern Ireland) cyclical social security expenditure in 1999-2000 by £1 billion, compared to what it would have been if the former convention had been retained (Treasury Committee, 1997, p. 117). The Treasury Committee was advised that cyclical social security falls about £250M (and all expenditure by about £350M) for each 100,000 fall in unemployment (*ibid.*, Q. 527) and so changing the convention accounts for more than all of the reduction in planned cyclical social security expenditure in 1998-99 shown in table 3.

Non-cyclical social security expenditure is planned to grow more quickly in real terms than any other programme within the control total, as table 4 shows. New restrictions on housing and council tax benefits are expected to save about £145M a year; and one parent benefit and lone parent premium (described in a 1985 Government green paper as 'a contribution to the additional costs of lone parents in bringing up children alone') were again not uprated with inflation, and are to be abolished for new claimants from April 1998. The main savings in social security expenditure, however, are projected to be the result of a 'drive against fraud'. Expenditure on fraud investigations and security activities is to be increased from an average £300M to about £457M a year for the next three years. The saving is deducted from planned expenditure not, as previously, in the year in which the fraud is detected, but over the average period the fraud would have

Table 4. Changes in expenditure plans within the control total.

		Real expenditure as percentage of 1995/96			
	Outturn	*Estimated outturn*	*Plans*		
	95-96	*96-97*	*97-98*	*98-99*	*99-00*
Social security[1]	72.7	103.2	105.0	107.0	108.9
Health	32.9	100.6	101.5	100.9	100.9
of which, NHS	*32.0*	*101.3*	*102.8*	*103.1*	*103.1*
DOE—local government	30.3	101.0	99.0	98.4	96.0
Defence[2]	21.5	96.3	94.0	97.2	97.7
Scotland	14.3	99.3	95.8	94.4	93.0
Northern Ireland	7.7	103.9	102.6	100.0	100.0
Wales	6.7	100.0	98.5	95.5	94.0
Education and Employment[3]	14.5	99.3	91.7	90.3	89.0
DOE—other	9.0	91.1	81.1	80.0	71.1
Home Office	6.5	98.5	100.0	98.5	98.5
Transport	4.4	109.1	113.6	97.7	90.9
Foreign Office	1.3	84.6	76.9	76.9	76.9
Overseas Development	2.4	95.8	87.5	91.7	91.7
Agriculture etc.[4]	2.8	153.6	125.0	114.3	107.1
Trade and Industry programmes	3.2	100.0	90.6	90.6	87.5
Nationalized Industries	0.2	-250.0	0.0	-100.0	-100.0
Legal departments	2.7	100.0	96.3	96.3	88.9
National Heritage	1.1	90.9	81.8	81.8	81.8
Chancellor's departments	3.3	97.0	90.9	90.9	90.9
Cabinet Office	1.2	108.3	83.3	83.3	83.3
European Communities	3.2	43.8	65.6	68.8	81.3
LA-Self Financed Expenditure	13.2	97.7	100.0	97.0	100.0
Control total	*255.2*	*99.6*	*99.8*	*100.5*	*101.1*

[1]Excluding cyclical social security				
[2]Includes sale of married quarters	–0.94	–0.70		
[3]Includes sale of students' loan book*	–1.02	–0.96		
[4]Includes expenditure on BSE	1.54	0.73	0.58	0.49

*Figures in this row show the reductions in planned spending for 97-98 and 98-99. The Chancellor said these were 'more than accounted for by the sale of this debt', so they are less than the proceeds of the sale (HCDeb., 26 November 1996, c. 159). By November 1996, there were some £2 billion of outstanding loans (DfEE, 1996).

Source: Derived from HM Treasury (1996), tables 5.7 and 5A.5.

continued if it had not been detected. This leads to estimated savings for the three years beginning 1997-98 of £2 billion, £2.4 billion and £2.5 billion. This sudden and rather large saving, like the extra tax revenues the Government also claims to expect by eliminating fraud, remains to be seen.

Another of the budget's other 'wizard wheezes', to use a description apparently sanctioned by the Government's Chief Economic Adviser (Treasury Committee, 1997, Q.82), is revealed in table 4. By a peculiar convention, privatization proceeds are treated as 'negative expenditure' in the calculation of GGE (see table 2). But, until 1996, these proceeds had not been subtracted from the expenditure, included in the control total and GGE(X), of the government department formerly responsible for the privatized assets. Now, however, the control total and GGE(X) have been reduced in this way, by subtracting from defence expenditure the proceeds of the sale of the Ministry of Defence's married quarters, and, from education expenditure, the proceeds of selling the right to collect the repayments of loans made to students. This anomalous treatment of asset sales reduces the control total in 1996-97 and in the two following years, compared to plans laid out in the 1995 budget, by, on average, £1.2 billion a year. And the planned proceeds in 1997-98 (shown in table 4) more than account for the £1.7 billion by which the Chancellor claimed he had cut the planned control total (see table 3).

Asset sales are not reductions in expenditure. This new treatment of them, the apparent optimism about the result of anti-fraud measures, the changed convention about forecasting unemployment, and the 1995 budget's overestimate of the inflation rate all help to clarify, and greatly qualify, the Chancellor's claim that the 1996 budget 'reduces public spending plans further'.

Priorities

The Chancellor also claimed that the budget provided 'more money for priority services': schools, combating crime, and the National Health Service. The Government does not, however, directly control expenditure on all of these programmes.

Expenditure on schools is, generally, the responsibility of local authorities, and so the Government's prioritization of it is, at best, indirect. The Department of the Environment provides grants to English local authorities, which are supplemented by council tax and other less important receipts to finance their total expenditure. The Secretary of State for the Environment outlined the Government's plans for it: 'Every year, the Government announce the sum of money which local authorities are expected to spend—the total standard spending or TSS. Next year's figure is £45.66 billion....an increase of £1.1 billion, and when the transitional costs of local government reorganization are taken into account...a cash improvement of 2.4%... In allocating this sum between services for 1997-98, I have decided to give the main priority to education. My proposal is therefore that education spending should increase year on year by 3.6% after adjusting for the introduction of nursery vouchers. Councils must decide how much to spend on education, but I am sure that parents, governors and teachers will wish to ensure that education remains the top priority for authorities' (HCDeb., 26 November 1996, cols. W145-146).

Table 3 shows the Government's plans for total local authority expenditure (which was about £2.5 billion greater than the Government's TSS in 1996-97). It is planned to fall in real terms in every year up to 1999-2000. Any increase in expenditure on priority services would therefore mean a greater fall in real terms for other services, compared with the fall in total expenditure.

There are cash increases in the 1997-98 TSS provisions for education (3.6%), police (3.4%), fire (4.2%) and personal social services (4.1%). These are all real increases too, i.e. they are greater than the forecast inflation measured by the GDP deflator. However, the costs (particularly wages and salaries) of providing a particular level of any one of these services may rise more quickly than the GDP deflator (which is expected to rise in 1997-98 by less than the retail price index) so that a 'real increase' in expenditure may bring no improvement in the service as its users perceive it. (The Government's arguments against the publication of service specific deflators are examined in Gillie, 1995.)

The Secretary of State for Education explained what the Government's prioritization of, and real increase in, expenditure on schools meant: 'So long as pay settlements are at affordable levels, and reflect our overall approach to public sector pay, our schools will be able to fund the increase in pupil numbers and other pressures which they will face next year' (DfEE, 1996).

That may seem a modest aim for a priority; she added 'It will of course be for local authorities to decide how to allocate the available funding but parents will expect them to give priority to schools'. Although the Government states that it regards education as a priority, and says that it expects local authorities to spend £18,088M on education in 1997-98, this is less (in cash terms) than the £18,160M they are estimated to be already actually spending in 1996-97, which is an 'overspending' of about £700M compared to the 1996-97 TSS provision.

In contrast, the amount the Government expects local authorities to spend on the police in 1997-98 (£6,391M) is greater than their 'overspending' expenditure on the police in 1996-97 by about £32M. But the TSS provisions for fire services and for Personal Social Services are not sufficient to bring cash spending up to existing 1996-97 'overspending' levels. Personal Social Services are likely to be under great pressure. The increase in the TSS provision of £310M to £7,846M is not enough to match local authorities' 1996-97 'overspending' (£8,096M) and the latest transfer of community care responsibilities from the Department of Health to local authorities is expected to require expenditure of more than £300M (Hale, 1996).

The Government has pledged to increase expenditure on the NHS in real terms every year, and so this was the other spending priority identified by the Chancellor. Total spending is planned to increase in real terms by 1.5% in 1997-98, and by 0.3% and 0.04% in the following years. Current expenditure accounted for 95% of the total in 1996-97, and 74% of current expenditure was on Hospital and Community Health Services (HCHS). HCHS current expenditure is planned to increase by 3% in real terms in 1997-98 and by 0.1% in the next two years. This election year increase is much greater than the 0.1% real increase in expenditure for 1997-98 planned in the 1995 budget.

The change in the Government's HCHS capital expenditure and other NHS capital expenditure is more dramatic. It is planned to fall by 16.5% in 1997-98 (much more than planned in 1995) following a similarly large fall in 1996-97. These falls are exacerbated by the recognition that 1995's estimates of investment under the private finance initiative have turned out to be too high. Although the Chancellor said in his budget statement that 'the PFI contract for the Norfolk and Norwich hospital scheme, worth close to £200M, was signed yesterday', it turned out that agreements with banks to finance the scheme had yet to be reached.

The Private Finance Initiative
No large hospital scheme has yet been finally agreed under the PFI. Nevertheless, the Government (partly, perhaps, with the IMF's strictures about the disproportionate reductions in public sector investment in mind) has been at pains to argue that reductions in planned government capital expenditure have been offset by increases in the estimated spending under the PFI, whereby the private sector is to provide capital assets for leasing to the public sector. This provision is proceeding more slowly than the Government forecast. Expenditure in the three years up to 1995-96 is now put at £0.7 billion (down from last year's estimate of £1.2 billion) and is now estimated to be £1.1 billion in 1996-97, rather than the £1.2 billion forecast last year. The 1996 budget included estimated PFI capital spending of £2.51 billion, £3.65 billion and £4.26 billion for the three years beginning 1997-98, and highlighted the total of £10.41 billion. However, the estimated spending for which deals have been signed is rather less, at £1.3 billion, £1.3 billion and £1.24 billion for the same years, totalling £3.85 billion, £3.22 billion of which are for transport projects—still dominated by the planned channel tunnel rail link (HM Treasury 1995, table 6.4; 1996 table 5.4; HCDeb., 11 December 1996, W125).

Taxation

The projected path of aggregate tax revenues was shown in table 1; table 5 shows tax changes announced in the 1996 budget. Including the confirmation of previously announced increases in road fuel and tobacco duties, but excluding an estimated 6% increase in council tax due to budget decisions, the budget increased taxes by £350M in 1997-98 (compared to what they would have been if the only changes had been to increase allowances, thresholds and excise duties by the increase in the retail price index). It also increased total taxes in each of the following two years. A tendency since 1993 has been to increase tax revenues by widening the tax base while reducing some marginal tax rates, a policy which generally reduces the effects of the tax system on people's behaviour.

This policy of 'fiscal neutrality' is not always appropriate, and taxes can be used in an attempt to change behaviour—particularly if that behaviour involves costs or benefits for other people not reflected in an individual's decisions. Increases in tobacco and road fuel duties can be justified on these

Table 5. Changes in tax and National Insurance Contributions.

	Changes from an indexed base; £M yield (+)/cost (-)		
	97-98	*98-99*	*99-00*
Income tax			
Basic rate reduced to 23%	-1,250	-1,800	-1,800
Personal & age-related allowances increased	-920	-1370	-1420
Lower (20%) rate band widened	-60	-140	-160
Car fuel scales increased	30	30	30
Relief for profit related pay to be phased out	100	700	1700
Inheritance tax			
Threshold raised to £215,000	-30	-55	-65
Capital gains tax			
Reinvestment relief extended	-5	-10	-15
Business taxes			
Small companies' corporation tax rate cut to 23%	0	-80	-110
Business rates transitional relief	-115	-100	-80
Change in capital allowances for long-life assets	45	325	675
Finance leasing of assets	80	150	150
Relief for drilling production oil wells		150	200
VAT anti-avoidance and revenue protection measures	560	320	320
Insurance tax 17.5% if sold with some goods and services	160	235	260
Excise duties			
Most tobacco duties up 5% in real terms*	140	150	155
Beer, most wine, cider and perry unchanged	-95	-100	-105
Duty on spirits cut by 4%	-50	-50	-50
Petrol and diesel up 3p a litre (including VAT)*	15	15	15
Ultra-low sulphur diesel 1p differential	-15	-15	-15
Road fuel gas cut by 25%		-5	-10
Fuel and gas oil up 5% in real terms	15	15	20
VED for cars increased and cut for low emission lorries	40	35	30
Other indirect taxes			
Insurance premium tax: main rate increased to 4%	325	455	470
Air passenger duty doubled to £10 or £20	120	385	415
Other tax measures	75	60	60
National insurance contributions			
Car fuel scales increased	0	10	10
Employers' NICs intermediate earnings thresholds frozen	100	100	100
Total	**-735**	**-590**	**780**
*Tax increases previously announced and now confirmed, but not included above:			
5% real increase in road fuel duties	850	935	1030
3% real increase in tobacco duties	235	245	260
Total (excluding increases to be confirmed after 1996)	**1,085**	**1,180**	**1,290**

Source: HM Treasury (1996), tables 1.4, 6.1, and 6B.1.

grounds, as can the encouragement to reduce pollution by reducing the duties on road fuel gas, ultra low sulphur diesel (which lowers their relative prices) and cutting the vehicle excise duty by up to £500 on lorries adapted to produce very low particulate emissions. The real reduction in the taxation of most alcoholic drinks is again intended to reduce the loss of revenue due to cross-border shopping where taxes on alcoholic drinks are lower, and to reduce differences in the rates of tax per unit of alcohol.

Changes in income tax illustrate the marginal rate reducing/base widening strategy. The basic marginal rate was reduced to 23%, and the marginal rate of some tax payers with low incomes is reduced to 20% by the widening of the lower rate band. The reduction of the income tax base due to the increase in personal allowances will be more than compensated by 1999-2000 by the phasing out of the tax relief on profit related pay.

'Securing the Tax Base'

The tax revenues gained by the reduction of the annual rate of capital allowances on machinery plant with a working life of at least 25 years, from 25% to 6%, has been seen as a pre-emptive strike at the taxable capacity of the privatized utilities, on which the Labour Party has pledged to introduce a 'windfall tax'. However, the Government presented it as one of a series of measures designed to 'secure the tax base' (phasing out of the relief on profit related pay was another, and more are listed in the last four lines of 'Business taxes' in table 5). Some of these measures have fairly predictable results. But the revenue effects of those designed to counter tax avoidance (legal) and evasion (illegal) are less certain. When the Labour Party produced proposals for reducing the avoidance and evasion of tax, the Chancellor dismissed them as 'not serious options for revenue raising' (HCDeb., 8 December 1994, c. 474).

But Customs and Excise are now to attempt to collect more VAT, receipts of which have been consistently less than forecast since 1989-90. Measures on VAT compliance and avoidance, on the shadow economy, excise fraud and evasion, and Single Market excise smuggling, are estimated to raise £2.25 billion over three years at a cost of £88M, a yield better than 25:1. This is the most remarkable return in the 'Spend to Save' package (HM Treasury, 1996, p. 106). The Inland Revenue is to deploy up to 2,000 more staff in the next three years 'to counter tax evasion and avoidance. Priorities will be the pursuit of bad debts, enquiring into the liabilities of large companies, investigating international transactions, and dealing with cases of tax avoidance and serious fraud' (Inland Revenue, 1996). This is estimated to raise an extra £1.95 billion revenue over three years, a yield of just over 10:1. One tax specialist threw doubt upon the effectiveness of these measures, and noted that 'critics may suspect that the approach is a rationalisation for retaining staff who would otherwise have been released as a result of computerisation and self assessment. If it is effective, other critics will wonder why the measures were not introduced sooner'.

The Distributive Effect of the Budget

Table 6 shows estimates, provided by the Institute for Fiscal Studies (IFS) and by the Treasury, of the effects of the budget measures on the distribution of post-tax incomes in 1997-98. The last two columns show the regressive impact of the increase in tobacco duties, which reduces by 0.3% the post-tax incomes of the poorest 10% of households, who spend a relatively high proportion of their income on tobacco. The overall pattern of gains, shown in

Table 6. Changes in post-tax incomes in 1997-98 due to tax changes announced in the November 1996 budget.

Decile	*£ per week*	*%*	*%*	
			Tobacco	*Other*
1 (poorest)	-0.48	-0.59	-0.3	-0.2
2	-0.27	-0.22	-0.2	0.0
3	-0.03	-0.02	-0.2	0.1
4	0.27	0.16	-0.2	0.3
5	0.78	0.39	-0.1	0.4
6	1.56	0.63	-0.1	0.6
7	2.16	0.74	-0.1	0.7
8	3.02	0.88	-0.1	0.7
9	3.76	0.94	-0.1	0.8
10 (richest)	5.74	0.89	0.0	0.8

Note: Council tax is not included in these estimates.

Source: Stark (1996) and HCDeb. (11 December 1996), W207.

two ways in the first two columns, reflects the changes to income tax. The widening of the 20% band by £100 more than was needed for indexation is worth £3 a year to all basic and higher rate tax payers; the increase of personal allowances by £200 more is worth £46 to basic rate and £80 to higher rate payers, and the cut in the basic rate is worth more to a tax payer who pays more tax at the basic rate. So the gains from the income tax cuts rise with income. The estimates in table 6 show that tax payers gain on average from a budget which increased taxes because the taxes on companies are not allocated to individuals although they must, of course, pay for them in one way or another. The effects of council tax changes are also excluded.

Concluding Comments

The Treasury Committee's report on the budget focused on the issue of credibility. One concern is with the Government's assumption that faster economic growth can be accompanied by falling inflation, so that its borrowing and inflation targets can both be met. Several different estimates of NAIRU (the non-accelerating inflation rate of unemployment) suggest that inflation will accelerate when the rate of unemployment falls below 7% or 8% (Davies, 1996, p. 24). The Government's assumption of faster economic growth is accompanied by a forecast of unemployment falling from about 2M to 1.6M, or 5.9%, above NAIRU. Estimates of NAIRU, like estimates of the 'output gap' and forecasts of inflation rates, are uncertain. Yet the Bank of England's view after the budget was that in 1997 RPIX would be above 3%, and then 'fall gently towards the 2½% target [and] begin to pick up again later in 1997 and into 1998 as the upswing in domestic demand and output gathered pace' (HM Treasury, 1997, para. 21). An increase in interest rates, designed to achieve the inflation target, would threaten the borrowing target if it reduced the rate of economic growth (by reducing tax revenues and increasing expenditure).

Other issues of credibility concern the tax increases and expenditure cuts announced by the Chancellor. If the growth forecasts are too high, then the borrowing target will not be met and it will become apparent that fiscal policy has not been tightened enough. Furthermore, the fiscal tightening actually announced may prove to be illusory, as some of the revenue raising and expenditure cutting measures depend upon the success of actions against illegal activities, the extent of which cannot be accurately predicted. Cuts in the Government's capital expenditure have not been compensated by private sector investment through the PFI and, as the IMF observed: 'Continuation of this approach would be undesirable as postponement of capital spending cannot be sustained and permanent cuts are likely to be detrimental to growth'. In any case, a rate of inflation higher than the Government forecasts will make it even more difficult to restrain the growth of government expenditure at the low rates projected by the Government.

Nevertheless, Labour's shadow Chancellor pledged a Labour government, if elected in 1997, to keep to the control totals already planned for 1997-98 and 1998-99 (Brown, 1997). A 'Comprehensive Spending Review' will continue the effort to implement spending priorities already attempted by the Conservative Government in its 'Fundamental Expenditure Reviews'. Expenditure on getting young and long-term unemployed people back to work, to be financed by the yet unspecified windfall tax on privatized utilities, is the only additional expenditure to which the Labour Party is committed. There is no specific commitment on the level of government expenditure after 1998-99, but there is a commitment to the 'golden rule' for borrowing over the cycle only to finance public investment (which would correspond to the proposed EMU stability pact).

The Labour Party is also committed to reduce the rate of VAT on domestic power and fuel to 5%, and not to extend it to food, children's clothes, books and newspapers, or public transport fares. These are the largest potential sources of VAT, although they are currently zero-rated. Other zero-rated expenditure was estimated to have reduced tax revenues by almost £4.7 billion in 1996-97, the most important being the zero-rating of the construction of new dwellings (£2.2 billion). Another £7.2 billion was reckoned to be forgone by the exemption of rent on domestic and commercial properties (£3 billion and £1.3 billion), private education (£1.05 billion), some betting and gaming (£0.7 billion) and other expenditure. (HM Treasury, 1996a). The commitment not to increase the basic and higher rates of income tax does not preclude the abolition of the NIC upper earnings limit, which would increase the top marginal rate on earnings (but not on other income) from 40% to 50%, or the reduction of the many income tax reliefs now available. The intention to encourage long-term saving and investment seems likely to preserve some of these, but there are others. The Conservative Government has announced the phasing out of relief on profit related pay (which cost the exchequer £1.5 billion in 1996-97) but not on child benefit (£0.7 billion) or the married couple's allowance (£2.8 billion), or mortgage interest relief (£2.4 billion) or the many other smaller reliefs. Corporate taxation is also, no doubt, under scrutiny, and a Labour government can be expected to continue the widening of the tax bases begun by the Conservatives. Those people concerned about fairness and the progressivity of the tax system might urge a Labour government to accept a Treasury Committee recommendation, that an estimate of the distributive impact of the budget should be routinely published in the *Financial Statement and Budget Report*. ■

References

Brown, G. (1997), *Responsibility in Public Finance* (Labour Party Media Office).

Davies, G, (1996), The economic forecast. In G. Davies *et al.*, *Options for 1997: The Green Budget* (Institute for Fiscal Studies, London).

Department for Education and Employment (1996), Shephard announces £875M more for schools, colleges & universities (26 November).

Gillie, A. (1995), Reporting government expenditure. In Gillie, A. (Ed) *The Big Spenders: A Review of the Government's Departmental Reports and Major Spending Programmes, 1995-96* (CIPFA, London).

Hale, R. (1996), Impact of the budget on local authorities. In *Corporate Strategy* (CIPFA, London).

HM Treasury, (1995), *Financial Statement and Budget Report 1996-97* (HMSO, London).

HM Treasury (1996), *Financial Statement and Budget Report 1997-98* (HMSO, London).

HM Treasury (1996a), *Tax Ready Reckoner and Tax Reliefs* (HM Treasury, London).

HM Treasury (1997), *Monthly Monetary Meeting: 11 December 1996* (HM Treasury, London).

Inland Revenue (1996), *Boost for Inland Revenue's Counter Evasion and Counter Avoidance Work* (26 November).

International Monetary Fund (1996), *United Kingdom—1996 Article IV Consultation, Concluding Statement*, HM Treasury News Release (26 July).

Stark, G. (1996), *The 1996 Budget: What it Does to British Families* (Institute for Fiscal Studies, London).

Treasury and Civil Service Committee (1995), *Third Report: The 1994 Budget* (HMSO, London).

Treasury Committee (1996), *Third Report: The 1995 Budget* (HMSO, London).

Treasury Committee (1997), *Third Report: The 1996 Budget* (HMSO, London).

3 Constitutional Issues

Robert Hazell

The Constitution Unit, University College London

In 1996 the traditional political polarization remained reversed. There was little to choose between the parties on running the economy, but great divergence of views on the constitution. In the pre-election year Labour and the Liberal Democrats restated and developed their wide-sweeping and radical programmes of constitutional reform, while the Conservatives responded by stoutly defending the status quo. This chapter begins with a review of the constitutional highlights, before turning to a forecast for 1997.

Labour's Proposals

The year began with Tony Blair setting out Labour's constitutional reform proposals in the John Smith memorial lecture in February. It was an appropriate way to honour his predecessor, because the constitutional reform agenda is one that Tony Blair has largely inherited from John Smith. Historically, constitutional reform is a Liberal or Liberal Democrat set of ideas, which Labour has gradually signed up to during the long years in the wilderness. The following measures are now all held in common between Labour and the Liberal Democrats:

- Devolution to Scotland and Wales.
- Regional government in England.
- Reform of the House of Lords.
- Referendum on electoral reform.
- Incorporation of the European Convention on Human Rights.
- Freedom of Information Act.

Tony Blair returned to these themes in a long article in the *Economist* on 14 September, when he developed the arguments for democratic renewal (a term he prefers to constitutional reform), focusing in particular on over-centralized government and undeveloped citizenship.

The one item on which he clearly remains unconvinced is electoral reform. In his article he stated bluntly: 'I personally remain unpersuaded that proportional representation would be beneficial for the Commons'.

On devolution, Labour made a significant adjustment to their policy in June, when they announced pre-legislative referendums before establishing assemblies in Scotland and Wales. In Scotland there were cries of betrayal; but it was, Tony Blair responded, a 'principled tactic', to provide the devolution legislation with a degree of popular entrenchment, and to make it easier to get through Parliament. In Wales such a tactic seemed only prudent, given the four to one rejection of Labour's proposals for a Welsh assembly in the referendum in 1979.

Policy documents in the autumn on English regional government and on incorporation of the European Convention on Human Rights confirmed Labour's phased approach to constitutional reform. Not until the second stage will there emerge directly elected regional assemblies, or a home-grown British Bill of Rights; and possibly not until a second Parliament. Interestingly, both documents were published by Jack Straw, shadow Home Secretary, raising the question of who would lead any of these reforms in a Labour government. A number of constitutional reforms—electoral reform, the House of Lords, Freedom of Information, a Bill of Rights—have no obvious lead department, with the Home Office and the Cabinet Office having competing claims. But without a lead department, and a strong Ministerial champion, they are most unlikely to happen.

The Conservative Response

John Major launched his counter-attack in summer 1996 with a speech to the Centre for Policy Studies in which he defended the evolutionary nature of the British Constitution:

Our constitution is not a piece of architecture that one can re-engineer by knocking down a wall here or adding an extension there. It's a living, breathing constitution. Its roots are ancient, but it has evolved.

He argued that Labour's plans for devolution would undermine the central role of Parliament; and defended a House of Lords with a strong hereditary element, on the basis that it worked. He sharpened his attack on three difficult issues in Labour's devolution plans:

The West Lothian question, for a start. Simply put, why should Scottish and Welsh MPs be able to vote on English matters, but English MPs be unable to vote on Scottish and Welsh matters? Would devolution mean a cut in the number of Scottish and Welsh MPs at Westminster? If not, why not?

At the moment, the Government spends more in Scotland and Wales than it raises in tax. Would that continue? And if so, who would fund it? Would we still have Secretaries of State for Scotland and Wales in the Cabinet?

Why give the Scottish parliament the power to raise tax, and make the Scots pay more tax than any part of Britain? Why should Scotland have a tax-raising parliament, but Wales only an assembly?

He concluded his speech by promising that, in the coming weeks, seven of his Cabinet colleagues would directly address constitutional issues in 'the most thorough debate on the constitution for a generation'. But the debate failed to ignite, with some Ministers not giving their promised contributions at all. A stronger debate took place in the House of Lords in July, when Lord Cranborne (Conservative Leader in the Lords) devoted two whole days to a set-piece debate on the Opposition's plans for constitutional reform. Many peers expressed concern about the powers of patronage which would accrue to the Government from an all-nominated House of Lords, if the hereditary peers were removed; and about the survival of the conventions which help to minimize conflict between the Lords and the elected chamber. In December, Lord Cranborne offered to formalize the Salisbury Convention, whereby the Lords will not block a bill which has featured in the Government's manifesto; but in return invited Tony Blair to honour the convention that constitutional bills should have their committee stage on the floor of the House of Commons. This is a convention which makes constitutional bills peculiarly vulnerable to filibustering; and one which the Constitution Unit has recommended a new government should review. In future, constitutional bills should follow the same committee stage procedure as the Finance Bill, with the clauses of principle being debated on the floor, but the detail being referred to a standing committee.

The Liberal Democrats

At their annual party conference in Brighton, the Liberal Democrats published their 'Constitutional Declaration and Great Reform Bill'. The Declaration set out a timetable for the development of a written constitution for the UK. In 1997, the Great Reform Bill would introduce, in a single all-encompassing measure, devolution, Lords reform, electoral reform and a Bill of Rights, all to be implemented during the first Parliament. In the next Parliament the House of Commons would be elected also to sit as a constituent assembly, to draw up a written constitution. Devolution would be far-reaching, with not merely the Scottish parliament but the Welsh assembly and regional assemblies in England having both legislative and revenue-raising powers.

Despite the breadth and ambition of the Liberal Democrats' vision, a close examination of the Great Reform Bill reveals a more careful and phased approach. Lords reform is now to be in two stages, starting with removal of the hereditary peers; and regional assemblies in England are now to be introduced only upon demand, following a local referendum. The Liberal Democrats have thus accepted the possibility of asymmetrical devolution, in place of a federal solution for the UK. Apart from the clear difference between Labour and the Liberal Democrats over the long-term goal, and over electoral reform, the remaining constitutional differences between the parties are now mainly ones of emphasis rather than of substance.

In November 1996, Robin Cook (Labour's greatest enthusiast for constitutional reform) and Bob Maclennan (the Liberal Democrats' President) announced that the two parties had established a Joint Consultative Committee on Constitutional Reform. Paddy Ashdown and Tony Blair had long wanted greater co-operation between their respective parties; and constitutional reform was the area of strongest overlap. It is unlikely so close to the election that either party will make any further policy shifts (although the Liberal Democrats must hope for further movement from Labour on electoral reform); but if the parties can agree upon a strategy, in terms of the overall timetable, and upon tactics in terms of changes to parliamentary procedure, that may represent a significant step forward.

Parliament: Self-Regulation Post-Nolan

In Parliament the cash for questions affair rumbled on, with further allegations of how the ex-Ministers Neil Hamilton MP and Tim Smith MP had accepted cash from Mohamed al-Fayed, the owner of Harrods, to ask parliamentary questions. The libel action brought by Neil Hamilton and the lobbyist Ian Greer against the *Guardian* was revived after the statutory bar in the Bill of Rights 1689 had been removed, by an amendment to the Defamation Bill which happened conveniently to be passing through Parliament. Then, days before the trial, the action was abandoned. Ian Greer's lobbying consultancy collapsed; and Neil Hamilton became subject to an investigation by the new Parliamentary Commissioner for Standards, Sir Gordon Downey, in the first real test of the machinery established following the Nolan Committee's first report.

The libel action had generated quantities of documentary evidence, which led to a bizarre twist in the story. One of the documents disclosed was a note by a junior Whip, David Willetts MP, which led to him being arraigned before the Commons Committee of Standards and Privileges for bringing undue pressure to bear on the chairman, Sir Geoffrey Johnson Smith MP. Following a critical report by the Committee, David Willetts immediately resigned as Paymaster-General. The new self-regulatory machinery had passed its first test; the second will be when the Committee considers Sir Gordon Downey's report into Neil Hamilton.

Meanwhile the Nolan Committee itself has quietly continued with its business. Following its report into appointments to national public bodies it has conducted a similar enquiry into appointments to local bodies and quangos; and in the summer it embarked upon an enquiry into standards in local government, including declarations of interest, the procedures for planning applications, and surcharges. The new Commissioner for Public Appointments, Sir Leonard Peach, took up post and issued draft guidelines, which in time should put to an end the accusations that quangos are stuffed with political placements. The Nolan Committee stands ready to conduct an enquiry into the funding of political parties, including the possibility of state funding; but with no encouragement from the present government, that would have to await a change of government at the next election.

Public Opinion

Constitutional reform is frequently dismissed as the preserve of the chattering classes, and something of little interest to the ordinary voter. Recent opinion surveys suggest this may no longer be the case; ordinary voters are losing faith in our system of government and the workings of Parliament, and look to constitutional reforms as a possible remedy. The decline in faith has been dramatic, and accelerating in recent years. Twenty-five years ago one in two people thought our system of government worked well. In 1991, the proportion was one in three; by 1995 it had shrunk to one in four (see table 1).

Public support for possible reforms has been tested in a series of polls commissioned by the Joseph Rowntree Reform Trust, in 1991 and 1995 from MORI, and in 1996 from ICM (see table 2). For simplicity, only the 1996 data is shown in table 2; but the previous polls showed similarly high degrees of support for most of the items in the Lib-Lab constitutional reform agenda.

Outlook for 1997

If the Conservatives are re-elected, constitutional issues will remain to the fore. European questions will continue to dominate. The Inter-Governmental Conference on the future of the European institutions will limp towards a conclusion, which is likely require legislation to

Table 1. Public opinion on the system of government in Britain, 1973–1995.

	Crowther Hunt 1973	*MORI 1991*	*MORI 1995*	*Change 1991–95*
Works well	48%	33%	22%	-11%
Could be improved	49%	63%	75%	+12%

Source: MORI (May 1995).

Table 2. Public attitudes to constitutional reform in 1996.

	Yes	*No*	*Evenly balanced/ don't know*
Need written constitution	74%	9%	17%
Need Bill of Rights	75%	8%	17%
Need Freedom of Information Act	77%	8%	14%
Reform House of Lords	55%	27%	19%
Government power too centralized	62%	15%	24%
Scottish parliament*	40%	33%	27%
Welsh assembly*	36%	34%	30%
Give English regions choice of regional assembly	63%	15%	22%

*The 1991 and 1995 polls showed higher levels of support for devolution: nearer 60% for a Scottish parliament (or independence), and 50-60% for a Welsh assembly. The 1996 figures may be lower because the questions were set specifically in the context of commenting on Labour policies.

Source: ICM (September 1996).

approve the necessary Treaty amendments: legislation like the Maastricht Bill in 1992, which could immediately reopen the European fault lines in the new Parliament. That would be as nothing compared with legislation to take the UK into EMU stage 3, but even if (as seems likely) the Conservatives stay out, EMU and its consequences for the inner and outer European core will dominate the rest of the Parliament. Staying out is almost as difficult an option as going in: if EMU looks to have even a chance of success, the City and business interests will be keen for the UK to be at the table.

Europe is forcing the pace on lesser items in the constitutional reform agenda as well. On freedom of information, the EC Data Protection Directive will force an early decision on an incoming government of whatever persuasion, because the UK must legislate in 1997 in order to comply with the directive by its implementation date of October 1998. The policy choice is whether to legislate narrowly to comply with the directive, and introduce limited access to personal files within areas of

EC competence; or whether to build on this and introduce a general right of access to personal files. A statutory right of access to personal files is something which the present government first promised in William Waldegrave's White Paper on Open Government of 1993; and which it may finally be forced to introduce to make sense of the EC Directive. For Labour the policy choice could go one step further, and embrace a comprehensive Freedom of Information Act. Given the obligation to legislate to comply with the EC Directive, the argument will go, freedom of information could be a promising candidate for early legislation, if the first session is not already too overcrowded.

One other constitutional issue which a returning Conservative government would have to decide is the future of the Nolan Committee. It was established for three years in the first instance, which expire in October 1997. The Committee was clearly intended to stay in being to monitor and review the implementation of its recommendations; but it is not clear whether the Committee is now a standing piece of constitutional machinery, or whether having fulfilled its initial remit it can be disbanded—and how much political fuss there will be if the Committee is wound up.

Labour's Priorities

Labour's constitutional reform agenda goes much wider, and could occupy much of the next Parliament; but for Labour, too, the dominating constitutional issue will be Europe. If, as is more likely than with the Tories, a Labour government decided to join the single European currency in the first wave, that would be seismic. Seismic in terms of its own huge importance, bigger even than Maastricht; but seismic also in terms of the other legislation it would bring in its wake. Not only would there need to be a bill to make the Bank of England more independent; there would also need to be legislation to transfer ownership of the foreign currency reserves, and to change the arrangements whereby the Government borrows on the money markets via the central bank, which would be outlawed under EMU.

This EMU and EMU-related legislation could pre-empt much of the first year's legislative programme. The only constitutional items on which Labour has given a commitment to legislate in the first year are

Scotland and Wales. That is a brave commitment, even with an 18-month first session. The referendums promised in Scotland and Wales will require separate legislation, which will need to be passed by July 1997 (or, at the latest, October) if the referendums are to be held in the autumn. More demanding will be the production of White Papers, which will need to be published in the same timescale, so that the voters in Scotland and Wales have a specific and detailed proposition which they are invited to endorse. The referendum in Wales might be held later than that in Scotland; that would help to prevent the debate in Wales being overshadowed by the Scottish debate, which is what happened in the 1970s, and might also generate a bandwagon effect which could boost support for a Welsh assembly.

The second major timetabling question for a new Labour government is whether they will need to reform the House of Lords first, in case the Lords block the devolution legislation.

They are unlikely to be diverted by Lord Cranborne's sabre rattling. At the end of the day the Lords should abide by the Salisbury Convention, and not block or wreck a bill which has featured in the Government's manifesto. If the Lords break with the convention, they will have signed their death warrant; and they cannot block legislation forever. The Government can always invoke the Parliament Acts, reintroduce the devolution legislation in the following session, bypass the Lords and submit the Bill direct for Royal Assent. The net effect could be to delay achieving Royal Assent only by some three to nine months.

Influence of the Liberal Democrats

What if Labour is governing with Liberal Democrat support; or is relying on the Liberal Democrats to help deliver the constitutional reform programme? It is unlikely that the Liberal Democrats will persuade Labour to adopt their Great Reform Bill, introducing devolution, House of Lords reform, electoral reform and a Bill of Rights in a single, all-encompassing measure; and it is true that such an ambitious measure would face a very difficult parliamentary passage, given the cumulative opposition which would be ranged against it. But Labour should not be too dismissive of the central idea in the Liberal Democrat proposals, which is that to deliver a major constitutional reform programme the new government must have commitment to the programme as a whole; and must see it as a coherent whole, and understand the linkages between the different items.

The other aspect which the Liberal Democrats have perceived very clearly is the need first to reform parliamentary procedure. The main obstacle is the convention that constitutional measures have their committee stage on the floor of the House of Commons. Time on the floor of the House is at a premium, with a total of only around 400 hours of legislative time available each session to the Government, during which it must secure the passage of some 40 to 70 programme bills. Previous constitutional bills have taken up as much as 100 or 200 hours of this precious legislative time: the Maastricht Bill holds the record at 185 hours, while the Scotland Act 1978 took 160 hours.

If a new government wishes to have any legislative time for non-constitutional measures, it needs early in the new Parliament to propose some changes to parliamentary procedure. The desire to secure the passage of a large constitutional reform programme should be seized as an opportunity to improve the legislative process for all bills; and to introduce wider parliamentary reform. Only when these procedural changes have been introduced can the constitutional reform programme sensibly be allowed to roll. ■

4 Central Government

Colin Talbot

University of Glamorgan Business School

In the run-up to a general election which is expected to produce a change in governing party, it is not unusual for reforming zeal to become even more rhetorical and less real than is usual. In the lead up to the 1992 election, even the Citizen's Charter was quietly put on the back-burner by a Whitehall which expected a Labour victory. Therefore it might have been expected that there would be a downturn in reforming initiatives in 1996. However, the continuing pressure on the Government to reduce both the PSBR and taxes without reducing public spending increased the pressure to make efficiency savings. And the creation of the novel role of 'Deputy Prime Minister and First Secretary of State' for Michael Heseltine gave this notably 'managerialist' minister the opportunity to pursue his reforming intentions for the civil service. In particular, the programme of privatizing small agencies gathered pace in 1996. There were signs of soft-pedalling from within Whitehall on some of the more radical initiatives—such as the privatization of HMSO and RAS. And there was a rebellion by agency chief executives over proposals to 'league table' agencies' performance. An individual act of rebellion came from the new Director General of the Prison Service who challenged the funding regime for his agency and forecast dire consequences if the combination of reducing funding and rising inmate populations continued.

Next Steps

Agencies—New Launches

Over 40,000 more staff were transferred into newly established executive agencies during 1996, bringing the total number of agencies to around 125 (this number changes frequently due to new launches and privatizations of existing agencies).

Reviews and Privatization

Two of the most controversial privatizations of civil service organizations took place in 1996—HMSO and the Recruitment and Assessment Service (RAS)—the former responsible for publishing government documents and the latter playing a major role in recruiting civil servants.

HMSO had been one of the first three executive agencies launched under 'Next Steps' in 1988. The intention to privatize was announced in September 1995 and the sale was completed in September 1996. A consortium called the National Publishing Group, led by Electra Fleming, paid £54M for HMSO and agreed to raise £71M to fund investment. (HMSO had a turnover

Table 1. Agencies launched in 1996.

	Launch date	*Staffing*
Defence Bills Agency	1 Jan 1996	655
Pay and Personnel Agency	1 Feb 1996	890
Defence Dental Agency	1 Mar 1996	836
Medical Supplies Agency	1 Mar 1996	250
Office for National Statistics	1 Apr 1996	3,040
Army Individual Training Organization	1 Apr 1996	10,392
Ministry of Defence Police	1 Apr 1996	3,860
Service Children's Education	1 Apr 1996	1,775
CCTA	1 Apr 1996	260
Property Advisers to the Civil Estate	1 Apr 1996	250
Forest Enterprise	1 Apr 1996	2,765
Construction Service	1 Apr 1996	725
Environment and Heritage Service	1 Apr 1996	345
Government Purchasing Agency	1 Apr 1996	60
Land Registers of Northern Ireland	1 Apr 1996	215
Northern Ireland Statistics and Research Agency	1 Apr 1996	185
Planning Service	1 Apr 1996	405
Roads Service	1 Apr 1996	2,325
Water Service	1 Apr 1996	2,310
Treasury Solicitor's Department	1 Apr 1996	380
Joint Air Reconnaissance Intelligence Centre	19 Apr 1996	480
Defence Secondary Care Agency	30 Apr 1996	2,045
Defence Codification Agency	17 Jun 1996	160
National Savings	1 Jun 1996	4,650
Naval Manning Agency	1 Jun 1996	260
Defence Intelligence and Security Centre	1 Oct 1996	435
Business Development Agency	1 Oct 1996	280
Rivers Agency	1 Oct 1996	500
Total staff		*40,733*

of £33M in 1995 and 2,700 staff.)

The sale was not without complications. A National Audit Office (NAO) report, published in April 1996, stated that HMSO had moved from a small surplus on its operating account for 1994 (£0.37M) to a substantial loss in 1995 (39.7M). This was due largely to provision for future pension costs and redundancies (£26.1M) and an extremely embarrassing £3M loss on trade with Uzbekistan. The Chief Executive was reported as saying that HMSO had been the victim of 'a sucker punch' in this deal, while NAO noted the dangers of trading in international markets for the first time (NAO, 1996a). The provision for the pension and redundancy payments while HMSO was still in the public sector could be seen as a subsidization of the proposed privatization by the Exchequer.

The other substantial problem with the sale was the statutory responsibilities of HMSO. Founded in 1786 and run by a Controller, HMSO was always what a 'non-ministerial department', i.e. a government department without a direct political head. (HMSO was accountable to Treasury Ministers, but was transferred to the Cabinet Office in 1992.) It had also been a trading fund since 1980. Although it lost its formal monopoly of providing stationary and printing to other government departments in 1982, it retained much of this business, as well as a monopoly on Parliamentary printing. Most important was its role in administering Crown copyright. This problem has been resolved by retaining a residual body with the HMSO title (the privatized organization is now known as the Stationery Office) to administer the Crown copyright and 'oversight of the Gazette' (OPS Press Notice, 1996). HMSO also retains the copyright on the back catalogue of publications and the new Stationery Office is licensed to reproduce them.

While the sale of HMSO seemed to provoke most attention in the House of Commons, it was the proposed privatization of RAS which provoked an extraordinary response in the House of Lords. Following a debate in March 1996, the Lords took the unusual step of establishing a Select Committee on the Public Service and asking it to report on the RAS privatization. The Report was debated at length and the Government's proposals came in for sustained criticism from a formidable cross-bench alliance opposed to the privatization.

RAS is a small organization (130 staff and a turnover of about £9M), but it has a substantial role in the future of the civil service. It undertakes the recruitment of entrants to the 'fast stream', which still supplies over half of the most senior staff in Whitehall. This is why so many members of the House of Lords, including many ex-civil servants, saw the privatization of the RAS as such a crucial issue potentially undermining the ethos of the civil service, the neutrality of the recruitment process and the notion of 'public service'. It was not only the policy of privatization that incensed the Lords—they complained bitterly that after assurances that the committee's report would be taken seriously, the Deputy PM had made it abundantly clear that the decision had been taken and would not be reversed. RAS was sold in September 1996 to Capita Group plc for £7.25M.

These sales brought the total number of agencies privatized to nine (seven of which occurred in 1996, see table 2)—with about 5,200 jobs transferred to the private sector. However, total privatization of whole agencies is not the only way in which vital service functions have been moved into the private sector. The National Physical Laboratory operation was transferred to NPL Management Ltd, which is owned by SERCO plc. Although this was a 'contractorization' rather than a privatization, about 540 staff were transferred out of the civil service. On 1 April 1996, a contract for the management of the Teachers' Pensions Agency (400 staff) was let for seven years to Capita Managed Services Ltd, who also gained a contract to run the customer enquiry, postal search and search accounts functions of Companies House from 1 July 1996. On 31 March 1996, the Social Security Resettlement Agency (85 staff) ceased to exist, having transferred its hostels mainly to the voluntary sector. In June 1996, Roger Freeman announced the decision to privatize that part of the Security Facilities Executive Agency (SAFE) which provides security guards for Whitehall—the so-called 'custody services' which employed about 700 staff and had a turnover of about £14M.

Competing for Quality, Efficiency Plans and Market Testing

In November 1996, the annual Competing for Quality (CFQ) Report claimed that the initiative was now saving the Exchequer over £700M per year. These savings came from 'abolition, privatization, strategic contracting out, market testing and internal restructuring outcomes where the review is done in the context of the Prior Options questions'. The 'expected gross annual savings' total of £700M is an intriguingly similar figure to the early

Table 2. Agencies privatized in 1996.

	Purchaser	*Date*	*Staff*
DVOIT	EDS	Dec 93	370
National Engineering Laboratory	Assessment Services Ltd	Nov 95	260
Transport Research Laboratory	Transport Research Foundation	Mar 96	415
Laboratory of the Government Chemist	LGC (Holdings) Ltd	Mar 96	265
Natural Resources Institute	Consortium: University of Greenwich; Imperial College; Wye College	May 96	465
		Aug 96	360
Chessington Computer Centre	Consortium: Management and Employee Buyout Team; Integris UK; Close Brothers	Aug 96	360
Occupational Health and Safety Agency	BMI Health Services	Sep 96	100
RAS	Capita Group plc	Sep 96	130
HMSO	National Publishing Group	Sep 96	2,835
Total staff			*5,200*

1980s claim that the efficiency scrutinies were saving the Exchequer £600M a year—although a later report admitted that in fact only about half these savings were actually being realized.

The claimed savings from CFQ have varied widely. Analysis of the figures given in *Government Opportunities*, when compared to departmental running costs, show some quite astonishing differences between departments (see figure 1 and table 3). Top of the league table, in terms of percentage savings on running costs, comes the Office of Public Service (OPS) with claimed savings of 22.4% of running costs; second is the Overseas Development Agency (ODA) at 11.5%. Most other departments lie in the range of about 3% to 8% savings from CFQ. The overall savings on these figures are 2.3% per annum (for the selected departments used here). In percentage terms, the Ministry of Defence (MoD) comes very low (1.4%), but contributes 35.2% (£244.6M) of the total CFQ savings.

These figures can be interpreted in a number of ways. It could be uneven implementation of CFQ because either it is more easy to implement, for logistical reasons, in some departments compared to others or because there has been uneven Ministerial, official, or other enthusiasm or resistance to the CFQ programme. The extreme variations of CFQ results do seem to pose some rather awkward questions.

Citizen's Charter

The Citizen's Charter was launched in 1991 and was met with a great deal of scepticism. Much press comment focused on the admittedly laughable excesses of the initiative, such as the infamous 'Cones Hotline' (a telephone number for motorists to ring to complain about unnecessary 'coning-off' of sections of roads by contractors—the hotline received only a few calls and was soon discontinued). 1996's report on the Charter, covering the first five years of the programme, records many claimed benefits. Interestingly, the report only covers the achievements of four main areas of central government activity (revenue, customs and excise, benefits and employment services) and the majority of information is about non-central government and even private sector services (education, health, the Post Office, road and rail users, tenants and other users of local government services, victims and witnesses, water, electricity and gas customers) (Prime Minister, 1996).

There have been serious criticisms of the Charter initiative from a number of quarters. Many in non-central government public services, especially local government, pointed out that they had already been involved in initiatives aimed at standard setting and consultation with their users long before the Government latched onto the idea. Moreover, they resented the subsequent imposition of national standards, via the Audit Commission, which they saw as unwarranted interference in local decision-making and contrary to the principles of much public sector reform emphasis of decentralization and responsiveness. Academic and other commentators pointed out the way in which the supposed 'principles' of the Charter initiative seemed to be something of a chameleon, changing as it developed—for example the early commitment to redress and compensation for poor service soon metamorphosed into simply being about effective complaints procedures.

After the initial wave(s) of publication of Charter documents, the initiative was clearly somewhat stalled until the launch of the Charter Mark scheme in 1992. This also got off to a slow start, with only 50 awards

Table 3. Savings from CFQ and running costs for selected departments.

	Expected gross gross annual savings (92-96)[1]	*Gross running cost limits (96-97)*[2]
Customs & Excise (C&E)	30.4	720.1
Department for Education and Employment (DfEE)	37.1	1276.9
Department of the Environment (DoE)	16.6	218.1
Department of Health (DoH)	17.9	276.2
Department of Transport (DoT)	24.3	376.1
Department of Social Security (DSS)	96.1	3,161.9
Department of Trade and Industry (DTI)	28.2	359.2
Foreign & Commonwealth Office (FCO)	21.1	519.1
Department of National Heritage (DNH)	1.3	26.1
HM Treasury (HMT)	1.9	58.1
Home Office (HO)	37.5	1,802.3
Inland Revenue (IR)	62.2	1,657.6
Lord Chancellor's Department (LCD)	3.4	437.3
Ministry of Agriculture, Fisheries and Food (MAFF)	9.7	304.7
Ministry of Defence (MoD)	244.6	1,7962.5
Northern Ireland Office (NIO)	11.2	787.4
Overseas Development Administration (ODA)	6.5	56.7
Office of National Statistics (ONS)	3.4	99.8
Office of Public Services (OPS)	19.8	88.5
Scottish Office	18.6	325.7
Welsh Office	3.2	72.7
Total	*695.0*	*30,587.0*

From: (1) *Government Opportunities Special Edition,* November 1996; (2) *Public Expenditure Statistical Analysis 1996-97*, table 3.8a. Organizational categories used in the two sources may not be entirely compatible.

available in 1992 and only 36 winners (and most of these from non-central government services). In 1993 and 1994, the number of awards available rose to 100 and the percentage of actual awards also grew (93% and 98% respectively). For 1995 and 1996, the upper limit (which had been heavily criticized as arbitrary) was removed entirely and the number of winners

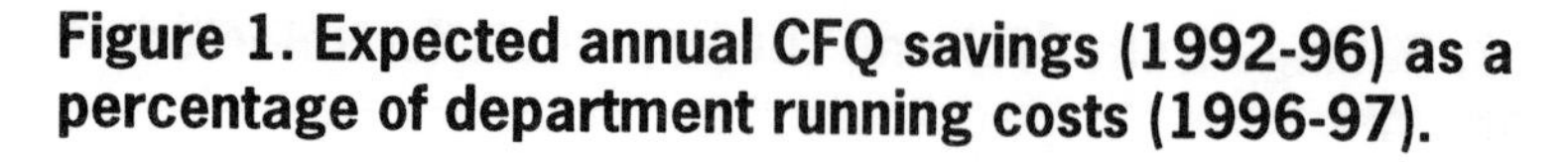

Figure 1. Expected annual CFQ savings (1992-96) as a percentage of department running costs (1996-97).

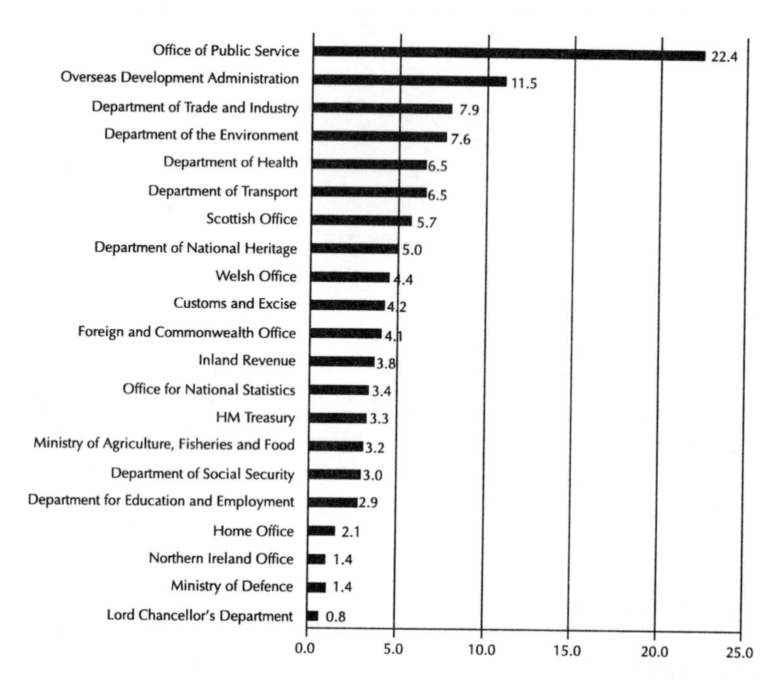

jumped to 224 and then 323 (of which 77 were renewed awards to existing Charter Mark holders—the award now lasts for three years). Almost 3,000 organizations were reported to have applied for Charter Marks and 645 organizations hold the award—a success rate of about one in five. Or put another, less charitable, way about 50% of those applying for Charter Marks fail to meet the standard.

Nevertheless, the scheme has now received support from both the National Consumer Council and from the left-leaning 'think tank', the Institute for Public Policy Research. The Charter, or more specifically the Charter Mark award scheme, does therefore seem to be having a significant impact—at least in terms of interest shown by organizations in applying for it. How far this is reflected in actual service improvements is obviously more arguable. The somewhat opaque way in which the Charter Mark judges are appointed and carry out their work raises suspicions about the objectivity of the whole process. Recently, outside authors (Deloitte and Touche in 1996) monitored the process to ensure consistency and thoroughness. Journalists

Figure 2. Charter marks.

Any public service providing a service direct to the public which has significant managerial independence is eligible to apply for a Charter mark. To win the award, organizations must demonstrate that they meet the following criteria:

- Setting challenging standards and telling users what those standards are and whether they have been achieved.
- Telling users about all services available, asking users what services they need and how they think they can be improved.
- Giving users a choice wherever possible.
- Providing a polite and helpful service.
- Providing an effective, user-friendly complaints procedure.
- Ensuring value for money.
- Evidence of improvement in the quality of service and new ideas for future improvement.
- Evidence that users agree that a good service is being provided.
- Evidence of planned improvements or innovations, which will improve services at no extra cost to the taxpayer.

(from the *Times* and the *Guardian*) were invited to accompany assessors on visits.

Governing Governance by Codes

While the three Es of economy, efficiency and effectiveness have been the driving force behind recent government reforms, there has also been a continuing pressure to safeguard the other Es of equity, equality, ethical behaviour and, of course, probity.

New codes proposed, implemented, amended or pending in 1996 included:

- The role of the civil service.
- Recruitment to the civil service.
- Public appointments covering some 8,300 posts in 230 executive NDPBs and 654 NHS bodies.
- Acceptance of appointments outside government by former civil servants.

- Guidance for civil servants on answering Parliamentary Questions.
- A revision of the code of practice on access to government information (pending).

In addition, following a recommendation from the new Public Service Committee of the House of Commons, the Government accepted in principle the need for a Resolution of the House setting out how Ministers should discharge their responsibilities to Parliament in providing full and accurate information, although they disagreed on the wording and (unusually) thought that this was matter which required cross-party consensus.

Civil Service Code

The Chancellor of the Duchy of Lancaster, Roger Freeman, introduced the Civil Service Code on 1 January 1996: 'The Government is committed to maintaining the essential values of the Civil Service, including integrity, political impartiality, and objectively and I believe the new Code is a major contributor to this. It is part of the hugely successful programme of Civil Service reform'. However, the Government had initially opposed the need for a new code, on the grounds that existing framework documents were adequate, when it gave evidence to the Treasury and Civil Service Select Committee (TCSC) in 1994. As early as 1986, the TCSC had argued for a new code and in their November 1994 Report they proposed a draft, rejecting the Government's defence of the current regime. This influential TCSC Report followed on from the well-publicized Report of the Public Accounts Committee earlier in 1994 which highlighted 26 instances where there were 'failings [which] represent a departure from the standards of public conduct which have mainly been established during the past 140 years'. Eventually the Government accepted as a basis for consultation, with amendments, the TCSC's new draft code in the command paper *Taking Forward Continuity and Change* (Cm 2748, 1995). The real history of the birth of the Civil Service Code thus makes the claim that it was an integral part of the civil service reform process somewhat dubious.

In a broader context, the new Civil Service Code can be seen as part of an increasing move towards formulating more specific and articulated, as opposed to the old 'constitutional conventions', rules about how the civil service should operate. It is perhaps inevitable that as almost three-quarters of the civil service becomes structured in its activities through framework documents, business and corporate plans, efficiency plans and the rest of the paraphernalia of documents which govern agencies that there will be a strong tendency to apply the same approach to the core. Such a tendency can also be seen in the adoption by most government departments of some sort of statement of aims and objectives over the past two years (although, ironically, this move has been largely stimulated by the commitment to get 'Investors in People' status for departments, which requires they have such a statement).

Civil Service Commissioners

The Civil Service Code includes an independent appeal procedure by civil servants to the Civil Service Commissioners (CSC) if they feel that they are being asked to do something which violates the Code. The CSC, in their first report since their new enhanced role, indicated that one appeal was currently being investigated (CSC, 1996). The Commissioners also issued a new Recruitment Code for departments and agencies, which included a requirement for them to produce summary information on their recruitment. The CSC will be auditing recruitment activities against the provisions of the Recruitment Code.

Controls and Scrutiny

NAO Reports: English Heritage and National Savings

The need for better rules and controls was demonstrated by two small crises highlighted in National Audit Office (NAO) reports. The first concerned the resignation of the Chief Executive of English Heritage, which is an executive non-departmental public body [NDPB] (NAO, 1996b). In July 1996, Christopher Green resigned from the above post after what the Comptroller and Auditor General, Sir John Bourn, concluded were 'clear failure[s] in the proper conduct of public business' although he accepted that no fraud was involved. The events at English Heritage were said to emphasize 'how important it is that chief executives and other senior staff [in NDPBs] are quickly made fully conversant with all aspects of public sector accountabilities'.

The second incident involved much more substantial sums—the

problems experienced by National Savings Agency (a 'non-ministerial department', which was launched as a 'Next Steps' agency in July 1996) (NAO, 1996c). The NAO identified uncertainties about total liabilities in the investment and ordinary deposits, unexplained balances, improperly matched cash flows and transactions, reconciliation and recording failures. These involved large amounts: for example a £2.1M error in the investment deposits; a £700,000 error in ordinary deposits; a £28M 'overdraft' in an account which could not theoretically be overdrawn. While these were probably accounting systems errors, the NAO pointed out the enormous risk of fraud that such inadequate systems imply and that National Savings could not exclude the possibility of there being actual, as opposed to merely accounting, errors.

Public Services Committee—Ministerial Accountability and Responsibility

The Public Service Committee of the House of Commons, formerly the Treasury and Civil Service Committee (a similar committee was also established in 1996 in the Lord's) made its second report of the parliamentary session covering *Ministerial Accountability and Responsibility*. The preceding investigation had begun as one focusing the role of Ministers in relation to executive agencies (following the Derek Lewis affair in the Home Office/ Prison Service), but the publication of the Scott Report widened the scope of the enquiry and the focus of the final report was on the broad question of Ministers' accountability and responsibility to parliament and the public. There were 34 recommendations mainly suggesting ways of improving existing codes and other arrangements (such as agency framework documents) for spelling out more clearly the roles and responsibilities of Ministers and civil servants. In many ways this echoed the theme mentioned earlier of increasing 'codification' of practices previously governed mainly by convention. The Government rejected the Committee's recommendations to make civil servants more directly accountable to Parliament, something which had been raised before by this Committee's predecessors.

Effects

Size of the Civil Service

The size of the civil service continues to decline, and it is now below a half million. Historically, the non-industrial (i.e. white-collar and scientific) civil service remains a substantial size (see figure 3), while the industrial civil service continues the rapid decline which commenced in the early 1950s and has continued at a remarkably stable pace ever since.

The total decline in the non-industrial civil service since the election of the Conservatives in 1979 has been from 547,000 in 1980 to 458,000 in 1996: 16% or about 1% a year. This overall average, however, masks the more rapid decline in the years of the first two Conservative administrations, the relative stability and even growth in the middle period and the more recent renewed downward trend, currently running at about 3–4% per year.

Development and Training White Paper

A White Paper entitled *Development and Training for Civil Servants—A Framework for Action* was published in July 1996. Some of the key proposals in the White Paper had been trailed by the Deputy PM in a speech in February 1996 in which he proposed: a new drive to get more scientists and engineers into senior posts in the civil service; measures to increase the proportion of graduates with numeracy skills recruited to the fast stream; more direct entries at middle-management level; and more interchange between public

Figure 3. Historic trends in civil service employment.

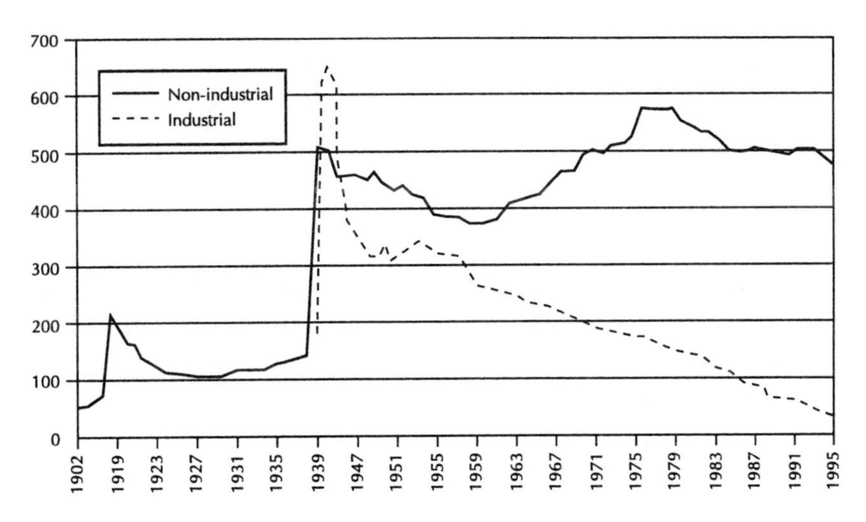

and private sectors. The latter was reinforced by the announcement by OPS in June 1996 of the setting up of 'a panel of senior businessmen to advise on interchange between the Civil Service and industry'.

The White Paper made proposals in three main areas:

- Committing all civil service organizations to achieving Investors in People status.
- Increasing the skills and awareness of civil servants.
- Giving civil servants greater responsibility for their own development and careers.

These relatively modest proposals, which did not include any commitment to increasing resources available for civil service training centrally but instructed departments and agencies to see that 'investment in the training and development of staff should be seen as a priority', are somewhat at odds with the introduction to the White Paper. These talks about globalization and increased international competition, competitive edges, the national skill base, continuous lifetime learning, and the civil service playing 'a vital role in promoting the prosperity of this country and the welfare of its citizens'.

The White Paper also represents another example of the tendency to impose centrally determined policies and priorities on the supposedly 'disaggregated' civil service. Besides the imposition of the necessity for applying for Investors in People status (which is clearly an operational matter and should be left to managers to decide whether it is useful or not), there are also proposals to impose a whole new set of action plans and performance measures:

- 'Departments and agencies will produce by 1 November 1996 their own action plans for implementing the approach set out in this White Paper'.
- 'Departments and agencies will set annual targets, quantified wherever possible, for improving their own performance in these areas; and monitor progress'.
- '[The Government] has identified a range of indicators against which it will seek to monitor progress'.

These are added to the already complex, unco-ordinated requirements placed on departments and agencies for a wide range of reporting procedures to the 'centre' (see Talbot, 1996).

Despite the impression which has been created of the civil service being swamped with recruits from the private sector, the White Paper implicitly acknowledges that this has not yet happened and sets some modest targets for 'improving' the situation: 'at least an additional 50 middle managers [in 1997] and 80 by 31 March 1998' and 'the Government would like to see external recruitment at this general level rise to at least 500 a year by the year 2000'.

Performance

The *1995 Next Steps Review* published in February 1996 covered the work of 109 agencies and the Inland Revenue (IR) and Customs and Excise (C&E). The *Review* included for the first time data presented in historical series about agencies' performance against their key performance indicators (KPIs) as well as, also for the first time, information about running costs.

The *Review* made some remarkably honest analyses of the data, although it maintained the incredible assertion that the increase in the percentage of KPIs 'met' (up to 83% from 80% the previous year) demonstrated the 'success' of agencies. This was despite the fact that its own analysis revealed that some 47% of KPI targets for 1995-96 had been set at levels lower than the previous years outturn, a further 21% at the same level and only 32% at levels higher than the previous outturn. Coupled with the shifting population of agencies and KPIs year-on-year, issues about what is being measured (there is substantial inconsistency in what KPIs seek to record) and concerns about audit, the 'headline' success figure is fairly meaningless. There are undoubtedly agencies which are making significant advances. However, academic analysts have varying views on whether the overall picture is positive or more suspect for exams (see Talbot, 1996). (In a puzzling, minor slip up, the *Review* and accompanying press release claim that it reports and analyses '1,400 key performance indicators'. In fact there are only 961 for 109 agencies plus IR and C&E, as against 765 for 94 agencies plus IR and C&E the previous year, so it is difficult to see where this '1,400' figure comes from.)

The *1995 Review* also grouped together data about similar types of agencies, which presaged a more radical proposed development in reporting agency performance driven by the Deputy PM's office. The intention to introduce some form of agency league table had been signalled at the agency chief executives conference in March 1996 and was greeted with some concern and controversy. In June 1996 the OPS 'Next Steps' Team circulated the text of a paper to chief executives which the Deputy PM was circulating to Ministers entitled 'Indexation of agency performance'. This set out 'options for producing an Index of agency performance'. Option 1 was simply to count the number of KPIs achieved. This was rejected on the grounds that it gives no indication of the seriousness of any over or under achievement; and 'since targets change, [it] does not allow for meaningful year on year comparisons'. Option 2 was to express outturn figures as a percentage of the KPI target and then produce an average score for each agency. This was rejected on the grounds that it would produce distortions and not reflect the priority given to some KPIs over others.

The option favoured involved a two-step process of first developing for each individual KPI a scoring system which might be based on a ratio between the target and outturn figures, and then aggregating the resulting individual KPI 'scores' through a system of weightings to reflect Ministerial priorities and produce a single number indicating the overall 'performance' of each agency.

This is not the place to develop a detailed critique of these proposals, but two points are worth noting. The first is 'why bother'? What is the point of comparing the 'performance' of, say, the Royal Mint (a small industrial organization operating in a largely competitive environment) with that of the Benefits Agency (a massive service delivery operation in an entirely non-competitive environment)? While league tables make some sense in education or health, where potential users (parents, purchasers etc.) might be able to use the data to make choices, the proposed agency league tables have no such obvious use. The approach adopted in the *1995 Review* of grouping data about the performance of similar types of agencies makes more sense than an overall league.

The second major flaw in the proposal is that it is based on accepting the existing 'bundle' of KPIs. These are an extremely mixed bag—some KPIs measure inputs, others processes and the majority outputs. Some don't 'measure' anything at all and are merely 'milestone' targets (for example Customs & Excise's 1995 target to 'implement the change programme').

Unless a great deal of work was done to develop a more systematic approach to the principles of setting KPIs, although not necessarily the detailed application, the existing set of targets would provide an extremely shaky foundation for any form of 'indexation'.

The Future

If the Conservatives are in for a fifth term, it can reasonably be expected that some of the recent trends—privatization of parts of the civil service; performance league tables; more CFQ activities; greater external recruitment etc.—will accelerate. If Labour win the election, some of these trends will be stopped or will slow down, although there is a surprising absence of specific policy statements in this as in some other areas from Labour.

Some of the changes, whoever wins, are unlikely to go away. Pressure for greater codification of our constitutional arrangements as they affect administration of government is likely and will probably eventually include moves to place many of these on a statutory or other legal basis.

The structural changes to the civil service, especially 'Next Steps' and many of the delegations which have taken place, are unlikely to be wholly reversed. An incoming Labour administration may take the opportunity to carry out a full-scale evaluation of the changes so far and pose that most important question—'what works?'—safe in the knowledge that they do not have to take responsibility for any negative findings from such an investigation and that they could reap considerable benefits from the positive recommendations it might produce. Certainly, given their commitments on taxation, spending and services the pressure for producing 'more for less' is unlikely to diminish under Labour even if the focus changes.

The structural reforms to the constitution which Labour proposes will have far-reaching consequences for public administration which have hardly been touched upon in recent debates. The advent of some form of Scottish and Welsh tiers of government, for example, will pose major issues about the forms of accountability and control of civil service bodies, NDPBs and other central government organizations within their territories. We already have one separate civil service within the UK's territorial boundaries (in Northern Ireland)—would we also create separate Welsh and Scottish services? Would some of the major current 'national' agencies (for example Benefits,

Employment, Prisons [in Wales], Inland Revenue and Customs & Excise) also be disaggregated and devolved along with other administrative units? Such changes might have other consequential organizational impacts. For example, devolving responsibility for Welsh Prisons (as is already the case in Scotland) would pose the issue of breaking up the Prison Service on regional lines and raise the possibility of a unified 'corrections' agency incorporating prison and probation services at a regional level, a possibility raised seriously by the former Director General (Lewis, 1996). ■

References

Civil Service Commissioners (1996), *Civil Service Commissioners' Annual Report 1995-1996* (Office of the Civil Service Commissioners, Basingstoke); and *Civil Service Commissioners Recruitment Code.*

Lewis, D. (1996), Speech at the University of Glamorgan as part of the Public Sector Management 2000 seminar (October 1996).

National Audit Office (1996c), *HMSO Trading Fund Accounts 1995—Report by the Comptroller and Auditor General* (NAO, London).

National Audit Office (1996b), *Report by the Comptroller and Auditor General on the Resignation of the Chief Executive of English Heritage* (NAO, London).

National Audit Office (1996c), *National Savings Agency: Financial Reporting—Report by the Comptroller and Auditor General* (NAO, London).

Prime Minister (1996), *The Citizen's Charter—Five Years On*, Cm 3370 (HMSO, London).

Talbot, C. (1996), *Ministers and Agencies: Control, Performance and Accountability* (CIPFA, London).

5 Northern Ireland

Michael Connolly

University of Glamorgan Business School

The story of 1996 is defined by the ending of the IRA cease-fire and the efforts by various parties to find a way to restore it and sustain the peace process. This took place against growing sectarianism within Northern Ireland society, something which made the search for a permanent cease-fire and settlement more important and yet more difficult to achieve. This occurred in the latter half of the year and was triggered by the marching season. While there were a number of serious acts of loyalist violence, the loyalist paramilitaries maintained their cease-fire, despite considerable pressure to end it. And, despite all, the talking between the British and Irish governments and the main parties within Northern Ireland continues. 1996 may be seen in retrospect to be a transition year, leading either to peace and a settlement, or to greater violence. However, it is likely that we will have to wait until the outcome of a British general election before we can clearly see which option will prevail.

The report from Senator Mitchell and his colleagues appeared early in 1996. The British Government accepted it, but with the additional caveat of an election to a forum which would pave the way to negotiations. This reaction was used by the IRA to justify their violence and they ended their cease-fire on 9 February 1996 by bombing Canary Wharf in London. Further IRA violence in Britain, on the European mainland and in both parts of Ireland occurred throughout the year. The blame for the breakdown in the cease-fire, together with the attempts to resurrect the peace process, reflected the political divisions. In a statement in February 1996, the IRA condemned the British Government, arguing that Sinn Fein had been promised meaningful talks, which had not happened as yet. The nationalist community, both north and south of the border, appeared to sympathize with this. While strongly rejecting the IRA violence and their attempt to justify the bombing, the Irish Government and the SDLP both maintained that the British Government had dragged its feet over inter-party talks. However, the continued IRA violence brought tensions within the broader nationalist community. In June 1996, the Manchester bomb in which over 200 civilians were injured in an attack on the city centre, together with the IRA murder of a police officer in the Republic of Ireland, put increasing pressure on the Provisionals. The latter killing, in particular, had an enormous impact on Irish opinion and John Bruton, the Irish Prime Minister, indicated unhappiness at his Government's continuing dialogue with the IRA, while President Clinton, and other prominent Irish-Americans, declared their irritation over continued violence and sought to increase pressure on Gerry Adams.

On the other hand, the unionists argued that their suspicious attitude to the IRA and their, and the British Government's, cautious approach to peace had been vindicated. A major concern throughout the year was to ensure that the loyalist paramilitaries did not react to the IRA violence by ending their cease-fire. In fact while there was evidence of loyalist involvement in murder, attempted murder and other similar activities, the formal cease-fires held. Those political parties associated with the loyalist paramilitaries were rewarded with a meeting on 22 July 1996 with the British Prime Minister and remained within the talks process.

In the early part of the year, there were frantic efforts to revive the cease-fire. A date for talks (10 June 1996) was announced (something which appeared to met one of Sinn Fein's key demands), but this was predicated on the outcome of an election to the Forum and adherence to the Mitchell principles. In essence, this involved the IRA restoring their cease-fire and any such announcement being seen as 'genuine' and 'permanent'. Central to this is the 'decommissioning' of paramilitary weapons. Unless progress is made on this topic unionists will not accept an IRA cease-fire as genuine, arguing that if the IRA is serious about a cease-fire being permanent, there is no reason for them to retain their weapons. And, if the unionists cannot be persuaded to meet Sinn Fein in negotiations, the process will have no future. The IRA rejects these demands, arguing that in effect this is a requirement that they surrender. And the wider nationalist community believes that it is a step too far for two reasons. First, weapons traditionally have not been handed over, but quietly buried and forgotten about: in other words decommissioning reflects a lack of understanding of the republican tradition. Second, there remains a fear of loyalist violence in the nationalist community, where many, especially in some of the working class areas in Belfast, with a long history of distrust of the police, see the IRA as their main protection.

Forum

The election (using one of the most innovative electoral systems ever used in the UK) for the 110-member Forum took place at the end of May 1996, with the Ulster Unionist Party (UUP) securing 30 seats, the SDLP, 21 and the DUP, 24. However, and crucially, Sinn Fein's vote increased to 15.5% and they won 17 seats, making them the fourth largest party. The various parties associated with the loyalist paramilitaries won sufficient votes to be involved, as did a number of other fringe parties.

The negotiating talks opened on 10 June with an acrimonious row over the responsibilities of George Mitchell, the American ex-Senator, as chair of the negotiating body. The DUP wanted Mitchell excluded, but the UUP finally accepted a reduced role for him. It was argued that this unionist debate over Mitchell's position was one of the factors propelling the IRA towards violence. The *Irish Times* (17 June) indicated that the lack of progress at the talks at Stormont Castle strengthened the Republican view that the talks were not worth entering. In any case, because of the continuing IRA violence, Sinn Fein were not invited to the talks, and refused to take their seats in the Forum.

Marches

The attempts at securing peace were dramatically affected by serious violence over Orange Order marches, especially the proposed rerouting of an Orange parade in Portadown in early July. The then RUC Chief Constable decided not to allow an Orange march to proceed through a mainly Catholic area (the Garvaghy Road) in the town. Loyalist fury was intense and considerable social disorder followed. Northern Ireland was brought close to breakdown as loyalists throughout Northern Ireland sought to support the marchers. The upshot was that, after four days, the march was allowed to proceed down the Garavghy Road, with the police forcibly removing protesting local residents. In turn, that generated intense nationalist anger and violence, with a bomb, the first in Northern Ireland since the cease-fire, being set off in Enniskillen. The justification offered by the Chief Constable for his reversal was that the alternative was major disorder and the possible attack on the Garavghy Road residents.

The Portadown incident had a series of tragic consequences:

•Relations between the two communities sunk to new depths.
•The British and Irish governments had a very public falling out.
•The moderate leader of the Catholic church declared that he felt betrayed by the reversal decision.
•Suspicions between the police and the minority community grew.
•The leader of main unionist party, David Trimble, was widely attacked by opinion in Britain (though not by the British Government, something which itself added to nationalist suspicion).
•The peace process stumbled, without quite falling down completely.

The SDLP withdrew from the Forum on 14 July 1996, leaving the unionist parties present alone in this body. Sinn Fein, who had been out of favour with the Irish Government since the Canary Wharf bombing and later the murder of the Irish police officer, were involved in talks with officials and the Fianna Fail leader, Bertie Ahern (16 July). More importantly the attempt to persuade the Catholic community that there was a point in politics and that the state was reformable was dealt a severe blow. To quote Mary Holland 'nobody should doubt the effect of the events of the past week have had on the Catholic community in deepening mistrust of the British Government and strengthening the extremists' hands' (*Observer*, 14 July). Garret Fitzgerald, a moderate nationalist and former Prime Minister of Ireland, declared that 'It is not easy for a government by a single act to abdicate its own moral authority, undermine confidence in the police, insult church leaders of the four principal faiths, and boost the acceptability of a terrorist organization'. But, he said, the decision on Drumcree did all of that (Independent, 13 July). Mo Mowlan, Labour Shadow Secretary of State for Northern Ireland, joined in the criticism of the Government over its handling of Drumcree. There were calls for the resignation of the Secretary of State by British newspapers and columnists, for example Anthony Bevins in the *Independent* on 17 July, again a comparatively rare phenomena.

In the western counties of Fermanagh and Tyrone boycotts by Catholics against Protestant shopkeepers were initiated. The *Guardian* (23 August) reported that some six weeks after the Drumcree incident these were still being maintained, though at a lower level. Other examples of continued sectarian tension include persistent Loyalist picketing of (with some associated violence) Catholic church-goers at Harryville, Ballymena (something which was condemned by Ian Paisley), and the burning of schools and churches in various parts of Northern Ireland.

It was obvious that a longer term solution to managing controversial marches had to be found. After initially refusing to hold a meeting of the Anglo-Irish Intergovernmental Conference, the Secretary of State confirmed a meeting in the Commons. Again he also agreed to an independent review of marches, having rejected this idea earlier. Ms Mowlan wrote to Sir Patrick on 17 July 1995 asking 'what preparations are being made to establish a mechanism for discussions between the community groups in advance of the marches next year?' In February 1996, she had written with proposals for an independent body to give advice on mediating and the routing of marches. Sir Patrick replied that operational handling of parades were a matter for the Chief Constable. An argument against such a body would be its relationship with the RUC. Could the police set aside its recommendations? If so, what would be the impact on its status? If not, would that place the police in very difficult situations? In any case an independent review committee, under Sir Peter North, vice-chancellor of Oxford University, was set up to examine the parades issue and is due to report in February 1997.

One solution to the parades problem is to encourage local residents and marching organizations to negotiate arrangements. In the case of Drumcree one of the issues raised was the inability of the residents and the Orange Order leadership, including David Trimble, to negotiate a solution. While the residents expressed their willingness to meet, David Trimble indicated that he was unwilling to meet with what he regarded as a Sinn Fein front organization, lead by a convicted republican. However, his position was somewhat undermined when it was revealed that he met and negotiated with a leading loyalist, Billy Wright, who in the words of the *Belfast Telegraph*, was 'known to be influential in loyalist paramilitary circles', especially the Ulster Volunteer Force (UVF). Trimble's justification for this meeting was 'exceptional circumstances', and the continuing loyalist paramilitaries' cease-fire (though the violence included the murder of a Catholic taxi-driver in Portadown). Nevertheless, it prompted accusations by the SDLP, Alliance Party, Sinn Fein and the Irish Government of double standards. The meeting caused a spilt within unionism, with other unionist leaders, including Ian Paisley, indicating that they would not meet with loyalist paramilitaries. In addition a number of prominent British politicians, including Mo Mowlan and David Steel, criticised Trimble by implication. Mo Mowlan declared that 'the consent to comply with the rule of law did not exist with the Portadown Orange lodge and they were not encouraged to do so by constitutional politicians and they should have done'. Indeed, the Rev Martin Smyth, an MP and then head of the Orange Order, was quoted as stating that he condoned the breaking of the law (*Belfast Telegraph*, 8 July).

The overall judgement in one paper was that Northern Ireland had barely matured since 1970s (*Belfast Telegraph*, 15 July 1996). Not surprisingly, the next major Loyalist march, which took place in Londonderry, a predominantly nationalist town, in August 1996 was seen as a matter of great concern. An attempt to find an acceptable compromise failed, and the Secretary of State rerouted the Orange march. Nevertheless the march went off relatively peacefully, though there was some violence in the town and in some other towns as marchers returned home. In many of these towns the issue was one of majority Catholic populations refusing to allow Loyalist marches through without negotiations first. The slogan 'no consent, no march' became a new rallying cry. The negotiations which did take place involved Sinn Fein, strengthening their hand in the wider negotiations.

Cease-fire

The talks ground on. Both governments were clearly frustrated by the lack of progress. Towards the end of the year a further initiative to promote an IRA cease-fire was undertaken by John Hume and Gerry Adams, who wrote to the Prime Minister making a number of proposals. Both the Taoiseach and Prime Minister agreed that Sinn Fein's participation in the talks require a 'credible cease-fire', adherence to the Mitchell principles and the ground rules for the all-inclusive talks. Where they disagree is on paragraph 8 of the ground-rules which state that the parties must establish a commitment to exclusively peaceful means. The Irish Government believe that if the IRA call an unequivocal cease-fire in 'words that are believable', and provided that there was nothing done that was inconsistent with this cease-fire or the Mitchell principles, then Sinn Fein could join the talks. John Bruton declared that a credible IRA cease-fire in December could mean Sinn Fein joining the multi-party talks by the end of January 1997. But the British Prime Minister declared that intelligence reports and not passage of time would determine his judgement, and thus the timing of Sinn Fein's entry into talks (*Irish Times*, 9 December).

RUC

There were important developments associated with policing in Northern Ireland. On 8 March 1996, the Secretary of State sacked two prominent members of the Police Authority for Northern Ireland—the Chair, David Cook, and Chris Ryder. Both had adopted a high profile in arguing that the RUC needed to reform itself if it was to become more acceptable to the Catholic minority. Ryder, in an article in the *Sunday Observer* on 10 March 1996, argued that two issues were central, namely the flying of the Union flag (especially on 12 July when Orange lodges are marching) and the oath of allegiance to the crown. Ryder argued that both of these contributed to the perception among the minority community that the RUC was not impartial. However, these views were rejected by the majority on the Police Authority and on 21 February there was a no-confidence vote in Cook and Ryder and a dozen members threatened to resign. The Secretary of State was therefore forced to sack Cook and Ryder. Ryder asserted that this decision sent 'the wrong signal about the possibility of change at a time when the concepts of accommodation, reconciliation and tolerance...needed to be rigorously defended' (*Observer*, 10 March).

The Government published a White Paper on the RUC on 1 May 1996. Sir John Wheeler, Minister at the Northern Ireland Office, was criticised by nationalists when he declared that a change in the name of the RUC was akin to a dismantling of the United Kingdom. 'As long as the people of Northern Ireland see themselves as citizens of the UK, they are entitled to have symbols and institutions which reflect that status' he declared. Issues such as the RUC's name, oath and flags have been left to the forthcoming negotiations. The White Paper recommends the transfer of control of the RUC's £600M budget from the Police Authority to the Chief Constable.

The violence stemming from Drumcree had its effect on the Police Authority with a member of the Authority putting down a vote of no confidence in the Chief Constable (19 July). The vote, in fact, was not taken, but the *Belfast Telegraph* indicated in a report on the 16 July 1996 that at least three members of the Authority were considering resigning over the handling of Drumcree. The chair of the Authority, Pat Armstrong, admitted that real damage had been done to the community's confidence in the RUC (*Belfast Telegraph*, 20 July). The Chief Constable had announced his resignation on 21 May 1996 and he was replaced by Ronnie Flanagan, formerly a senior officer with the RUC.

Economy

The return to violence prompted pessimism on the economy. The July 1996 violence, with the bombing of the hotels in Fermanagh, impacted on the tourist industry. Investment is expected to fall over the next 12 months (*Financial Times*, 27 November).

The public expenditure settlement announced by the Secretary of State in December reflected the ending of the cease-fire. The planned public expenditure for the next three years is £822M in 1997-98, £826M in 1998-99 and £836M in 1999-2000. For the first time since direct rule, there will be a cut in expenditure, since the growth forecast falls 1.8% short of the predicted inflation rate. The gap in public expenditure per head between Northern Ireland and England has narrowed in recent years, while the differential in favour of Scotland has grown. The budget settlement saw cutbacks in housing, education and training, something which brought considerable criticism on the Secretary of State. He justified his decision by arguing that it was necessary to restore the law and order budget. The ending of the cease-fire and incidents such as Drumcree generated extra burdens on the security forces. Hence almost £12M extra is being provided for security and compensation, with an additional 377M allocated to the Police Authority over the three year period up to 2000. ■

6 Scotland

Arthur Midwinter

University of Strathclyde

As the debate about devolution is becoming politically important, the Scottish public finances are being closely examined. The country has a high proportion of public employment, and the Scottish Office has estimated that the Scottish fiscal deficit in 1995 was £8.6 billion. This level of fiscal deficit has been challenged by the Scottish National Party which claims that, since 1979, Scotland has a combined surplus of £91 billion. Arthur Midwinter gives the background to Scotland's fiscal problems and suggests ways forward for the new government.

This chapter is concerned mainly with public expenditure under the control of the Secretary of State for Scotland, which accounts for 48% of General Government Expenditure (GGE) in Scotland. Some 28% is social security spending. Within the Public Expenditure Survey (PES), framework the Secretary of State for Scotland's programme (known as the Scotland Programme) falls into two categories. The Scottish Office Block is determined on a formula basis, where there is a requirement for a standard policy across Great Britain or the UK, and applies to changes in GGE provision for comparable expenditure in Whitehall departments (Heald, 1994). Within this total, the Secretary of State is free to pursue Scottish priorities, but differences tend to be marginal (Keating, 1985). Non-block spending is negotiated on a programme basis with the Treasury. The Scottish block comprises 96% of the Scotland Programme.

In the Thatcher years, spending priorities fell in areas outwith the Scotland programme. The Major Government since 1990 has been more sympathetic to Scotland, developing a modest strategy to recognize Scotland's distinctive place in the Union (Scottish Office, 1993). The squeeze on public spending in recent years, however, has led to planned reductions since 1994-95. Scottish Office spending rose in 1992-93 and

Table 1. The Scottish block; real terms (£M, 1994-95).

	90-91 outturn	*91-92 outturn*	*92-93 outturn*	*93-94 outturn*	*94-95 outturn*	*95-96 estimated outturn*	*96-97 plans*	*97-98 plans*	*98-99 plans*
Central government expenditure									
Industry, enterprise and training	291	587	555	545	598	593	566	538	531
Roads and transport	240	230	251	248	259	226	217	193	202
Housing	325	374	360	340	344	188	228	229	230
Scottish Homes loan repayments							-76		
Other environmental services	95	106	91	62	58	68	413	372	352
Law, order and protective services	357	392	411	438	434	442	444	436	424
Education and sport	422	516	588	1,126	1,208	1,234	1,245	1,240	1,217
Arts and libraries	36	38	56	59	76	78	73	71	68
Health	3,445	3,467	3,846	3,847	3,948	3,996	4,004	4,004	4,005
Social work services	19	35	40	41	44	47	55	55	53
Other public services	158	177	175	173	175	179	161	156	151
Total central government expenditure (including public corporations)	5,388	6,102	6,373	6,879	7,142	7.051	7,329	7,295	7,234
Local authority capital expenditure	939	917	929	899	904	964	579	570	557
of which housing (HRA)	232	224	152	174	188	283	170	166	163
Police	13	8	13	8	9	15	17	16	14
Fire	10	10	10	13	10	7	13	12	12
Provision to match receipts from ESF and ERDF	42	31	38	134	148	159	160	166	181
Central government support to local authorities current expenditure	4,709	5,385	5,551	5,377	5,401	5,352	5,096	4,879	4,728
Total Scottish Block	11,077	12,433	12,885	13,288	13,594	13,164	13,164	12,928	12,728

1993-94, but this was mainly due to increased provision for local authority grants to sustain first the community charge and then the council tax. In 1993-94, the further education sector was transferred to the Scottish Office's responsibility from local government, and care in the community from Social Security to local government (see table 1). During this period, Ministers made spending on health, industry, and law and order priorities, whether in terms of allowing growth in real terms or maintaining programmes in the recent period of retrenchment. As in the 1980s, local government has faced the greatest spending reductions with grants falling from 42.5% of spending in 1990, to 40.6% in 1995, and a further fall to 37.3% in place for 1998-99. Local authority capital expenditure also faces reductions, although government strategy assumes that this shortfall will in part be compensated for by the private sector through the Private Finance Initiative (see table 2). The Scottish Office continues to seek improvements in efficiency and value-for-money as required by the Government.

The Fiscal Deficit Issue

Political concern about the Scottish fiscal deficit has grown since the devolution issue arose in the 1970s. The Government's approach excludes any income from North Sea oil, and apportions a share of the British fiscal deficit to Scotland. Not surprisingly, this action was challenged by the Scottish National Party, who questioned the assumptions over oil revenues and the treatment of privatization income. The Scottish Office (1996) duly responded by concluding:

The estimates themselves should be regarded as indicative rather than precise. In addition, a variation in the choice of alternative plausible assumptions would inevitably change the precise arithmetic of the fiscal deficit. However, it would not be sufficient to alter the broad orders of magnitude or to invalidate the principal conclusions reached here. In 1994-95, Scotland had a substantial fiscal deficit, which, depending on whether no oil revenues or all revenues (and output) were allocated (and on whether or not privatization proceeds were included) ranged from 14% to 8.5% of Gross Domestic Product at market prices.

The SNP response, drafted by two former Scottish Office economists,

Table 2. Programme shares of Scottish Office block (%).

	1990	*1995*	*1998*
Industry	2.6	4.5	4.2
Roads and transport	2.2	1.7	1.6
Housing	2.9	1.4	1.8
OES	0.9	0.5	2.8
Law OPs	3.2	3.5	3.3
Education	3.8	9.4	9.6
Arts and libraries	0.3	0.6	0.5
Health	31.1	30.3	31.4
Social work	0.2	0.4	0.4
Other public services	1.4	1.4	1.2
LA capital	8.5	7.3	4.4
ESF/ERDF	0.4	1.2	1.4
Central grants	42.5	40.6	37.3

was to apply the Government's own methodology over time, back into the period of fiscal surplus for the UK, to show that by these calculations, the Scottish fiscal surplus was £81 billion since 1979! They then built in their own assumptions over oil income, and increased the surplus to £91 billion. Such exercises do not really help to understand the Scottish public finances. Scotland's expenditure relativities are well established in independent research, showing a spending level of around 20% above the UK average, and 30% for the programmes to be devolved to a Scottish parliament (Heald, 1994). Even if the UK public finances were in balance, Scotland would still be benefiting from fiscal transfers, consuming 10.3% of the UK public expenditure with 8.8% of the population, and raising 8.9% of the revenues or 9.6% if all the revenues for North Sea Oil are included. There would, therefore, be a loss of resources from the Scottish Office on independence, irrespective of the UK budget position.

Problems with Labour's Agenda

These fiscal transfers could also become a problem for Scotland in the event of a Labour victory leading to the establishment of a Scottish parliament. The Scottish parliament will be financed by an assigned budget, based on the current position, with tax-varying powers of up to 3p on income tax (Midwinter and McVicar, 1996). Some advocates of a Scottish parliament suggest a new needs assessment study is necessary to secure stable funding under devolution, and the present Scottish relativity, at 130% of the UK average, could be under threat:

Although it would be unwise to guess at the detailed outcomes of the Expenditure Needs Assessment Exercise, the Scottish Parliament would have to recognize the probability that the relative need index would be lower than the actual relative. In such an eventuality, the design of the formula for a concentrated reduction of block grant over a period of years would be a critical issue (Heald, 1990).

It is likely that such a shift would be politically unacceptable in Scotland, requiring considerably greater cutbacks than under the present fiscal squeeze. The last such exercise suggested Scotland's spending was 8–9% higher than its needs, although: 'The results are by no means final. The departments who have carried out the study agree that the methods of assessment are a long way from providing a wholly definitive means of expressing the relative expenditure needs of the four countries' (HM Treasury, 1976).

The key point is that despite the political rhetoric about Scotland's spending advantage being justified on grounds of higher need, the current formula is not based on any precise and rigorous assessment, but simply on historic spending with marginal changes reflecting population shares. This position rests on its political acceptability to the British Cabinet. Once these spending powers pass to a devolved parliament, there can be no guarantee this approach will continue.

The Labour Party is being very cautious about its spending plans, making few firm expenditure commitments. This was put neatly by columnist Ian MacWhirter writing in the *Scotsman* on 21 November 1996:

Brown's case is essentially this. Do not believe anything any Labour politician says. Promises, pledges, hints and words are all so much hot air. Teachers can forget their sabbaticals. Scotland can forget about the cost of setting up its

Parliament; the multiple referendums will have to be financed by flag days, as will the minimum wage. The only things that are kosher are in the Labour manifesto. These amount to the very minimal promises on the back of that credit card that Labour distributed after the conference. Class sizes will be cut by abolishing the assisted places scheme. Youth employment will be abolished by the windfall tax on the privatized utilities. Waiting lists will be reduced thanks to cuts in NHS bureaucracy. And that is that. Read my lips says Brown: 'No new money'.

There are few assisted places in Scotland, and even if the bureaucracy in NHS could be eliminated, it would not release very much to reduce waiting lists. In short, Labour is promising little.

By contrast, it is more specific about reforming resource allocation mechanisms. It will end the internal market in the National Health Service (NHS), which has never fully developed in Scotland anyway, looking often like an alien Thatcherite imposition, and irrelevant in rural Scotland in particular. This would no doubt have popular support in Scotland, where scepticism of the market-based approach to health care remains high.

In local government, Labour promises to end capping and compulsory competitive tendering; to return business rates to local government; and to expand the Account's Commission role to auditing 'quality' as well as value for money. The economic rationale for capping and the nationalization of the business rate was always unconvincing. Labour has however already promised to consult with business before returning the taxes to local control. The independent evidence remains overwhelming that business rates had little effect on investment and employment decisions (Birdsey and Webb, 1984; Crawford and Dawson, 1982; Cuthbertson *et al.*, 1979). Returning non-domestic rates to local government would bring important gains in the accountability and autonomy of local government, raising the locally controlled element of revenues from 13% to nearly 30% in Scotland, thus reducing the gearing effect of high grant.

The prospects for quality audit are less convincing. Labour appears to have the same naive belief in the capacity of financial techniques and technology to analyse quality or efficiency. At best, such indicators are benchmarks which assist political judgements. They are not precise, not foolproof, and not politically neutral. They require interpretation and value judgements.

The big gap in Labour's agenda is its failure to address underfunding. This is not simply a Scottish issue, but has had a bigger impact in Scotland because the local government reorganization occurred in a context of underfunding. By underfunding I mean that the Government has been feeding in wholly unconvincing efficiency assumptions over pay and the costs of the new local authority system, thus failing to provide sufficient resources to fund existing programmes, while claiming their financial policy does not require cuts in service delivery. Such a position is untenable and Labour must address it if they wish to be taken seriously as practising sound finance in the public sector. Unfortunately, they seem to be seeking to avoid spending commitments for fear of being attacked as a 'tax-and-spend' party. Sound finance does not only mean controlling spending, it also means providing adequate finance for the programmes you wish to provide. Labour must face up to this issue, or their claim to defend the welfare state will be seen through in Scotland. ■

References

Birdsey, P. and Webb, T. (1984), Why the rate burden on business is a cause for concern. *National Westminster Bank Quarterly Review* (February).

Crawford, M. and Dawson, D. (1982), Are rates the right tax for local government? *Lloyds Bank Review*, No. 145.

Cuthbertson, K. C., Foreman-Peck, J. and Griapos, P. A. (1979), Local authority fiscal policy and urban employment. *Applied Economics, 11*.

Heald, D. (1990), *Financing a Scottish Parliament—Options for Debate* (Scottish Foundation for Economic Research, Glasgow).

Heald, D. (1994), Territorial public expenditure in the United Kingdom. *Public Administration, 72*, pp. 147–176.

Keating, M. (1985), Bureaucracy devolved. *Times Education Supplement, Scotland* (5 April).

Midwinter, A. and McVicar, M. (1996), Uncharted waters? Problems of financing Labour's Scottish parliament. *Public Money & Management, 16*, 2, pp. 47–52.

Scottish Office (1993), *Serving Scotland's Needs: The Government's Expenditure Plans 1993-4 to 1995-6*, Cmnd 2214 (HMSO, Edinburgh).

Scottish Office (1995), *Government Expenditure and Revenues in Scotland* (HMSO,

Edinburgh).

Scottish Office (1996), *Serving Scotland's Needs: The Government's Expenditure Plans, 1996-7 to 1998-9*, Cmnd 3214 (HMSO, Edinburgh).

Treasury, HM (1976), *The Assessment of Public Expenditure Needs in England, Scotland, Wales and Northern Ireland* (London).

7 Wales

Alys Thomas

University of Glamorgan Business School

A number of events and developments brought Wales into national focus in 1996. Early in the year the Sea Empress oil-tanker disaster raised important environmental and economic issues for west Wales, while the announcement of the Korean Lucky Goldstar company investment near Newport provided an apparent vindication of the inward investment strategy of the Welsh Development Agency and the Welsh Office. The opening of a second Severn Crossing provided another boost for economic development along the M4 corridor. In political terms, the face of local government was transformed as the unitary authorities came into being on 1 April and the debate surrounding Welsh devolution stepped up a gear with the proximity of the general election.

The Economy

Although Wales has the second lowest per capital Gross Domestic Product (GDP) of all the regions of the UK (15% below the UK average in 1994), the Government has claimed success in diversifying the Welsh economy and in attracting inward investment (Welsh Office, 1996). A Welsh Office white paper, *The Competitiveness of Wales*, asserted that the Welsh economy has particular strengths based on two main features: the encouragement of indigenous business, and its success in attracting inward investment from overseas. With regard to the latter it argued that this had contributed to the diversification of the Welsh industrial base and that, with only 5% of the population of the UK, Wales has consistently attracted 10–20% of all inward investment projects. Within the first three months of 1996 over 2,000 new jobs were announced with Korean and Japanese projects in south Wales, but the real coup came in July with the announcement that a Korean firm, Lucky Goldstar, wanted to set up a plant near Newport. The project is estimated to create 6,100 jobs, representing the largest inward investment project ever in Britain. It amounted to almost 50% more in terms of jobs created by 53 new company investments in the previous year (*Western Mail*, 10 July 1976). Nevertheless, this investment was not free of controversy. It was alleged that the Welsh Development Agency (WDA) had given a grant of £76M to Lucky Goldstar which would deplete the land reclamation budget (*Independent*, 14 July 1996). The Secretary of State for Wales announced an increase of £37M to the annual budget of the WDA in November 1996 (*Hansard*, 2 December 1996). Furthermore, concerns were being expressed in north and mid Wales that the bulk of new inward investment was being focused on the M4 corridor and other parts of Wales were losing out (Thomas, 1996).

The white paper acknowledged that parts of Wales, including the upper south Wales valleys and rural west Wales, remained unemployment blackspots. In March 1996, the Secretary of State for Wales had published *A Working Countryside for Wales*, a white paper for rural Wales which encompassed a wide-ranging review of the Government's rural policies. The paper reaffirmed the central role of the Development Board for Rural Wales (DBRW) and the WDA. The former has been set a target for 1996-97 of creating or safeguarding 1,100 jobs with existing mid Wales employers and of creating 400 by new investment into the area, of which not less than 30% should be outside Powys. The WDA has been set a target of safeguarding or creating 12,500 jobs in Wales, of which not less than 20% should be outside the eastern M4 and A55 corridors. The paper stressed the need for rural diversification, for sustaining local commerce such as village shops and post offices and the importance of developing such initiatives as 'teleworking'.

However, rural Wales fell under two extraordinary blows during the course of the year. In February, the *Sea Empress* oil-tanker struck rocks as it was approaching Milford Haven and lost an estimated 73,450 tonnes of oil, less than 3,000 tonnes of which were recovered. The impact of this on the economy of south west Wales looked ominous, tourism being a major employer in an area hard hit in recent years by defence closures. A report by Cardiff Business School calculated a loss of between £21M and £30M to the local economy during the year, and a loss of between 1,100 and 1,400 jobs during the holiday season. Tourism was worth £1.8 billion to the local economy in 1994 and employed 9% of the population.

Commercial fishing and shellfish fisheries, worth £5M to the economy, and agriculture were also affected (Mihinnick, 1996). Furthermore, the BSE crisis has hit rural communities hard—12% of the total UK beef herd is in Wales and beef is worth £22M to the Welsh economy. A report by Cardiff Business School and the Institute of Rural Studies at Aberystwyth calculated that approximately 2,000 jobs could be lost as a result of the BSE crisis (*Hansard*, 13 November 1996).

Public Expenditure

The Welsh Secretary of State announced his overall spending plans for the Welsh Office over a three-year period on 26 November, coinciding with the Budget (see table 1). The point was made that the Government had again recognized the need for higher per capita spending in Wales than in England and the block grant formula had applied to this end (Welsh Office press release, 26 November 1996). However, in the run up to the budget it had been reported that the Secretary of state had to fight to make a case for the preservation of the Barnett formula.

The Secretary of State for Wales announced his breakdown of spending for 1997-98 in mid December, the most notable increase being a rise of £94M (around 4%) in health spending. However, *Tai Cymru* (Housing for Wales) received a reduction in capital provision from £88.8M to £60M; £566M was made directly available for education in Wales, including £177M for further education and £237M for higher education. Nevertheless, the Chief Executive of the Welsh Higher and Further Education Councils expressed the view that the settlement in Wales for post-16 education compared badly with that announced by the Chancellor for England (*Western Mail*, 13 December 1996). Economic

Table 1. Welsh Office spending plans (£M).

	1997/98	*1998/90*	*1999/2000*
Cash terms	6900	6800	6900
Real terms (1995-96 prices)	6600	6450	6340
Percentage change	-0.9%	-2.3%	-1.6%

Source: Welsh Office (November 1996).

development saw an increase, the Secretary of State identifying it as priority, a rise of £37M to the annual budget of the WDA had been announced in November 1996 (*Hansard*, 2 December 1996) and it made clear that increases to the WDA were with a view to covering additional expenditure with relation to the Lucky Goldstar investment (*Hansard*, 12 December 1996). The Secretary of State indicated that the extension of PFI would allow 'the money available to go even further' and it is anticipated that capital spending of around £350M will be generated over three years (*Hansard*, 12 December 1996).

With regard to local authority spending, aggregate external finance was set at £2,578, an increase of 2.6%. This represents £844 for each person in Wales. Total standard spending was set at £2, 931M, including £169M for community care and £341M for police authorities. The Secretary of State also announced an £18.3M 'damping' scheme to ensure that increases in council tax should not exceed 15% (*Hansard*, 12 December 1996). The Opposition argued that the settlement for local government was inadequate and that sharp increases in council tax would be inevitable. In this they were supported by the Welsh Local Government Association, which expressed concern that it would have serious effects on services already coping with the problems of reorganization (*Western Mail*, 13 December 1996).

Devolution

A new Labour Party document *Preparing for a New Wales*, which fleshed out the principles outlined in 1995, was approved by the Welsh Labour Party conference in May 1996. The document emerged after Labour's 1995 proposals had come under heavy criticism from groups both within and outside the Party and reflected attempts to meet some of the concerns voiced over the course of the year. With regard to the actual work of the Welsh assembly, the report focused on economic development, European affairs, health and broadcasting and further indicated that the role of the high spending executive bodies created by primary legislation should be reviewed and, if necessary, reformed.

Labour asserted that there would remain 'an important and clearly defined role for the chief executives of these bodies and their staff' in implementing the policies of the assembly and advising on policy

Table 2. High-spending Welsh quangos identified by Labour (total gross expenditure 1994-95, £M).

Countryside Council for Wales	£21.23
Curriculum and Assessment Authority for Wales	£7.043
Development Board for Rural Wales	£27.152
Further Education Funding Council for Wales	£172.5
Land Authority for Wales	£23.045
Tai Cymru (Housing for Wales)	£139.575
Wales Tourist Board	£14.358
Welsh Development Agency	£157.066

Source: Cabinet Office (1995).

development, but with an assembly in place they would function in a 'publicly accountable atmosphere'.

There was some discussion within the Labour Party about whether *Shaping the Vision* in fact alludes to specified powers for primary legislation relating to certain issues such as local government reorganization, the Welsh language and reforming the quangos (see table 2). *Preparing for a New Wales* provided a measure of clarification on the latter issue stating that 'the Commission has now accepted that there is a need for these defined powers to be devolved and that they should be stated in the Act establishing the Assembly'.

The method of election to the Welsh assembly has been a prominent subject of debate, the original proposal to retain the first-past-the-post system having been criticized on the grounds that Labour appeared to be looking to its own interests in that the system would be likely to return a majority based on the Party's strength in south Wales. It was also felt that an assembly returned by a form of proportional representation (PR) would better reflect the pluralistic nature of Welsh society. *Preparing for a New Wales* did not directly tackle the issue of PR, but the criticisms about Labour domination levelled at its omission in *Shaping the Vision* provided a significant sub-text to much of the document. It stated that the assembly would 'move away from the more negative aspects of the Westminster Parliament' and operate on a 'consensual basis' through an internal structure resembling a local authority committee system and further proposed to establish advisory regional committees for the purpose of ensuring a 'close working relationship between the assembly and Welsh local authorities'. In short, the Policy Commission had shown itself sensitive to concerns about the first-past-the-post system, but with strong anti-PR feeling within the Party, the structural devices of a consensual committee system and regional committees were presented as the best guarantee of a balanced assembly.

However, in June 1996, closely following the publication of the Constitution Unit's report of a Welsh assembly, Tony Blair announced the decision to seek approval for the creation of a Welsh assembly in a referendum and, at the same time, announced that the Policy Commission would be reviewing the question of using a form of PR for elections to the assembly. This was formally approved by the Welsh Executive of the Labour Party some day later. There were strong suspicions by some in the Party that the Welsh leadership had been excluded from the deliberations leading to this policy change, supported by the fact that the Shadow Secretary of State, Ron Davies, had been on the radio the day before the announcement stoutly arguing that a general election mandate would be sufficient to let the Labour government proceed with its devolution proposals. The Policy Commission announced its support for an alternative vote system in January 1997.

The Conservatives perceive their opposition to a Welsh assembly as a vote winner in Wales and have employed a number of lines of attack. The 'privileged channel of access' argument has been invoked with the claim that Wales' voice in Westminster would be muted if an assembly was in place. It is further argued that devolution might pose a threat to inward investment from abroad and that foreign investors would not want to deal with 'an extra layer of bureaucrats, with an extra layer of politicians, with an extra layer of interference' (*Western Mail*, 13 June 1996). Support for such arguments is also forthcoming from sections of the business community, with CBI Wales claiming that its members believe by a ratio of two to one that a Welsh assembly would damage the Welsh economy (Haywood, 1996).

Recent opinion poll evidence has given little clear indication that a referendum would deliver an overwhelming endorsement of a Welsh assembly. An Institute of Welsh Affairs/Beaufort poll in November 1995 showed 41% in favour, 19% against and 40% 'don't know' and an HTV/ NOP poll in March 1996 indicated that 45% favoured an assembly, 31% opposed it, but 24% were undecided (Balsom, 1996). A poll by the Conservative party in October was the only one to produce a substantial majority opposed to the establishment of an assembly and unlike most other polls produced a much lower percentage of undecided respondents (*Western Mail*, 8 October 1996). A *Western Mail* & Deloitte poll of the business community in December 1996 indicated 57% of respondents opposed to the establishment of an assembly (*Western Mail*, 5 December 1996).

Plaid Cymru has been calling for a 'preferendum' which would list a number of options, ranging from an assembly along the lines proposed by Labour to its own idea of a 'powerhouse parliament' (*Western Mail*, 15 October 1996). In October 1996, the Institute of Welsh Affairs published a report, *The Road to the Referendum* in which it argued that the concept of a 'referendum' was unlikely to be acceptable to the Government but argued that the question should be framed in such a way as the result should be unambiguous; for example 'An assembly: yes or no?' It further argued that the result of the referendum should be decided on a simple majority and that the count should take place on an all-Wales basis at a single centre. It stressed that the referendum should take place within four to five months of the general election (time allowing for the referendum legislation to pass through Parliament) and that the campaign should not overlap with that in Scotland. These recommendations picked up on problems which had emerged during the 1979 campaign.

Looking to the Election

Should Labour win the general election and the promised referendum once again rejects an assembly, the Party has given little indication of how it would deal with the so called 'quango state'. On the other hand, if an assembly is set up, the implications for public services in Wales are far reaching and an inevitable period of upheaval and transition will ensue.

The future of the Barnett formula in determining expenditure in Wales may well come under scrutiny. The Conservatives argue that an assembly will create resentment in England and the Welsh will no longer be able to enjoy higher per capita spending. On the other hand, the increasingly competitive race for regional economic development has already led some England regions to question the 'advantages' enjoyed by Wales in the form of a government-funded development agency and higher public expenditure. It must be questioned whether Wales can retain these even in the absence of an assembly. ■

References

Balsom, D. (1996), Taking the temperature of home rule. *Welsh Agenda* (Summer).

Cabinet Office (1995), *Public Bodies* (HMSO, London).

Constitution Unit (1996), *An Assembly for Wales—Senedd I Cymru* (UCL, London).

Haywood, E. (1996), Devolution? The views of Welsh business. Presentation on behalf of CBI Wales, QMW Public Policy Seminar: Devolution to Wales—Parameters for a Welsh Assembly.

Mihinnick, R. (1996), The treasure hunters—life after the *Sea Empress*. *Planet,* 117 (June/July).

Thomas, H. V. (1996) *The Place of North Wales.* Gregynog Paper, Vol. 1, No. 1 (Institute of Welsh Affairs).

Welsh Office (1996), *A Working Countryside for Wales,* Cm 3180 (HMSO, London).

Welsh Office (1996), *Meeting the Challenge—Competitiveness in Wales* (HMSO, London).

Welsh Office (1996), *A Statistical Focus on Wales* (HMSO, London).

8 Local Government

Richard R. Barnett and Paul Carmichael

University of Ulster

Given the continuing financial squeeze on local authorities, councillors could be forgiven for devoting their attention to their pressing statutory obligation of setting a budget. Certainly, the forthcoming financial year promises a continuance of the familiar unremitting pattern of tight settlements from Whitehall. Financial difficulties have been accompanied, and in many instances compounded, by new configurations of local government introduced throughout Scotland and Wales, a process of reorganization whose costs have far exceeded Ministers' optimistic predictions. Parts of non-metropolitan 'shire' England have also witnessed the introduction of reorganized structures of local government as the Local Government Commission's recommendations are implemented. However, throughout 1996 and early 1997, as the general election approached, increasing thought has been devoted to the prospects for local government, as an institution, as well as to what role the concept of regional government might play. This process has been given added piquancy by the possibility of a new government committed to radical change.

Finance

For the immediate future, finance remains the primary preoccupation of local government. If the 1995 Budget occasioned severe difficulties for local authorities, then the settlement outlined in November 1996 offered a repeat prescription. Local councils had sought £47.2 billion (an increase of £2.3 billion) to reflect their actual level of spending and new commitments. However, in cash terms, Total Standard Spending (TSS)—the Government's view of the appropriate amount of spending for local government as a whole—is planned to rise by 2.5% (£1.13 billion) to £45.66 billion (see table 1). Moreover, TSS is rising twice as fast as Aggregate External Finance (AEF)—central government's support for TSS. By implication, therefore, short of making deep cuts, the difference must be met by local taxpayers. Furthermore, since both TSS and AEF are declining in real terms over the next two years, the effect has been to force *c*.£4 billion onto council tax bills.

The arguments over the size of central government support are accompanied by disputes over its distribution. Although a technical point, this has important implications for individual councils. Despite arguments over the determination of Standard Spending Assessments (SSAs)—the Government's view of the appropriate amount of spending for an individual local authority—no major changes to the weightings for sparsity, density and area cost adjustment were sanctioned. This has important ramifications for those individual authorities or authority types for whom not only is the TSS (the national sum of individual SSAs) worrying, but for whom the distribution is allegedly iniquitous. (For a consideration of the technicalities of TSS and SSAs, see Barnett and Carmichael, 1996.)

The tough nature of the 1996 Budget was underscored by the simultaneous requirement for local authorities to find 'new money' (*c*.£633M) for schools (as part of the Government's attempts to placate dissent amongst its backbenchers and bolster stubbornly low opinion poll ratings in the pre-election period) and to meet the growing burdens of the community care programme. If the prospect for yet more belt-tightening through 'efficiency' gains appears daunting, then it will surely

Table 1. The financial settlement for local government, budget 1996 (£ billion).

Total Standard Spending (TSS)	*1996-97 settlement*	*1997-98 plans*	*1998-99 plans*
Cash terms	44.53	45.66	46.54
Real terms	44.53	44.76	44.73
Aggregate External Finance (AEF)			
Cash terms	35.23	35.77	35.96
Real terms	35.23	35.07	34.56

Sources: CIPFA; HM Treasury; *Local Government Chronicle.*

be rendered more so by the 'present confusion of responsibility between central and local government [which] gives perverse disincentives to local authorities to seek, or at least disclose, efficiency gains lest it reduces the grant they receive from central government' (Hulme, 1997, p. 8). The likelihood of higher inflation than central government has forecast (or, more crucially, has allowed for in its grant settlement), along with underfunded statutory obligations to implement the awards of the pay review bodies for professional occupations in local government (teachers, police and fire personnel), will provide finance officers and councillors with continued headaches.

Consequently, council tax payers can expect real-terms increases in bills. Householders in a typical band 'D' property can now expect to pay £690 per annum (up over £40)—an average rise of 6%, according to the Institute of Revenues Rating and Valuation. In Scotland, where reorganization costs of £281M are four times the Government's provision, the figures are even worse. In return for these higher bills, council taxpayers can expect a diminished level of service provision. A spate of redundancies has also been part and parcel of the continuing fallout from the financial woes of local government.

The Local Government Review in England

The protracted review of local government in England is in its final stages. While, in Scotland and Wales, a case was made for a unitary configuration of local government, the reform process in England operated under altogether more novel criteria. Originally, in commissioning its reforms, the Government had sought to satisfy complaints about the 1974 structure which were 'almost diametrically opposed. The traditionalists' objection to the 1974 reorganization was that it went too far, while advocates of unitary authorities argued that it did not go nearly far enough' (Leach, 1994). Predictably, the outcome has been one which has managed to satisfy few.

The Local Government Commission completed the last of its county reviews in January 1995. Parliament has now endorsed all of the Secretary of State's recommendations, some of which modified those of the Commission, and some of which rejected them. In some instances, the Government asked the Commission to 'look again' at their initial

Table 2. Summary of the UK's changing structure of local government.

Year	*Shire district*	*Shire county*	*New unitary*	*Metro-politan districts and London boroughs*	*Scotland*	*Wales*	*Northern Ireland*	*UK total*
1994	296	39	0	69	65	45	26	540
1995	294	38	1	69	65	45	26	538
1996	286	35	13	69	32	22	26	483
1997	273	35	26	69	32	22	26	483
1998	253	34	46	69	32	22	26	482

Sources: Local Government Chronicle; Department of the Environment.

proposals on the grounds that they had not been wholly consistent with the application of the statutory criteria governing the exercise. Consequently, the Commission produced revised recommendations, all of which were accepted. In the event, contrary to early rumours of their extinction, England's shires have survived broadly intact. With the exception of Avon, Cleveland and Humberside, themselves artificial constructs of the 1974 reorganization, the only county to be abolished (save for ceremonial purposes) was Berkshire. Elsewhere, the map of shire England has been peppered with new unitary authorities based on the large towns and cities. In summary, 14 shire counties were left unchanged, five were abolished and the remaining 20 experienced some form of alteration. The result has been the creation of 46 unitary authorities: 27 in the old shires (including restoration of Herefordshire and Rutland); a new unitary Isle of Wight; and a further 18 in the abolished shires (Avon, Cleveland, Humberside, along with the Royal County of Berkshire, now reduced to a ceremonial unit). The rest of the system in the shire counties remains two tier (see tables 2 and 3). Full implementation is to be completed by 1998.

In effect, what has emerged has been an augmented version of the last Labour Government's White Paper *Organic Change* (HMG, 1979). This had contained proposals to restore key powers (lost in 1974) to the

Table 3. Summary of structural changes within England.

County (with number of districts pre-review and date for implementation of any change)	*New structure (listing district councils on which unitary authorities are based)*	*Ceremonial arrangements*
Avon (6) (April 1996)	*4 unitary authorities*	Avon abolished
	(a) Bristol	A separate Lieutenancy created or Bristol
	(b) North Somerset (formerly Woodspring)	N. Somerset and Bath and N.E. Somerset deemed part of Somerset
	(c) Bath and North East Somerset formerly Wansdyke and Bath)	
	(d) South Gloucestershire (formerly Northavon and Kingswood)	S. Gloucestershire deemed part of Gloucestershire
Bedfordshire (4) (April 1997)	*1 unitary and two-tier:*	
	(a) Luton	Luton to be deemed part of Bedfordshire
	(b) Remaining area two-tier	
Berkshire (6) (April 1998)	*6 Unitaries:*	
	(a) Bracknell Forest	Royal County of Berkshire to be retained
	(b) Newbury	
	(c) Reading	
	(d) Slough	
	(e) Windsor and Maidenhead	
	(f) Wokingham	
Buckinghamshire (5) (April 1997)	*1 unitary and two-tier:*	
	(a) Milton Keynes	Milton Keynes to be deemed part of Buckinghamshire
	(b) Remaining area two-tier	
Cambridgeshire (6)	*1 unitary and two-tier:*	
	(a) Peterborough	Peterborough to be deemed part of Cambridgeshire
	(b) Remaining area two-tier	
Cheshire (8) (April 1998)	*2 unitaries and two-tier:*	
	(a) Halton	Halton and Warrington to be deemed part of Cheshire
	(b) Warrington	
	(c) Remaining area two-tier	
Cleveland (4) (April 1996)	*4 unitaries:*	Cleveland abolished
	(a) Hartlepool	Hartlepool and Stockton (north of the River Tees) deemed part of County Durham
	(b) Middlesbrough	Redcar and Cleveland

County	*New structure*	*Ceremonial arrangements*
	(c) Redcar and Cleveland (formerly Langbaurgh-on-Tees) (d) Stockton-on-Tees	Middlesbrough and Stockton (south of the River Tees) deemed part of North Yorkshire
Cornwall (6)	*Status quo*	
Cumbria (6)	*Status quo*	
Derbyshire (9) (April 1997)	*1 unitary and two-tier:* (a) Derby City (b) Remaining area two-tier	Derby to be deemed part of Derbyshire
Devon (10) (April 1998)	*2 unitaries and two-tier:* (a) Plymouth (b) Torbay (c) Remaining area two-tier	Plymouth and Torbay to be deemed part of Devon
Dorset (8) (April 1997)	*2 unitaries and two-tier:* (a) Bournemouth (b) Poole (c) Remaining area two-tier	Poole and Bournemouth to be deemed part of Dorset
Durham (8) (April 1997)	*1 unitary and two-tier:* (a) Darlington (b) Remaining area two-tier	Darlington to be deemed part of County Durham
East Sussex (7) (April 1997)	*1 unitary and two-tier:* (a) Brighton and Hove (b) Remaining area two-tier	Brighton and Hove to be deemed part of East Sussex
Essex (14) (April 1998)	*2 unitaries and two-tier:* (a) Southend (b) Thurrock (c) Remaining area two-tier	Southend and Thurrock to be deemed part of Essex
Gloucestershire (6)	*Status quo*	
Hampshire (13) (April 1997)	*2 unitaries and two-tier:* (a) Portsmouth (b) Southampton (c) Remaining area two-tier	Portsmouth and Southampton to be deemed part of Hampshire
Hereford & Worcester (9) (April 1998)	*1 unitary and two-tier:* (a) Unitary Herefordshire on pre-1974 boundaries (b) Worcester remains two-tier	Hereford and Worcester to be abolished Separate Lieutenancies to be created for Herefordshire and Worcestershire

County	*New structure*	*Ceremonial arrangements*
Hertfordshire (10)	*Status quo*	
Humberside (9) (April 1996)	*4 unitaries:*	
	(a) East Riding of Yorkshire (formerly East Yorkshire, Beverley, Holderness and part of Boothferry)	Humberside abolished
	(b) City of Kingston upon Hull	Hull deemed part of East Riding of Yorkshire
	(c) North Lincolnshire (formerly Glandford, Scunthorpe and part of Boothferry	North and North East Lincolnshire deemed part of Lincolnshire
	(d) North East Lincolnshire (formerly Cleethorpes and Great Grimsby)	
Isle of Wight (2) (April 1995)	*1 unitary:*	
	Whole island	No change
Kent (14) (April 1998)	*1 unitary and two-tier:*	
	(a) The Medway Towns (Rochester and Gillingham)	The Medway Towns to be deemed part of Kent
	(b) Remaining area two-tier	
Lancashire (14) (April 1998)	*2 unitaries and two-tier:*	
	(a) Blackburn	Blackburn and Blackpool to be deemed part of Lancashire
	(b) Blackpool	
	(c) Remaining area two-tier	
Leicestershire (9) (April 1997)	*2 unitaries and two-tier:*	
	(a) Leicester City	Leicester to be deemed part of Leicestershire
	(b) Rutland	Rutland to be separate Lieutenancy
	(c) Remaining area two-tier	
Lincolnshire (7)	*Status quo*	
Norfolk (7)	*Status quo*	
Northamptonshire (7)	*Status quo*	
Northumberland (6)	*Status quo*	
North Yorkshire (8) (April 1996)	*1 unitary and two-tier:*	
	(a) York (on extended boundary)	York deemed part of North Yorkshire
	(b) Remaining area two-tier	
Nottinghamshire (8) (April 1998)	*1 unitary and two-tier:*	
	(a) Nottingham City	Nottingham to be deemed part of Nottinghamshire
	(b) Remaining area two-tier	

County	*New structure*	*Ceremonial arrangements*
Oxfordshire (5)	*Status quo*	
Shropshire (6) (April 1998)	*1 unitary and two-tier:* (a) Stoke-on-Trent (b) Remaining area two-tier	The Wrekin to be deemed part of Shropshire
Somerset (5)	*Status quo*	
Staffordshire (9) (April 1997)	*1 unitary and two-tier:* (a) Stoke-on-Trent (b) Remaining area two-tier	Stoke to be deemed part of Staffordshire
Suffolk (7)	*Status quo*	
Surrey (11)	*Status quo*	
Warwickshire (5)	*Status quo*	
West Sussex (7)	*Status quo*	
Wiltshire (5) (April 1997)	*1 unitary and two-tier:* (a) Thamesdown (to be renamed Swindon) (b) Remaining area two-tier	Swindon to be deemed part of Wiltshire

Source: Department of the Environment.

larger borough authorities in England (the 'big nine' of Bristol, Derby, Hull, Leicester, Nottingham, Plymouth, Portsmouth, Portsmouth, Southampton and Stoke-on-Trent), Cardiff and Swansea in Wales, as well as Scotland's four largest cities (Aberdeen, Dundee, Edinburgh and Glasgow), most of which were Labour controlled. Just as Labour criticized the Heath Government's reform only to propose modest revision, the Major Government has settled for an implementation of *Organic Change—Plus*. In other words, while Labour's agenda focused on returning powers to a limited number of cities, coupled with modest boundary augmentation, the Conservative's reforms have conferred unitary status on a larger group of districts in an extension of the 'doughnut solution' to some county towns and/or principal town(s) as unitary authorities within an otherwise two-tier county.

For all its faults, the reviews by the Local Government Commission raise a number of public policy issues, some of which have implications beyond the immediate impact of the structure of local government. John Banham, the Commission's first chairman, asked whether the very nature of the Commission's work and its extensive consultation have enhanced the legitimacy of the outcome. Simply, irrespective of the way in which Government (and Opposition) manipulated the findings in order to derive maximum political capital, perhaps there is something to be said for inviting the reportedly alienated, cynical and distrustful general public to become involved in the process of informing decision-makers in their deliberations over how to proceed. Certainly, with the atmosphere suffused with calls by politicians for 'greater public involvement', 'getting closer to the public' and 'restoring the public's faith in government', the process of consultation as practised by the Commission might well be a model for any future structural reform.

In addition to issues relating to the legitimacy of the *process*, there are important questions to be answered concerning whether the *outcome* was 'correct'. Banham appears in no doubt that this was so, and that the Commission was successful in 'correcting the mistakes of 1974, improving the operation of the two-tier system, creating a more effective base for community government, in the form of local town and parish councils, *and* developing a process to enable local government to adapt to the future [all of which] seems a reasonable outcome' (Banham, 1995, p. 5).

Of course, if it is the right outcome, one is left wondering why similar exercises could not have been undertaken in Scotland and Wales (to say nothing of Northern Ireland). Banham concluded that Commission's work was 'All in all, not a bad outcome...better than we had any right to expect'. Crucially, he noted that the Commission's inability to consider the regional dimension unnecessarily limited and harmed its work. However, Banham's sentiments are clearly centred on the 'next stage' of a process of governmental change, namely, the regional dimension. First, they concern the functions of any regional tier, for instance, strategic planning, health, economic development, transport infrastructure and co-ordination of EU regional funding. Second, there is the vexed question of finance concerning the funding of any regional tier. Assigned revenues, central government grants, regional taxes, precepts on constituent local councils or a combination of all or some of these needs to be determined. Equally, the principle of equalization in the allocation of public funds which presently operates between the UK's component countries requires updating to accommodate any English regional dimension. Third, the political composition of regions could vary—either indirectly elected in a form of confederal arrangement involving the constituent local authorities or directly elected as a full autonomous tier (and, if so, by what method of election and with what frequency). Crucially, what would be the form of any centre-regional relationship? (For a fuller discussion, see Constitution Unit, 1996a, b.)

Developments in Parliament

Under the auspices of two distinguished peers, Parliament has focused on local government in the last year. From October 1995, under the chairmanship of Lord Hunt of Tanworth, the former Cabinet Secretary, a cross-party House of Lords Select Committee of Inquiry reviewed central-local government relations. Despite an altogether narrower remit than those of the preceding Layfield and Widdicombe Committees, the Report of the Hunt Committee, entitled *Rebuilding Trust*, published in July 1996, constituted a wholesale rejection of the aggressive anti-local government stance taken by the Conservatives since 1979. Moreover, it declared that John Major's 'concordat' of 1994 had done little to improve relations between local government and Whitehall. Having a remarkable congruence with the Labour Party's current plans on local government, it argued for: signing of the European Charter of Local Self-Government as an 'important symbolic first step towards better relations'; government controls over local councils' self-financed expenditure to be relaxed; SSAs to be simplified; capping to cease as a standard procedure—if needed, SSAs ought not be the criteria for determining caps; business rates to be returned to local authorities to help raise the proportion of income derived locally to *c.*50%; introduction of a statutory power of local competence; simplification of CCT regime and a switch to a voluntary scheme; new laws to allow internal management reforms; improved machinery in Whitehall for managing local government; and, establishment of a permanent local government committee of MPs (LGC, 1996). In its response, the Government indicated that it was prepared to accept some of the recommendations and would act accordingly. However, on the substantive concerns over finance—grants, taxes, business rates, and capping, as well as a power of local competence, CCT, and signing the European Charter, the Government remained unmoved.

The second major investigation was that by Lord Nolan who turned his attention to local government in what was the biggest enquiry for a decade (since Widdecombe). Given the prominence accorded to Nolan's investigations into *Standards in Public Life*, this was a rare recognition of the importance of the role of local government within the polity. Lord Nolan is looking at the rules on surcharging; the declarations of interest; codes affecting officers; and, the role of auditors and ombudsmen. The Committee is due to report by summer 1997.

In their own way, while these reports serve to place local government under the political spotlight, they represent only a partial exposure of a much wider issue. Moreover, irrespective of the findings, the concerns voiced by Banham over the interaction of local authorities with any regional tier of government leave many questions unanswered. It is with these questions in mind that we now turn to the potential agenda for change.

Prospects for 1997—An Agenda for Change?

The process of local government reorganization has served to consolidate further what was already the most centralized system of government in Western Europe. Both the main parties have encouraged this. When last in government, Labour's fudging of Layfield effectively left ajar the door to the 'centralist' option. Once in office, the Conservatives could exploit this.

Apart from some small countries, the idea that there should be no regional tier of government (notwithstanding an ever more crowded panoply of regional governance) is viewed with puzzlement and concern by many connected with local government. Currently, in Scotland, Wales, Northern Ireland, metropolitan areas of England, Greater London, and now, thanks to the 1992–95 review process, most large towns and cities in 'shire' England, there is only one tier of local government. Arguably, the absence of regional government might be defensible if local government was sufficiently differentiated in its structure. Even Britain's consolidated structure could, perhaps, be accepted as rational if those authorities enjoyed considerable powers of autonomy. However, as the seemingly ineluctable logic of Layfield's (1976) predictions of centralization is fulfilled, even those authorities which still preside over large budgets are finding their ability to exercise real discretion progressively curtailed, while their fiscal autonomy in respect of raising revenue via local taxes has been virtually emasculated through the universal application of capping of spending.

With such an inauspicious background, what might one anticipate from a new government? In the short term, probably very little. Quite simply, after the upheavals of structural reorganization, the appetites of civil servants and those in local government for a further round of changes has been blunted. As a result of their efforts to control the behaviour of a small number of allegedly errant Labour councils, successive Conservative Governments have succeeded only in weakening the institution of local government within the polity. All told, some 150 laws affecting the independence of local authorities have been enacted since 1979, severely constraining what was, at best, only ever a modest level of autonomy. It is possible that a fifth period of Conservative Government would herald a push for an extension of the unitary principle, especially if the rumoured removal of education from local government comes to pass. Otherwise, however, the Conservatives have consistently stressed their credentials as the party of the *status quo*. Local government could expect no favours from a new Conservative administration, while local councillors, most of whom are non-Conservative, would in any event, be undoubtedly shell-shocked by yet another defeat for their respective national parties. On regional government, too, while the Conservatives have introduced their own regional initiatives based on integrating Whitehall's administrative machinery in the provinces (via the Government Offices for the Regions), there appears to be no prospect of full devolution to regional authorities.

Recently, while the Conservatives have been at their nadir in local government, mainly as a result of 18 years in power at Westminster, Labour and the Liberal Democrats have enjoyed their strongest ever position. As the second largest party in local government and, given their history, the Liberal Democrats might be expected to be the most enthusiastic in their willingness to countenance change and, indeed, the most radical proposals for regional and local government have emanated from them. As part of their long-held enthusiasm for federalism (both as 'Home Rule All Round' within the UK and as a 'Europe of the Regions' within the European Union), they promise to actively encourage citizens to support the establishment of regional government. Local authorities would be strengthened through the progressive shift to a Local Income Tax (LIT) and granting of general competence. A revival of England's *c.*8000 parishes—currently spending under £200M, is a distinct possibility.

While Labour has criticized much of the Conservative's agenda since 1979, unlike the more radical proposals of the Liberal Democrats, recent pronouncements by leading Labour figures have been aimed at dampening expectations. Chiefly, with its newly professed commitment to fiscal rectitude, Labour promises only to maintain a strict control of public expenditure in the hope of blunting any enthusiasm for a relaxation of the Conservative's fiscal controls, lest it should unleash a torrent of additional local government spending. Nonetheless, if, to recast Crosland's phrase, the 'Party is still over', there remain prospects for some change under a Labour Government, albeit of a different nature. Tony Blair is understood to share, in part at least, Michael Heseltine's vision for a restoration of civic pride and rekindling popular interest, not least by the introduction of popularly elected mayors in the large cities. However, it will be difficult to hear the arguments for further change in local government above the general welter of demands for a new Labour government to act (spend) on a range of priority areas. Moreover, set against the stated intentions of Labour (shadow) chancellor, Gordon Brown, on the need for continued tight public spending rounds the costs of a further round of reorganization appear difficult to justify. Nonetheless, as part of the wider devolution debate, even if Labour has retreated from its more ambitious earlier plans for regional government, the Party is still disposed to offering London and the English provinces the possibility of voting on the possible introduction of a regional tier of government in their area. Given that there are a number of valid models of how any process of regionalization might proceed, precisely how Labour's *a la carte* regionalism would work in practice remains to be seen.

Conclusion

Irrespective of the outcome of the general election, those in local government appear resigned to accept further 'consolidation', both structurally and financially. Structurally, all the parties' 'visions' for local government involve changes to the *status quo*, albeit to varying degrees. Financially, with the new consensus on taxation and expenditure levels, there seems every prospect of continuing hard times. However, this need not imply that the outcome is meaningless. Even within these fairly constrained parameters, the general election outcome can still exert a major influence, as much in terms of the environment in which local councils operate. Both Labour and the Liberal Democrats are far more disposed to pursue the recommendations of the Hunt Committee, for example, than the Conservatives. Equally, while the Conservatives are clearly committed to minimal change, on regional government, the only likelihood of real change would come with a Labour or Labour-led coalition government. Both would appear equally minded to consider further change, given the commitments to devolution for Scotland, Wales, Greater London and those English regions which 'express a demand' for such. ■

References

Banham, J. (1995), Whitehall farce—or disaster averted? *Public Finance Foundation Review*, No. 6 (May).

Barnett, R. R. and Carmichael, P. (1996), Local government. In Jackson, P. and Lavender, M., *Public Services Yearbook 1996-97* (Pitman, London).

Constitution Unit (1996a), *Regional Government in England* (London).

Constitution Unit (1996b), *Devolution in the Round* (London).

HMG (1979), *Organic Change in Local Government*, Cmnd 7457 (HMSO, London).

Hulme, G. (1997), Public expenditure bulletin: 1996 budget. *Public Finance Foundation Review*, No. 13 (February).

Layfield, (1976), *Report of the Committee of Inquiry into Local Government Finance* (HMSO, London).

Leach, R. L. (1994), Restructuring local government. *Local Government Studies, 20*, 3.

LGC (1996), Interview with Lord Hunt. *Local Government Chronicle* (19 July), pp. 16–17.

9 Pay in the Public Sector

Chris Trinder

CIPFA, London

1997 is the fourth year of the public sector paybill freeze and the longer the policy continues the more it may come into conflict with the need to recruit, retain and motivate high quality staff. The difficulty of reconciling the 3.3% pay rise recommended for teachers by their pay review body with limited local authority funding resulted in the Government introducing larger amounts of deferment of the pay awards for teachers and the other pay review body groups—nurses, doctors, armed forces and senior civil servants—than had been necessary in 1996. The current policy is intended to continue into the new Parliament, so the same problems (only in a more aggravated form) will emerge in 1998. Moreover, as the economic recovery continues, the contrast with private sector 'real' earnings and employment growth becomes more marked and the need for a new medium-term public sector pay strategy clear.

Employment

In mid-1996 there were 5.15M people employed in the UK public sector. This was approximately one in five of the total workforce in employment at that time; 1.7M worked part time and 3.45M full time; 41% were men and 59% women. Over the two years from 1994–96, public sector employment fell by 182,000 and almost all of this fall was in full-time male employees. Over the same period, private sector employment increased by 646,000. The recession of the early 1990s affected the public and private sectors equally, but the current economic recovery is seeing major differences between the two sectors and these are expected to widen still further if the public sector paybill freeze is maintained while the economy grows faster than its long-term trend rate in 1997 and 1998.

The public sector is very heterogeneous, both in the types of jobs

Table 1. UK public sector employment (1979-1996), major categories (full-time equivalents).

	Central government					Local authorities			
Year	*HM forces*	*NHS*	*Civil service*	*Others*	*Total*	*Education*	*Police (including civilians)*	*Town hall manuals & others*	*Total*
1979	314	977	724	173	2,188	1,110	172	1,086	2,368
1980	323	1,001	700	172	2,196	1,087	176	1,080	2,343
1981	334	1,038	684	169	2,225	1,058	180	1,068	2,306
1982	324	1,047	659	168	2,198	1,041	180	1,053	2,274
1983	322	1,047	643	169	2,181	1,034	182	1,085	2,301
1984	326	1,036	619	168	2,149	1,027	182	1,111	2,320
1985	326	1,030	596	192	2,144	1,021	182	1,122	2,325
1986	322	1,018	597	179	2,116	1,029	184	1,139	2,352
1987	319	1,016	584	172	2,091	1,043	186	1,148	2,377
1988	316	1,017	577	174	2,084	1,046	190	1,143	2,379
1989	308	1,013	567	196	2,084	992	191	1,082	2,265
1990	303	1,008	889	206	2,076	990	194	1,094	2,278
1991	297	904	558	208	1,967	982	197	1,112	2,291
1992	290	750	567	216	1,823	970	199	1,088	2,257
1993	271	424	551	221	1,467	840	201	1,064	2,105
1994	250	158	529	204	1,141	818	201	1,059	2,078
1995	230	69	512	198	1,009	806	201	1,055	2,062
1996	221	76	512	129	938	800	202	1,035	2,037

Sources: Office for National Statistics (1997), *Employment in the Public and Private Sectors*; *Economic Trends* (March).

people do and the methods by which their pay is determined. Table 1 shows, on a Full-Time Equivalent (FTE) basis, the major employment categories in central government, local authorities and public corporations between 1979 and 1996.

The civil service and armed forces have both been reduced in size by about 30% since 1979. The reduction in the size of the National Health Service is largely due to NHS trusts being classified as public corporations. In local authorities, there were also reductions in 1996 in all the major categories except for the police.

Pay Determination

Table 2 sets out the current arrangements for determining pay in each of

	Public corporations			
Total general government	*Nationalized industires*	*NHS trusts & others*	*Total*	*Total public sector*
4,556	1,818	216	2,034	6,590
4,539	1,785	222	2,007	6,546
4,531	1,656	206	1,862	6,393
4,472	1,538	198	1,736	6,208
4,482	1,444	197	1,641	6,123
4,469	1,390	188	1,578	6,047
4,469	1,118	118	1,236	5,705
4,468	1,043	127	1,170	5,638
4,468	850	119	969	5,437
4,463	775	119	894	5,357
4,349	703	110	813	5,162
4,354	659	108	767	5,121
4,258	488	202	690	4,948
4,080	452	356	808	4,888
3,572	426	601	1,027	4,599
3,219	370	887	1,257	4,476
3,071	352	950	1,302	4,373
2,975	321	957	1,278	4,253

the main public sector negotiating groups. A variety of institutional arrangements apply at present, and they are continually evolving. The acceptance of uniform, across-the-board, national pay rises for nurses and teachers in 1997, and the Government's response in February 1997 to the Bett Inquiry into personnel management and pay in the armed forces rejecting the recommendation to make performance related pay more widespread, demonstrates that the national agreements are still exerting a major influence on pay levels and pay structures in significant parts of the public sector.

The Pay Review Bodies (February 1997)

The pay review body reports on nurses, schoolteachers, doctors and

Table 2. Current institutional arrangements for pay settlements.

Public sector negotiating group	*Number of employees (000s)*	*Expected settlement date*	*Current arrangements*
Central government			
Armed forces	210	Apr 1998	Pay review body
Nurses	500	Apr 1998	Pay review body
Civil service	500	Apr/Aug 1997	Local pay bargaining
Local government			
Teachers	500	Apr 1998	Pay review body
Police	200	Sep 1997	Indexing formula
Town hall staff and local authority manuals	1,200	Apr 1997	National agreement

dentists, armed forces and senior salaries were published in February 1997. Recommendations were made for pay increases for 1.4M public servants to take effect from 1 April 1997. The Government's response was to allow 2% to be paid from the due settlement date, with the balance taking effect from 1 December 1997. The effect of this staging is to reduce the paybill cost in the financial year 1997-98, but to maintain the baseline to which new recommendations would apply in 1998-99. For teachers and nurses, the recommended increases were 3.3% and for armed forces they averaged 3.2%.

Because the 1996 pay awards were also staged, the changes in pay in 1997-98 include the knock-on effect of last year's staging, as well as the 1997 new money. This means that the 100,000 or so teachers who are on spine point 9 of their pay scale, and have remained there throughout 1996 and 1997, will have been paid £20,700 in April 1996, £20,901 in December 1996, £21,318 in April 1997 and £21,591 in December 1997. Their pay, and hence the cost of employing them, was therefore 3% higher in April 1997 than in April 1996, but this was made up of 1%

of the 1996 delayed award and 2% of 1997 new money. If their average pay in the financial year 1996-97 is compared with their average pay in 1995-96, then the rise was 3.1%, despite review body recommendations of 3.75%; and for 1997-98 over 1996-97 the rise was 3.1%, despite review body recommendations of 3.3%. If, in April 1998, the recommendations are honoured in full from the due settlement date then the adding together of the knock-on effect of this year's staging and next year's new money will mean these shortfalls are corrected for with a lag, but the public expenditure funding totals for 1998-99 are even more stringent than in 1997-98 so if the full cost could not be afforded this year it is difficult to see how it will be affordable next year either.

The effect of staging pay awards is also deemed to be unfair. It permanently reduces the value of the pension for those who retire before the full amount comes into effect, and every pound which it saves the Government is a pound out of the pay packet of nurses, etc.

Public Sector Paybill

The public sector paybill is determined by the amount of employment, the earnings increases of those employed and policies on employer pension contributions and national insurance, as well as funding of early retirement and redundancy. In 1995 the public sector paybill was £95.79 billion: a rise of 1.5% on the calendar year 1994. This increase was 2%

Table 3. Nurses' pay from 1 December 1997 (£ per year).

Grade A	Nursing auxiliary	8,010-9,800
Grade B	Nursing nurse	9,485-10,800
Grade C	Enrolled nurse	10,800-12,805
Grade D	Senior enrolled nurse	12,385-14,165
Grade E	Staff nurse	14,165-16,410
Grade F	Deputy sister	15,715-19,250
Grade G	Ward sister	18,535-21,440
Grade H	Senior nurse	20,710-23,680
Grade I	Clinical tutor	22,925-25,975

Recent developments: The 1997 recommendations were for a 3.3% rise in the national rates.

Table 4. Schoolteachers' pay (England and Wales) £ per annum.

Spine	*April 1996*	*December 1996*	*April 1997*	*December 1997*
0	12,342	12,462	12,711	12,873
0.5		12,831	13,089	13,254
1	13,083	13,209	13,473	13,644
1.5		13,599	13,872	14,049
2	13,866	14,001	14,280	14,463
2.5		14,379	14,667	14,853
3	14,622	14,763	15,057	15,249
3.5		15,156	15,459	15,657
4	15,414	15,563	15,876	16,077
4.5		16,020	16,341	16,548
5	16,335	16,494	16,824	17,037
5.5		16,983	17,322	17,544
6	17,316	17,487	17,838	18,063
6.5		18,003	18,363	18,597
7	18,357	18,534	18,906	19,146
7.5		19,083	19,464	19,713
8	19,458	19,647	20,040	20,295
8.5		20,262	20,667	20,931
9	20,700	20,901	21,318	21,591
9.5		21,540	21,972	22,251
10	21,981	22,194	22,638	22,926
10.5		22,845	23,301	23,598
11	23,288	23,514	23,985	24,291
11.5		24,435	24,924	25,242
12	25,146	25,392	25,899	26,229
12.5		26,226	26,751	27,090
13	26,823	27,084	27,627	27,978
13.5		28,146	28,710	29,076
14	28,965	29,247	29,832	30,213
14.5		29,898	30,495	30,885
15	30,267	30,561	31,173	31,569
15.5		31,242	31,866	32,274
16	31,632	31,941	32,580	32,994
16.5		32,649	33,303	33,726
17	33,054	33,375	34,044	34,476

Recent developments: The 1997 recommendations were for a 3.3% increase. The heads' and deputies' pay spine was increased by 3.3% at all points. The awards were paid in two stages in April and December 1997.

Table 5. Police pay from September 1996 (£ per year).

Constable	14,916-23,607
Sergeant	22,785-26,574
Inspector	29,466-32,937
Chief inspector	32,067-34,299

Recent developments: A formula links pay rises for police officers to the median increase in private sector non-manual settlements over the previous year. The increases in 1996 were 3.5%.

Table 6. Town hall staff pay until 31 March 1997 (£ per year).

White collar		*Manual workers*	
Scale 1	6,693-10,194	Grade 1	7,748
Scale 2	10,194-10,686	Grade 2	8,065
Scale 3	10,884-11,646	Grade 3	8,378
Scale 4	11,874-13,233	Grade 4	8,707
Scale 5	13,581-14,892	Grade 5	9,018
Scale 6	15,375-16,404	Grade 6	9,344
Senior officers	17,055-19,818		
Principal officers	19,269-28,800		

Recent developments: The 1996 agreement for 2.9% increases from 1 April for all 1¹/4M white collar and manual workers.

Table 7. Armed forces' pay from December 1997 (£ per year).

Private	9,180-15,998
Corporal lance corporal	12,501-20,152
Sergeant/staff sergeant	18,429-25,634
Warrant officer	20,801-28,861
Lieutenant	19,341-21,371
Captain	24,659-28,667
Major	31,270-37,460
Lieutenant colonel	44,114-48,757
Colonel	51,272-56,674
Brigadier	62,930

Recent developments: The 1997 recommendation were for pay increases averaging 3.2%.

below the rate of inflation over the same period, but does mean that despite the freeze on running costs in civil service departments, other parts of the public sector (notably health and education) are allowed to see limited increases in their paybills. Nevertheless, the latest figures from the official annual earnings survey show that on average public sector pay increased less fast than private sector pay in each of the last three years. The private sector increase April 1993 to April 1996 was 11.6% compared to a 10.5% in the public sector. With a public sector paybill of £95.79 billion, each 0.1% shortfall is equivalent to £96M, so a 1.1% shortfall over the past three years amounts to £1.05 billion of extra public expenditure.

Two-Tier Public Sector

In the early 1980s headteachers in large secondary schools were paid the same wage as Brigadiers in the armed forces: £18,250 per annum. At the end of 1997, the most any headteacher can aspire to is £57,399 (the very highest point on their pay spine), but all brigadiers will be paid £62,930 per annum, which is 10% higher. After the Clegg comparability awards on civil service pay in May 1980, an executive officer at the maximum of the scale was paid £6,745 per annum, virtually identical to a police constable with 15 years of service who was paid £6,741 per annum. Now the average police constable's pay is 50% higher than the civil service executive officer's. There are possible causes for divergent trends within the public sector. For example, that the nature of the jobs has changes, but the explanation which most well fits the evidence for the two-tier public sector is more the effect of the different institutional arrangements, set up originally with the best of intentions, but over time dividing public servants into deserving and undeserving groups, and giving the former first claim to the limited funds and leaving what little is left to be fought over by the others. The detrimental effects on motivation and morale for those in the latter category can undermine the Government's need for high-quality well-motivated staff to deliver the efficiency gains so vital for more output without more inputs.

The New Parliament

The main problems with the current public sector pay policy are:

- A two-tier public sector has developed, with some groups (such as the police) doing much better than other groups (such as town hall staff).
- The cycles in public sector pay continue, with public sector pay rises being below those in the private sector in 1994, 1995 and 1996, thus building up pressure for a catch up sometime in the future.
- Public sector pay rises are not being properly funded, thus resulting in clampdowns on non-pay expenditure, particularly towards the end of each financial year.

The new Parliament offers an opportunity to put in place new policies that are fairer and more efficient.

The main ingredients should be, first, to ensure the policy is medium term. Short-term policies can be short-sighted and short-term savings can cost the taxpayer more in the long run. The need is to design a framework, similar to the medium term financial strategy or the inflation target, which makes the pay policy work better over the long run. This means paying the appropriate rates to recruit, retain and motivate high quality staff at the appropriate time thus avoiding the need for bounce back compensation awards after the damage has been done. It also means trying to introduce more elements of pay that reward good performance by individuals without having to pay everyone more.

Second, the strategy must build on existing institutions. There are strengths in the current arrangements which should be preserved. At the same time, the policy must recognize the devolved financial management which has already taken place in large parts of the public sector and the implications this has for local pay variations. It should also be noted that public sector workers are more likely to be part-time females.

Third, the approach must be holistic. The Government might save on public sector wages only to have to pay more in terms of unemployment benefits. The policy must make sense in overall public expenditure terms. ■

10 Regulated Industries

Peter Vass

Centre for the study of Regulated Industries (CRI), CIPFA, London and School of Management, University of Bath

Major developments in the UK's privatized industries during 1996 and early 1997 are examined in this Chapter. New privatizations included Railtrack and British Energy; water services in Scotland were taken out of local authority control, while in Northern Ireland the water service was made a Next Steps agency. There were important developments in the practice of regulation, particularly focused on the periodic reviews of price caps. Finally, Peter Vass calls for the objectives of regulation and competition policy to be more clearly stated and applied; for accountability and transparency to be improved; for better communication of the role of profit in an incentive-based regulatory system; and for the Government's policy for environmental and service standards to be more clearly articulated.

1996 saw the culmination of the privatization of the network industries and utilities which had begun with BT in 1984. Railtrack, the owner of the rail infrastructure, was sold in June 1996, closely followed by British Energy in July. The British Energy sale achieved what had not been possible in 1991, which was to privatize the nuclear generators, although the Magnox stations which are nearing the end of their generating life and have substantial—and unknown—decommissioning costs remain in public ownership. The number of franchises sold for running passenger train services slipped behind the Government's schedule, but in terms of the interest shown, probably exceeded commentators' expectations and demonstrated that the transfer of all rail operations, notwithstanding the high level of public subsidy and practical difficulties, could be achieved. The letting of all franchises was completed in February 1997. Two new regulators were appointed, the Chairman of the Civil Aviation Authority and the Director of Passenger Rail Franchising, but with no change of their role. The first energy regulator, combining gas and electricity, was achieved in Northern Ireland (OFREG). Table 1 sets out the present position (January 1997).

The Post Office remains in public hands. Whether or not this progresses towards privatization will depend on the outcome of the General Election and developments in the European Union aimed at achieving liberalization of network services in order to achieve a single market in goods and services. In Scotland, the water service was transferred from local government to three publicly owned water authorities from 1 April 1996, and in Northern Ireland the water service took on executive agency status.

Controversy over the activities of the other well-known regulatory office, OFLOT, which controls the national lottery, has diminished. Nevertheless, Labour has said that if it forms the next government it will examine whether the regulatory contract with the operator, Camelot, can be changed in order to reduce their profit. The other key issue is whether the next government will be seen to use lottery funds as a substitute for public money in the drive to cut public expenditure.

Europe

1996 has shown increased acceptance by mainland member states of the European Union for the policy of liberalizing national network and utility services. There has been considerable resistance to the UK 'experiment' in the past, but the evidence of efficiency improvements, without loss of

Table 1. The regulated industries.

Sector	*Privatization date*	*Regulatory office*	*Regulator*
BT	1984	OFTEL	Don Cruickshank
BG	1986	OFGAS	Clare Spottiswoode
BAA	1987	CAA	Malcolm Field
Water (E/W)	1989	OFWAT	Ian Byatt
Electricity(GB)	1990–1996	OFFER (GB)	Stephen Littlechild
Electricity (NI)	1993	OFREG (NI)	Douglas McIldoon
Rail infrastructure	1996	ORR	John Swift QC
Rail franchising	1996-1997	OPRAF	John O'Brien

security of supply, the threat of competition from other regions (particularly South East Asia) and the need to meet the convergence criteria for monetary union, has persuaded member states to change. This has given more power to the European Commission (and particularly DGIV, the competition directorate) to argue that liberalization must occur because the Union is founded on the idea of a common market in goods and services. National monopolies are inconsistent with this. Resistance has also been broken down because practical ways have been found to ensure that public service obligations can be maintained and financed (for example by a levy on all competitors in the market).

An electricity directive to allow cross-border trading and third party access to networks has been agreed, Deutsche Telecom has been privatized, France Telecom is being prepared for privatization, and telecoms alliances are being forged in preparation for a free market in 1998. There are similar developments in all member states. The next step will be to agree a directive to liberalize the gas market. It is proving difficult to get agreement on the postal services without a very long transitional period.

Periodic Reviews

The number of privatized industries, and the range of different businesses to which price controls apply, means that we can now expect some periodic reviews by economic regulators to be starting, progressing or concluding in each year. This will only be reduced once effective competition is introduced (prices controlled by the market-place and customers free to move to other suppliers). For the remaining natural monopoly businesses (the transport systems of pipes, wires, connecting nodes and rails), the frequency of periodic reviews may diminish over time as experience of regulation grows (particularly in forecasting); the amount of inefficiency in the system is squeezed out; and regulatory price control formulae include more self-correcting mechanisms with annual adjustments to compensate for explicit 'windfall' gains or losses (OFGAS has proposed a more cost-reflective control this year to ensure that undue profits are not earned when sales forecasts prove wrong). If so, the period between reviews might be extended (from five to ten years perhaps), which may be necessary to maintain the incentive for companies to go on trying for efficiency improvements which should be progressively more difficult to achieve as companies approach the frontier of productive efficiency. At present, however, the uncertainties caused by the introduction of competition have meant that the period between reviews is being shortened for some businesses to three or four years. Ian Byatt, the water regulator, announced that the next water review would be after five years in 1999 and he has mooted reducing the period of review to four years.

Communications

BT's regulation is the first to move towards deregulation because competition has increased in the 12 years since its privatization, and because the rate of technical change is so high that its natural monopoly is being eroded. OFTEL has therefore reduced significantly the percentage of BT's turnover which is controlled by price caps from 65% to 25% (it is concentrated on the 80% of residential customers who have lower bills), and plans to remove retail price caps in 2001, subject to the development of competition. Access prices for other suppliers wanting to use BT's networks would continue to be regulated. To ensure that the powers are in place to stop BT acting anti-competitively, for example through discriminatory pricing, OFTEL has amended the licence with a fair trading condition.

The debate continues, however, as to whether it is appropriate for sectoral regulators to take on the role of a competition authority (with the power to outlaw proposed predatory schemes in advance or to fine for first offences), or whether this should be left to the Office of Fair Trading. This will depend in part on whether the UK's system is reformed to bring it more in line with European practice. BT opposed the development of OFTEL's competition powers, but OFTEL said that the fair trading condition was inextricably linked with the price cap proposals, and that BT could not have one without the other. A compromise was reached, however, in which OFTEL's fair trading powers lapse in 2001 and the Director General agreed to publish the advice he received from an expert panel.

The main retail price cap for BT was amended from -7.5 to -4.5 until 2001 (OFTEL 1996). The value of X, which determines the percentage real cut in prices each year after allowing for inflation (typically known as the RPI-

X formula), was therefore reduced in 1996 for the first time. This is important for public understanding of the price cap system. Many people had begun to believe that each X would necessarily be tighter than the last—and that tightening it is a necessary 'virility' symbol for a tough regulator. However, this cannot go on indefinitely, otherwise prices would fall below the long-run cost of supply once the industry was operating near the frontier of efficiency. It is a moot point as to when that is achieved (if ever, given innovation and technical change), but it is reasonable to expect that in the long run the value of the efficiency component of X would fall to nearer the 1–2% per year range.

The review of BAA's airports in the South-East went through both the Monopolies and Mergers Commission (MMC) and Civil Aviation Authority stages smoothly, and took account of the prospective planning permission for Heathrow Airport's Terminal 5 and the loss of duty-free sales from 1999. Adjustments will have to be made if Terminal 5 doesn't come to fruition. The main price cap was changed from an X of -1 to -3 for Heathrow and Gatwick overall, and to +1 for Stansted, until 2002 (CAA, 1996).

Energy

The greatest difficulties were experienced in the energy sector, where the problems of the structure of the industry at privatization, and the price caps set by the Government at that time, continue to cast their shadow forward and affect the regulatory debates today.

Northern Ireland Electricity (NIE) faced its first periodic review since privatization. The National Grid Company (NGC), which was demerged late in 1995 from the 12 regional electricity companies and floated as a separate company on the stock exchange, faced its second periodic review. British Gas faced two periodic reviews, one for the retail price cap for domestic gas supply and one for its activities in storing and transporting gas—whether for its own gas supply business to the domestic and commercial sectors—or for competing suppliers who need to use British Gas' pipes. Both of these reviews, however, were complicated by the introduction of competition in the domestic gas market—the pilot scheme in the south west having started in April 1996—and the restructuring of British Gas to separate the competitive business of supply from the natural monopoly gas pipeline business.

In 1996, following the earlier internal split into separate businesses—but still as part of British Gas—resulting from the MMC review in 1993, British Gas decided that in the interests of efficiency, regulatory stability and business focus that it would demerge into two separate companies, the domestic trading business, Centrica, and BG plc which would include the pipeline business, Transco International and the global gas businesses and production and exploration. The demerger took place in February 1997 with the new corporate titles. Progress is being made with renegotiating the unremunerative 'take or pay' gas purchase contracts which British Gas had entered into when it had a long-term domestic gas supply monopoly. These contracts oblige British Gas to pay for the gas at above current market prices, which would not have been a problem if BG had retained its domestic monopoly. The erosion of this monopoly occasioned by the Gas Act 1995, along with excess gas supply, has stranded these contracts; which will be a liability left with the new trading business.

The pressures on the energy regulators to be tough have been high. In addition to the public perception that both gas and electricity companies had profited unduly from government mistakes on industry structure and price controls at privatization, OFFER's credibility was still in question from having had to reopen the electricity distribution review in 1995, and OFGAS's room for manoeuvre was limited to some extent by the promises which had been made about falling gas prices due to the introduction of domestic gas competition. This has to be allied, however, with the role the regulator plays in encouraging new entrants—given particularly that the Gas Act 1995 now requires the regulator to 'secure' competition; an interesting contrast with the other sectoral regulators whose duties are to 'promote' or 'facilitate' competition. Given the new entrants' promises on price cuts to the consumers who switch to them, their profitability is in part related to the extent which transport charges can be kept to a minimum.

Stephen Littlechild, the electricity regulator, after four consultation papers, stuck to making a tough settlement for NGC, cutting X from -3 to -20 in 1997 and then -4 thereafter until 2001 (OFFER, 1996). The NGC indicated it was unlikely to accept, but in the end decided against appealing to the MMC. It was rationalized in terms that an appeal—while fully justified in principle—would tie up too much senior management time, which needed to focus on developing its businesses in telecoms (through Energis, its company which can take advantage of the national grid lines to carry new fibre optic cables) and overseas. Nevertheless, it is interesting to note that, in spite of OFFER being accused of forecasting based on 'using only the rear-view mirror' (i.e. too much account was taken of out-performance in the past rather than of the real potential for efficiency savings in the future), as soon as the settlement was agreed the NGC announced efficiency improvements which seemed to show that achieving the forecasts was quite possible, and that there would be a margin for increased return to shareholders.

It is a problem for the public's acceptance of the incentive regulatory system that the regulated companies statements prior to a settlement have to be interpreted in the context of negotiations, rather than as a statement of what in fact can be achieved. To the public—used to public ownership and accountability—this suggests something untoward when, in fact, it is a necessary part of an adversarial, incentive regulatory system. The same issues arose last year when Northern Electricity was accused of misleading the regulator in the light of information from their defence to the proposed take-over by Trafalgar House.

For Northern Ireland Electricity and British Gas, the regulators' proposals proved too much. British Gas was able to agree the retail price cap for the domestic market which maintained the value of X at -4 until the year 2000 with a forecast profit margin of 1.5% on turnover, although there will be separate price caps for each tariff to protect different classes of customer. Pass through of gas purchase costs was reinstated, subject to economic purchasing (OFGAS, 1996a). However, for its capital intensive gas transportation business—which yields most of the company's profit—the combination of forecasting and methodological disagreements meant that it decided to go to the MMC. The proposal from OFGAS was to cut X from -5 to -20 in 1997 and to -2.5 thereafter until 2002; which equates to an annual cut of 6.5% p.a. (OFGAS, 1996b). There was considerable pressure on both sides to settle, not least because the Government wanted cuts in gas prices secured for the longer term before the General Election, but given the acrimonious background to the regulatory relationship between British Gas and OFGAS, the refusal to settle took on the aura of a test case.

OFREG had proposed tightening X to -31 in 1997 for NIE overall and then -2 thereafter until 2002. There are three separate price caps for the power procurement, transmission and distribution and supply businesses, which are of the same order of magnitude as the average for NIE as a whole (OFFER (NI), 1996). With NIE now also referred to the MMC there is a chance for the MMC to formally establish the appropriate methodology to be used when resetting X. Nothwithstanding, it is interesting to note the increasing use of dramatic first year cuts in X by regulators. To the extent that this can show the customer the benefits of a regulatory system which gives companies the incentive of profit to improve efficiency, then we might find public consent to the system improving in the future.

Methodology

Establishing methodology is a role which has fallen unexpectedly to the MMC. The MMC is not normally bound by precedent and, by treating each case on its merits, may appear to base its conclusions on a different approach from time to time. The regulated utilities, however, provide such essential services, and have such a high public and political profile, that the method and basis for resetting X is particularly scrutinized. The process of public consultation by a regulator, followed by a dramatic acceptance or rejection of the regulator's proposals, also serves to focus and heighten public awareness (or ignorance!) of the issues.

The problem has been, however, that the Government, when appointing regulators at privatization, gave little or no guidance on the process and methodology for resetting X. Regulators have developed their own methodologies, which may or may not be consistent depending on the context in which they are interpreted. The key differences of opinion on asset valuation and depreciation, however, result from decisions taken by the Government at privatization. Given the lack of clarity on 'regulatory bargains' made at privatization, it has been left to the MMC to evolve the core methodology through its reports on successive appeals by the companies against the regulators' proposals. The most notable report in this regard was that on Scottish Hydro, where the framework of the truncated cash flow model was revealed (MMC, 1995).

The truncated cash flow approach is the means by which the regulator can ensure that the price caps are based on allowing a forecast revenue which is equal to the forecast present value of costs (O'Neill and Vass, 1996). If the cash flows are discounted at the cost of capital to the firm, then an efficient company will be able to finance itself, which meets one of the statutory obligations on the regulators. However, three further aspects have to be taken into account in setting the current period's allowable revenue:

- The need to carry-over out-performance from the previous period in order to maintain, or give sufficient, incentives to efficiency.
- The possibility of clawing back economic profit earned in the previous period because it was 'illegitimately' achieved (i.e. reducing allowed revenue).
- The need to take account of the discount at which assets were sold at privatization.

The lack of guidance from the Government on the fundamental structure of the incentive regulatory scheme has meant a wide diversity of practice on the carry-over of out-performance. It is also complicated by the fact that regulators have not distinguished between carry-over which is designed to maintain incentives to efficiency and carry-over which is to honour the 'expectations' of investors as to the allowed rate of return (and dividend stream) at privatization. It is further complicated by proposals (notably from Ian Byatt, the water regulator) to recognize any voluntary acceleration of the return of benefits to customers by the companies through under-utilizing the maximum allowable price caps with an addition to allowable revenue in the next period. This is in order to preserve the incentive to efficiency.

The most dramatic instance of claw-back is the proposed windfall profits tax by the prospective Labour Government. This proposal elicits strong opinions, ranging from just desserts for the 'fat cats' to constitutional impropriety through state confiscation of private assets. If truly one-off, however, it would not damage future incentives to efficiency (it is simply a transfer of wealth from shareholders to the public purse). Of greater long-term interest for the regulatory system is the growing awareness that profits can be boosted by slipping the capital programme on which allowable revenue was based. The NIE proposals included an explicit claw-back (with interest accrued) of allowed revenue in respect of capital expenditure not undertaken. It is vital, however, to distinguish between reductions in capital expenditure which are due to efficiencies on schemes actually undertaken and reductions from simply deferring capital expenditure (although the BAA and OFGAS reviews show this to be difficult in practice). Only the latter should be subject to potential claw-back. The NIE proposals are, therefore, an important methodological development to be tested by the MMC. Both the rail and water regulators have announced their concerns about the progress of capital investment and made it clear that recovery of allowed revenue will take place unless the agreed targets are achieved. Railtrack responded by announcing a £16 billion investment programme over ten years, and some water companies will not increase prices by the maximum allowed in 1997.

For British Gas Transco, however, the major methodological issue is the treatment of the discount at privatization and the impact this has on the allowed depreciation and hence cash flow profile. It is probably accepted by all sides that the rate of return should only be paid on what investors paid for the assets at privatization, not on their notional modern equivalent asset replacement value. However, what has not been satisfactorily determined is whether the depreciation charge should be based on the acquisition value or the replacement value. The former will, other things being equal, mean lower prices today and higher prices tomorrow; the latter will tend to equalize prices over time. OFGAS proposes basing depreciation on the acquisition costs, and hence securing lower prices today for Transco services (OFGAS had originally planned to make this even more dramatic by focusing all the privatization discount on the regulated assets).

This has opened OFGAS to the charge of cross-subsidizing all gas supply businesses (given equal access) from the natural monopoly transport business with a view to justifying the benefits of supply competition. Also, British Gas argue that there is too much regulatory risk in relying on the regulator allowing prices to increase in the future, and hence the cost of capital should go up. Finally, reducing the level of depreciation in early years reduces the incentive to make capital efficiencies.

Unfortunately, although British Gas can argue persuasively that current consumers should pay the current costs of their use of assets (i.e. depreciation), it remains unclear what the implications are for the rate of return. In theory, if current replacement cost depreciation is to be charged, then the discount at privatization should be carried through in perpetuity as an annuity deduction from allowable revenue in each period. Some pronouncements, however, imply that the discount would also be written out, allowing a full return on the replacement value of assets. It will be for the MMC to clarify these issues. What is clear now, however, is that the question of the depreciation profile is mainly about inter-generational equity in charging customers and not the shareholder-customer conflict which is often suggested.

Table 2 shows the sequence of the main price caps for all regulated industries since privatization to date. It should be noted that where the controls also include (wholly or partly) a revenue cap, then the outturn price cap for the year may be different from that estimated by the regulator as shown in the table. In practice, price caps may also have been presented in terms of base cuts on last year's tariffs (for example P_0 cuts in the first electricity distribution review for England and Wales).

Industry Structures and Competition

Competition in the capital markets has continued following the Government's decision to allow take-overs and mergers by lifting its controlling (golden) share. However, developments have begun to intrude on competition policy and political sensitivities in the build up to the election. Multi-utilities have started to develop in order to achieve economies of scale and scope (for example United Utilities, Hyder and Scottish Power), but this argument was not successful with respect to Severn Trent Water's and Wessex Water's contested bids for the take-over of South West Water. Previous water mergers have been allowed if there was an additional price cut for customers to compensate for the loss of a company comparator which the regulator could use to judge efficiency. A price cut was offered so it is surprising that the MMC ruled against allowing either bid to proceed. The regulator noted South West's defence, and the improved efficiency they say they can achieve, and will hold them to these promises in future reviews, but the bidders can perhaps feel aggrieved that having been the catalyst for that information being revealed they, and customers in the region, are to be denied the opportunity to benefit from it.

Caution about the public interest must have been underlined for the MMC because the President of the Board of Trade had recently turned down their recommendation to allow National Power and Powergen to proceed with their bids for Southern and Midlands electricity respectively. Although a vertical reintegration, this had previously been

Table 2. Summary of main price caps since privatization.

BT	
November 1984–July 1989	RPI-3
August 1989–July 1991	RPI-4.5
August 1991–July 1993	RPI-6.25
August 1993–July 1997	RPI-7.5
August 1997–July 2001	RPI-4.5
(Wholesale network access charges to be determined by May 1997.)	
Airports	
April 1987–March 1992 (BAA)	RPI-1+S
April 1992–March 1994 (BAA)	RPI-8+S
April 1994–March 1995 (BAA)	RPI-4+S
April 1995–March 1997 (BAA)	RPI-1+S
April 1997–March 2002 (BAA)	RPI-3+S+D (H'row, Gatwick)†
†Differential should increase by 1% each year.	RPI+1+S+D (Stansted)
Loss of duty-free allowance D, +7$^1/_2$, 1999-2001.	
April 1988–March 1993 (Manchester)	RPI-1+S
April 1993–March 1998 (Manchester)	RPI-3+S
(Where S = Security cost pass through at 95%.)	
British Gas Trading (supply)	
December 1986–March 1992	RPI-2+Y
April 1992–March 1997	RPI-5+GPI-Z+E
Redetermined January 1994	RPI-4+GPI-Z+E
(Where GPI = Gas Price Index; Z = 1% pa; E = Energy efficiency schemes.)	
April 1997–March 2000	RPI-4+Y
BG (Transco)	
October 1994–March 1997	RPI-5
(Where the average price per therm in the base year, 1993-94, is 14.16p.)	
April 1997–March 2002 (proposed)	RPI-20 (1997)*
(Equates to -6.5% p.a. for full five years.)	RPI-2.5 (1998–2002)*
Electricity supply	
April 1990–March 1994 (England and Wales)	RPI-0+Y
April 1994–March 1998 (England and Wales)	RPI-2+Y
April 1990–March 1995 (Scotland)	RPI-0+Y (Hydro)
	RPI-0.3+Y (Scottish Power)
April 1995–March 1998 (Scotland)	RPI-2+Y
April 1992–March 1997 (Northern Ireland)	RPI+0+Y
April 1997–March 2001 (proposed)	RPI-43.9+Y (1997)*
	RPI-1.5+Y (1998–2001)*

(Y covers pass through of distribution, transmission and generation costs. Note: the temporary cap on generation prices in England and Wales ended in 1996. There is a price cap on the power procurement business in Northern Ireland.)

Distribution (England and Wales)

April 1990–March 1995	RPI+0.0 to +2.5 (av. +1.3)
April 1995–March 1996†	RPI-11; -14 or -17 (av. -14)
April 1996–March 1997†	RPI-10; -11 or -14 (av. -11.5)
April 1997–March 2000†	RPI-3

(† Equivalent to an average reduction in X from +1.3% p.a. to -9.5% p.a. for the full five years. The caps were redetermined from April 1996 from RPI-2.)

Distribution (Scotland)

April 1990–March 1995	RPI-0.3 (Hydro) RPI-0.5 (Scottish Power)
April 1995–March 2000	RPI-1 (Hydro) RPI-2 (Scottish Power)

Transmission

April 1990–March 1993 (NGC)	RPI-0
April 1993–March 1997 (NGC)	RPI-3
April 1997–March 2001(NGC)	RPI-20 (1997) RPI-4 (1998–2001)
April 1990–March 1994 (Scotland)	RPI-0.5 (Hydro) RPI-1 (Scottish Power)
April 1994–March 1999 (Scotland)	RPI-1.5 (Hydro) RPI-1 (Scottish Power)

Northern Ireland Electricity (transmission and distribution)

April 1992–March 1997	
Fixed component (75%):	RPI+3.5
Variable component (25%):	RPI+1.0
April 1997–March 2002 (proposed)	RPI-31 (1997)* RPI-2 (1998–2002)*

Water (England and Wales)

April 1990–March 1995	Various K factors; av. RPI+5
April 1995–March 2000*	RPI+1.4: weighted average
April 2000–March 2005*	RPI+0.4: weighted average

(*Equals RPI+0.9 over 10 years; +1.0 for water and sewerage companies; -0.4 for water only companies. Infrastructure charges now limited to £200 per service connection.)

Railtrack

April 1995–March 1996	RPI-8
April 1996–March 2001	RPI-2

(The majority of franchisees' passenger fares will also be capped; three-fifths of fares to RPI from 1996 for three years, then RPI -1% for four years.)

---

*Proposal referred to MMC, which reports in Spring 1997.

allowed in Scottish Power's take-over of Manweb and in Eastern Group's acquisition of generating capacity. In theory, vertical reintegration may be efficient and not cause problems with the abuse of monopoly power if there is effective supply competition. Indeed, in the long run, commentators are expecting between five and eight vertically integrated energy companies to emerge as the dominant players; so the DTI decision could be seen as contrary to market developments and politically influenced by the forthcoming election. Nevertheless, since full domestic competition in supply is not due until 1998 in gas and electricity, there is a defensible case for stalling on vertical reintegration, particularly as the RECs have argued strongly to postpone the introduction of supply competition.

One consequence, however, has been the domination of foreign take-overs, with US companies having acquired over 50% of the regional electricity companies. Table 3 shows the present position. It will be

Table 3. Take-overs of regional electricity companies.

RECs at privatization	*Acquired or proposed by*	*Bid date*
US bids		
Seeboard	Central and Southwest (CSW)	September 95
SWEB	Southern Company	September 95
Midlands	Avon (GPU and Cinergy)	May 96
Northern Electric	Calenergy	October 96
East Midlands	Dominion Resources	November 96
London	Entergy	December 96
Yorkshire	American Electric Power (AEP/PSC)	February 97
Other bids		
Manweb	Scottish Power	July 95
Eastern	Hanson	July 95
Norweb	Northwest Water (United Utilities)	September 95
SWALEC	Welsh Water (Hyder)	December 95
Other		
Southern	Bid by National Power blocked by Secretary of State	

important for the next government to clarify its overall competition policy and the constraints which that will place on regulated industry restructuring. The public is concerned about vertical reintegration in electricity, and we are already seeing evidence of amalgamation in rail (in addition to which, the rail regulator has warned competing rail operators to improve their accuracy and impartiality in selling tickets). A clearer vision of the expected market structures which might emerge through the introduction of competition is required. But because the public have a confused view of the respective responsibilities of the sectoral regulators, the Office of Fair Trading, the MMC, the Secretary of State for Trade and Industry and Parliament (including the Departmental Select Committees and the Public Accounts Committee), the prospect for criticism about arbitrary and politically inspired decision-making remains.

In the Telecoms sector, the process of making European and global alliances continued for both Mercury and BT, and reflects the breakdown of the barriers between traditional telephony, broadcasting and other multi-media services. BT's proposed merger with the US company MCI is a gigantic global venture, and has triggered regulatory investigations in the UK, the US and by the European Commission. It is likely to take more than a year before any go-ahead is given. In the transport sector, it is expected that groups will control a range of franchises, and bus companies have been to the fore in acquiring rail franchises. This could be a good thing if it integrates the planning of services over various travel modes, but may become a problem if local monopoly power is achieved and regulation is not effectively integrated across the travel modes.

The main proposal for regulatory integration has been to combine the gas and electricity regulators, but not until after 1998, the date for full supply competition. In the meantime, regulators have shown they can work together to ensure that multi-utility groups of companies cannot play off one regulator against another, for instance, in developing transfer pricing guidelines and amending licence provisions.

Policy Agenda for the Next Government

Whichever party comes into power after the General Election it will, in practice, be faced with the considerable inertia of past decisions. For Labour their pro-competition policy statements will limit the capacity for radical changes to the regulatory system, and for the Conservatives continuity would have been the order of the day. There are a number of policies, however, which either party could usefully pursue. They would be the same policies, but whichever party introduced them could argue they represented a distinctive feature of the party's political philosophy. Such policies would, if successful, encourage long-run stability in the regulatory system which, given an incentive-based regulatory system, would benefit shareholders and customers.

The objectives of regulation must be clearly stated. The primary objective is customer protection against the abuse of monopoly power, with the longer term objective of encouraging efficiency to reduce the long-run cost of supply. It would be worth considering whether the legislation which sets out the duties of regulators makes this objective clear enough, given the perception that regulators balance the interests of the companies against the interests of consumers. In practice this is not the case, there simply being a constraint on regulators to ensure that (an efficient) company can continue to supply, which of itself is in the long run interests of consumers. Competition is a means to an end, not an end in itself, and clarity of competition policy is essential. It could avoid the sort of dramatic reversal of policy which occurred in January 1997 when the Government announced that extensive direct competition in the water industry would not proceed after all.

Accountability and transparency must be enhanced with clear sources of reference on the general methodology to be adopted for resetting X. The Government might wish to consider issuing a statement on the framework for economic regulation, given experience to date, and to ally that with an improved process for Parliamentary accountability. This may be adequate when it comes to the line accountability of the regulator to the Minister of the sponsoring department and the associated House of Commons' departmental select committee, but there needs to be a focus for occasional cross-sectoral reviews of the incentive regulatory system as a whole. Rather than establish a special select committee for regulation (on the lines of the old Nationalized Industries Committee), it might be better to expand the Public Service Committee's remit, since it shadows the Cabinet Office and deregulation.

The question of making expert resources and advice available to select committees in this complicated area may also have to be addressed in the light of the National Audit Office's report on the work of the regulators for the PAC. Debate has continued on whether individual regulators should be replaced by panels or, at the very least, should have a non-executive board of expert advisers. In practice, all regulators have built up panels of advisers already. Of more concern is the continuing question of whether too much information remains unpublished because it is judged to be commercially sensitive. Confidentiality hinders accountability and transparency of decision making, and is a weak argument where there is natural monopoly. This should not obscure, however, the regulators' improving record on the extent of consultation and the publication of data to meet open government provisions.

Better communication of the role of profit, and the shared benefits between owners and customers of a periodic price capping system, is required if the public is to consent to the current system. There is a role for government, regulators and the regulated companies in achieving this, and it will involve the enhancement of the process and procedures for customer representation. Profits made from a regulated monopoly are likely to be judged an abuse, and so without improved public understanding of an incentive system which makes additional profit the quid pro quo for even lower prices in the future, there is a danger of public demands for change destabilizing regulation. Whether annual formula profit sharing, as proposed by Labour, is the answer is a moot point, although regulators in general have come out against it this year (Vass, 1996). But without regulatory stability, and a clearer statement on the methodological principles which helps ensure consistency for future periodic reviews, it is unlikely that the better alternative to annual formula profit sharing, which is voluntary acceleration of benefit transfer by the companies to customers when they are earning economic profits, will become widespread. The regulatory contract has to be real (Elphick, 1996).

Finally, following the introduction of a requirement for a cost-benefit test on new environmental standards, which was included in the 1996 Environment Act, the policy for environmental and service standards should be more clearly articulated. Standards should be set (broadly) at a level where the incremental benefit to the public and consumers equals the incremental cost. Nevertheless, lack of clarity on this issue has bedevilled the debate this year on whether the water companies should do more to stem leakage, and the public is not persuaded by the concept (however rational) of 'economic' leakage. It is just seen as wasteful (and lack of investment and maintenance as probably one of the reasons why the 'fat cats' can pay themselves so much!). Unfortunately, the issues become complicated because as demand for water grows, today's economic leakage becomes tomorrow's 'uneconomic' leakage, given the cost of acquiring new water resources. It is this wider context which makes the debate on water metering so controversial. The role of economic regulators and the Government has to have a clearly understood demarcation, and the balance between command and control standards versus market solutions or tax levies will need to be reaffirmed, otherwise public confidence will continue to be weakened by the default of a clear vision which integrates market and non-market processes. ■

References

CAA (1996), *Economic Regulation of BAA London Airports 1997-2002*, CAP 664 (October).

Elphick, C. (1996), *Sharing Out Performance* (CRI Discussion Paper 14, CIPFA, London).

MMC (1995), *Scottish Hydro-Electric plc—A Report under Section 12 of the Electricity Act 1989* (May), (HMSO, London).

OFFER (1996), *The Transmission Price Control Review of the National Grid Company: Proposals* (October).

OFFER (NI) (1996), *Price Control Reviews for Northern Ireland Electricity plc: The Director General's Proposals* (July).

OFGAS (1996), 1997 *Price Control Review—Supply at or below 2,500 therms a year—British Gas Trading: The Director General's Final Proposals* (November).

OFGAS (1996b), *1997 Price Control Review—British Gas' Transportation and Storage: The Director General's Final Proposals* (August).

OFTEL (1996), *Pricing of Telecommunications Services from 1997: OFTEL's Proposals for Price Control and Fair Trading* (June).

O'Neill, D. and Vass, P. (1996), *Incentive Regulation—A Theoretical and Historical Review* (CRI Research Report No. 5, CIPFA, London).

Vass, P. (1996), Profit sharing and incentive regulation. In Vass, P. (Ed), *CRI Regulatory Review 1996* (CIPFA, London).

11 The Future of Regulation

Catherine Waddams Price

Centre for Management under Regulation, University of Warwick

The two crucial questions for regulating monopolies over the next five years are: ensuring the best balance between incentive and equity; and the extent to which competition should be introduced. The price cap system of regulation will be 13 years old in 1997, and it has reached puberty in many senses. All the industries have seen at least one revision of the initial price cap, so that the levels no longer reflect primarily the initial privatization settlements which were so generous to shareholders. Equally, the structure of many industries, particularly BT and BG privatized in the mid 1980s, has changed almost beyond recognition with the introduction of competition into new areas. This changes the nature of regulatory policy from a deterministic approach to an entire industry, to a dual regulation: of an 'essential' facility where monopoly remains; and of the conduct of incumbent and entrants where markets became competitive.

The division between competitive and non-competitive parts of the privatized industries is now much more clearly defined, and development of regulation for those parts which 'competitions cannot reach' more important than ever. But these developments bring part of the privatized industries, and their regulators, much closer to the jurisdiction of general rules of competition, both British and European. It is therefore difficult to divorce the agenda for the nationalized industries from wider issues of competition policy. Moreover, the central role of the industries themselves in supplying both inputs to industry and 'essential' services to households raises broader questions of efficiency and equity, as well as sectoral issues on, for example, energy policy.

Price Cap: Dividing the Spoils

The issues of regulation and industry structure and competition are closely related, but let us start with a consideration of price cap regulation and its development since its 'infancy' since 1984. Price cap was introduced in the context of unhappy experiences with traditional rate of return (cost of service) regulation in the USA, and with the expectation that it might be a temporary measure. Very little attention was given to determining how the level of price cap should be chosen to succeed the initial constraint, which was set by the Government as part of the privatization bargain. If only successive price caps could be determined so apparently arbitrarily, much of the regulators' work and a great deal of political and industry angst would be saved. When the industries were privatized they were generally believed to be operating inefficiently, and so some positive efficiency target in the form of lower (real) prices seemed appropriate. Because of the Government's interest in the revenue raised from flotations, these targets were generally not unduly demanding, often reflecting productivity improvements already being realized in the last years of public ownership.

It was the incentive element of the price cap which has proved both its greatest success and its most controversial element. The industries achieved productivity gains greatly in excess of those required by the initial price caps, mainly by shedding labour, and exceeding the expectations of even the nationalized industries' most stringent critics. The combination of liberating the capital markets from public sector constraints and giving managers a direct interest in the profitability of their company exposed the enormous scope for lower costs within the previously nationalized industries. Questions of equity arose in determining whether the companies should keep these gains and, if so, for how long. In the short term, under pure price cap, all went to the company and could be clawed back for consumers in a variety of ways when the cap was revised. In theory, regulators could try to recover some of the past gains from the company, though most regulators deny that their decisions are in any sense retrospective, and are indignantly challenged by companies when their actions are perceived to be backward looking. As an intermediate step, the regulators can redefine the base prices to which the cap should apply by requiring a step reduction in price to reflect the new level of efficiency revealed by productivity improvements over the preceding period (so that the firm keeps the gains until the new price cap is introduced). Or the regulator can increase the rate of price reduction required in the new period so that the prices at the end of the period to which the new cap refers reflect both the efficiency gains made in the 'old' cycle and those which the regulator thinks are reasonable in the current period. Clearly the company benefits from efficiency gains for longer under the last than under the second regime, though the rate of price decrease required could make allowance for such interim gains. In price reviews conducted during 1996, the gas and electricity regulators used the step-price reduction approach, and the telecoms regulator the accelerated reduction approach. However, these price cuts did little to abate the public criticism of the levels of profit declared by the industries.

Much of this outrage is undoubtedly inherited from the ambivalent attitude to these industries when publicly owned: they were criticized for inefficiency if they made losses and for monopoly exploitation when profitable. Given their semi-autonomous status and unclear directions, along with political interference at both macro and micro levels, the size of the inefficiencies which have been revealed is hardly surprising in retrospect. The question is how far price cap regulation was responsible through its high powered incentives for these revelations, and perhaps more important, whether continuing high powered incentives are needed to realize further potential efficiencies. Here is a clear trade off between equity and efficiency. Managers will be more enthusiastic about realizing efficiencies the higher the proportion of these benefits and the longer the period over which they accrue to the company. More immediate profit-sharing schemes have been proposed; these link current profits and price levels, requiring additional price reductions if companies' profits exceed a predetermined level. Such schemes would reduce these incentives, but might make the system seem fairer. Perhaps the most worrying 'incentive' effect is the temptation to disguise the size of the profits, particularly around any level that might trigger profit sharing. This would result in considerable expenditure of effort and money on hiding profits, which might provide excellent opportunities for accountants but would produce little real economic gain.

The arguments for profit sharing on equity grounds are likely to appeal most to those who put more weight on consumers' welfare compared with the profits of companies, so it is not surprising that such proposals have come from within the Labour Party. But the concerns about incentives outlined above might also suggest alternative ways of redistributing the gains from eliminating inefficiency. One form of profit sharing already exists through corporate taxation and, if this proves unsatisfactory, a more general reform of that system might be appropriate. Little can be done to redress some extravagantly generous privatization deals such as were made with the water companies, but at least these are known in advance and can be taken into account by the regulator in determining the price cap. Of course companies do indulge in just the sort of tax avoidance behaviour which would attend profit-sharing schemes. But unless incentives can be skilfully balanced so that a company's action's effect on its tax is counteracted by its profit-sharing liability, which seems unlikely, the fewer such 'thresholds' the better. (Such a counter balance was found in the incentives provided to British Gas in the internal transfer price of the gas supplies which it owned in Morecambe Bay. A high price could be passed through to consumers via the price cap formula, but would increase British Gas' liabilities for petroleum revenue tax.) Some estimates of the additional gains for consumers from profit sharing suggest that bringing them forward, rather than allowing them to be recouped at the next price review, would have only marginal effects on consumer benefits (Vass, 1995).

Regulation for Quality—Universal Standards

However, the price cap system itself may need other forms of review, in the interests of both efficiency and equity. The main concerns are quality of service and the extent to which companies should be allowed freedom to rebalance prices within an overall constraint on average charges. The issue of freedom to rebalance prices is closely bound up with introducing competition, and another traditional role for nationalized industries in charging similar prices to all consumers regardless of their different costs of supply. The quality issue has been a longer-term concern of price cap regulation.

If the product to be price capped could be clearly and unambiguously defined and costlessly monitored, there would be no problem in regulating for quality. But, where this is not the case, the firm may increase profits within the cap by reducing the quality of the product or the service which accompanies its delivery. Moreover, even if the regulator can monitor quality, there is a problem if the integrity of the system requires a single level of quality (for example of the water in a distribution system, or reliability of supply for electricity): the regulator may have to choose that single quality with little information on which to base the decision.

Competition may give consumers the opportunity to choose between different qualities of service (for example incoming calls only facilities for telephones, interruptible residential supplies for electricity) which may have implications for social cohesion and social policy. There was a huge public outcry at the report of experiments to determine how much individuals valued security of electricity supply, since some commentators suggested it was outrageous that any consumer, especially those on lower incomes, should receive a supply inferior to that of others. It seems even stranger that the poor especially should be forced to pay for a higher level of quality than they would opt for, given a choice. But in challenging the notion that the utilities provide a universal service to all consumers, the new patterns in liberalized markets will pose a political and economic challenge to the incoming government.

Introducing Competition

Similar issues will emerge in pricing. Liberalization will change the behaviour of the incumbents as they respond to new entrants, though not quite in the simple way of making prices more cost reflective as is often suggested. It is true that liberalization will eliminate straightforward cross-subsidy where consumers are charged less than the directly attributable marginal costs of their supply. But the sum of these is generally much less that the total costs of supply, and there are probably few prices presently charged which do not cover these *direct* costs.

Even outside the natural monopoly distribution networks there are economies of scope, for example in an accounting system for supplying different types of consumer. Many of the costs of supply are joint and cannot be unambiguously attributed to any particular group. Recovery of these joint or common costs will be radically affected by competition. A monopolist will not necessarily want to charge these costs in equal proportions to all consumers; while a company supplies the entire market to maximize profits, most of these non-marginal and common costs are recovered from consumers who will reduce their demand least in response to price increases. This is also very similar to the most 'efficient' economic pricing structure, since demand is disturbed least from the pattern in which all consumers face only their marginal costs of supply. But if the market is liberalized and new suppliers can enter, they will naturally be attracted to just those markets where prices are considerably above marginal costs. The incumbent will react to defend these markets by lowering prices, and shifting the recovery of common costs more evenly across products and consumers. We have seen just this behaviour in the residential markets already opened to or preparing for competition: increasing line rentals for telephone; discounts for those who pay by direct debit in gas and electricity; agitation from regional electricity companies about the structure of their tariffs.

In gas and electricity, in particular, those who pay frequently by prepayment meters or other schemes are more costly to supply, but their demand is also more responsive to price changes, suggesting that on efficiency grounds alone they should bear a smaller part of common costs. The flat tariff structure which the privatized utilities inherited from their nationalized predecessors, with low mark-ups over marginal costs for these consumers and higher mark-ups for less price responsive consumers paying by direct debit, also coincided with a profit-maximizing pricing pattern. This is one explanation for the minimal tariff restructuring undertaken by privatized utilities in markets which were not threatened with competition.

But with competition the situation changes as the most profitable consumers become a target for new entrants: the direct debit payers in energy, the high users in telecoms, so the incumbent needs to lower prices to them to retain profitable markets. The price cap enables rebalancing within the average (subject to the constraints on standing charges which have proved binding in telecoms but not in gas) and we have seen considerable alterations. In telecoms, where competition has been at least a threat since privatization, line rentals have increased by 23% and call charges fallen by 40% in real terms since 1984. In gas, charges for those paying by direct debit have fallen 7% below those for credit consumers in the past two years, and 12% below prepayment charges. On average, electricity prices have fallen about 4% more for direct debit than for credit consumers.

Such rebalancing may reduce not only efficiency but equity. The distributional implications arise from the fact the consumers who are now bearing a higher proportion of the common costs are also low-income households. Those in receipt of state benefits will not receive any automatic adjustment; indeed since average prices which form the basis of benefits and pensions will fall under the aggregate price cap, benefits will also fall. This is properly a matter for central government, dealing with income distribution.

But the aversion of both the Labour and Conservative parties to addressing such problems directly suggests that it will have to be finessed through the regulators themselves. Various strategies have already been instituted.

From 1997, OFTEL has removed the price constraint from the one fifth of residential consumers who make most use of the telephone, thereby effectively tightening the cap for the less frequent users by narrowing the base over which prices could be averaged. The gas regulator has imposed separate caps on each element of the tariffs in place in 1997, preventing an *increase* in any element, though not differential rates of decrease within the cap. But, if competition and price rebalancing become fierce, there is a real danger that universal service will be maintained only at very high costs to those consumers who can least afford to pay, and the Government might need to take action to alleviate hardship. This is particularly worrying at a time when the system of paying fuel bills direct from benefits is under threat. The challenge is to safeguard those most at risk, without jeopardizing the benefits which liberalization can bring to the market as a whole.

Regulatory Institutions

So far we have discussed the outcome of the regulatory agenda for the next government rather than the regulatory structure itself, which was the subject of considerable debate in the last Parliament. The main issues have been whether the regulatory bodies should be merged, and whether the individual 'directors of supply' should be replaced by commissions. Some argue that the variety of styles of regulation which have developed within the typically vague statutes which instituted the offices of regulation calls for harmonization. But the system has clearly benefited so far from the evolution of different models of regulation, and such variety is likely to continue to be a strength rather than a weakness. The real problem is in co-ordinating regulators not at the executive level but at the policy level and this is a crucial issue for the incoming government. The nationalized industries performed a myriad of (mostly unacknowledged) functions:

- Providing regional employment.
- Cross-subsidizing between different geographical areas through equalized pricing.
- Subsidizing frequent payment schemes for consumers who needed them.

These functions are threatened by private ownership and liberalization. Commentators on the nationalized industries may have regretted lack of clear government guidance on their objectives, but the vacuum left by their privatization is potentially much more serious. The industries themselves are left unclear about the extent to which it is proper for them to undertake non commercial activities, and the regulators have no powers or duties beyond encouraging competition and preventing undue discrimination.

Some suggest a much more radical overhaul of the whole system. John Kay has promoted the idea of consumer-oriented corporations subject to financial constraints, though his proposals seem more convincing for bodies such as the BBC than for the utilities; where products are sold direct to consumers it is difficult to see how obligations could be defined in terms of different consumer groups, and even more difficult to see how such a corporate structure could operate in a competitive market. Although consumer co-operative ownership has worked reasonably well in places like Denmark, this has often been combined with heavy state regulation and continuing monopoly, and it is not clear that they would fit happily within the UK capitalist structure.

The Challenge

So the real challenge for an incoming government is to define much more clearly the role of the formerly nationalized utilities in the economy. This requires specification not only of the parts to be played by the regulators themselves (whether separate or united, individuals or commissions) but a clearer definition of both general competition policy and sectoral plans such as energy and environmental policies. Whatever the UK's future relation with the EU we shall be forced to confront these issues as these policies are formulated on the mainland of Europe. Contrary to the British tradition of unwritten constitutions and minimalist definition, these issues need to be addressed by the incoming government. An open and explicit discussion is likely to result in an outcome which is both more politically acceptable and economically efficient than the confusion and policy vacuum which was implicit in many of the nationalized industries, and is increasingly exposed by privatization and the liberalization of their markets. These are not new issues, but they are becoming increasingly urgent. ■

12 Private Finance Initiative

Douglas Hogg

CIBC Wood Gundy, London

Douglas Hogg, until Summer 1996 Chief Executive of the Private Finance Panel, looks at the problems and prospects for the Private Finance Initiative in the UK. He explains the excessive expectations that people have put on the Initiative and concludes that the way forward is in creative, derivative forms of the PFI.

The Private Finance Initiative was launched in Autumn 1992 by the then Chancellor, Norman Lamont. Mr Lamont said that:

- Self-financing projects undertaken by the private sector would no longer need to be compared with theoretical public sector alternatives.
- The Government would actively encourage the private sector to take the lead in joint ventures with the public sector.
- The public sector would have greater opportunity to use leasing where it involved significant transfer of risk to the private sector and offered good value for money.

PFI has quickly established itself as the 'belle of the ball', offering the Government the opportunity to increase investment in the short term, deferring government expenditure over the long term. Its initial focus was one of ensuring the deal is 'off balance sheet' and offers 'value for money'. The Private Finance Panel was established in 1993 to initialize and catalyse activity, to highlight and explain the benefits of the PFI, not just to do the deals! The Panel has fulfilled that vision of its remit and accelerated the PFI with the close support and sponsorship of HM Treasury. The Private Finance Panel's summary list of 'agreed' projects,

Table 1. Agreed* PFI projects (value in £M); end 1996.

Government department	*Value*
Home Office	266
Department of Transport	4,991
Department of Social Security	390
Department of Health	489
Ministry of Defence	408
Scottish Office	84
Welsh Office	22
Northern Ireland Office	26
Department of the Environment	215
Inland Revenue	50
HM Treasury	190
Department of National Heritage	45.5
Lord Chancellor's Department	10
Department for Education and Employment	11
Total	7,197.5

Source: Private Finance Panel (London).
*'Agreed' projects are where the preferred bidder has been announced and negotiations regarding the final contract are underway. Most, but not all, of the projects on this list have been signed.

with values in £M, is shown in table 1.

The initial expectation of the PFI was, and to a large extent continues to be, as *the* means by which much needed short-term capital investment can be made whether in new assets, refurbishing existing ones, or helping to maintain the country's capital stock. PFI has proved itself able to do this in areas where project finance has long been practised, notably transportation of one sort or another. From the 'shadow' tolling mechanisms used on the roads programme, PFI has been translated into other areas of public service where there is no 'real' or 'user' revenue stream. For example, in prisons, where a shadow payment mechanism attaching to the availability of prison cells creates a similar structure.

Couple the shadow toll mechanism with the opportunity to generate capital through surplus assets and the opportunities for PFI can be extended even further. However, every transaction must be properly tested to ensure that it is genuinely off balance sheet and not borrowing through the back door, whether by leasing or otherwise.

The 'off balance sheet' argument in relation to individual projects can become very circular. The Private Finance Panel and Treasury have published guidance to help people identify what may or may not be a suitable PFI project—for example, where there is a high capital cost and very low annual operating cost, with no surplus assets to leverage private sector capital, the transaction can look more like borrowing than anything else. Having said that, other problems dog the application of PFI—hospitals, for example, where the total 'capital to operating cost' over a 30-year life is 1:10, i.e. only about 10% of the total cost is on capital. And there are many other issues that need to be addressed:

- Who has a track record in building complex projects of these sorts?
- Who understands how the market-place will evolve over 30 years?
- Who understands how to operate hospitals?
- What are the political uncertainties?

In short, there are enormous uncertainties about how the *business* (if that is what it is) will evolve over such a long period of time that the private sector may just not be willing to play and put up the many, many millions of pounds needed to fund these transactions.

PFI is not the panacea to the absence of capital available to government right across the needs of the public sector in all its forms. A continued expectation that PFI can provide this sort of 'cure' is unrealistic and is unfair in judging how successful the PFI has been, is and will be. To continue to do so would be like 'setting the controls and heading for the centre of the sun'. We are quickly reaching the point where the Government should be able to draw a line in determining the limits of PFI 'as we understand it today'. However, many of the techniques that are being developed and used can be evolved to enable further private sector involvement in the more challenging and sensitive areas like education and health, where there is a desperate and growing need for capital expenditure.

There are an enormous number of constraints and difficulties opposing the progress of PFI in government; this chapter concentrates on the two important ones:

- How you define a potentially successful PFI project—otherwise known to some as 'scoping the project'.
- The difficulties in financing successful projects.

Defining PFI Projects

Traditional capital procurement focuses on the asset which needs to be replaced or refurbished. Not surprisingly, the focus for a potential PFI project is one that takes a similar approach. This is wrong, not least because we are now talking about a *service* rather than an *asset*. An asset may only be a part of a service, for example the catering facilities for a prison—the *asset* will be the kitchen, the service the feeding of prisoners; but as a structure for a deal this may not work and it may be necessary to think more holistically as has been done in terms of providing the full 'inmate service', i.e. full prison facilities. However, there are prisons where the catering is provided by the private sector but the prison itself run by the public sector—otherwise known as contracting out. We begin to get into difficulties, PFI begins on the one hand to look like privatizing infrastructure—my example of a private prison—or contracting out if one were simply to contract out the catering services. Thus, PFI becomes an option alongside existing initiatives, including contracting out and privatization.

The price, however, for failing to properly define a project or service—whether it is part of a larger service or not, is greater than simply failing to ultimately deliver the project because it won't work. Assuming that we had defined our project as kitchen services and provided a new kitchen, our (say) 10-year contract might then interfere some years later with another project which might require the replacement of the prison as a whole. In other words, too narrowly defining a project today may torpedo a potential project tomorrow. And worse still, for those responsible for defining potential PFI projects, it is not just a matter of looking at whether a transaction may be workable, but also whether it is going to enhance or interfere with future plans where PFI may also be a part of the solution.

The Challenge for Financiers

Before identifying a potential PFI project, it is vital to have a clear understanding of whether the private sector is going to be able to fund it off balance sheet. The initial focus across the public sector was one that concentrated on the off balance sheet treatment and ensuring value for money—risk transfer and value for money were the key tests defined by the Treasury and others as needing to be overcome.

However, there was little, if anything, available in the way of well-known and well-practised techniques for determining risk transfer and value for money. How do you measure the value for money of the cost of a service over 30 years, versus a public sector capital procurement over three? Little, if any, information exists on the budgeted versus outturn costs of running assets over decades—in both the public and private sectors. Yet this is what people have to try to do before a PFI transaction can qualify. A part of that process of course involves risk—is the higher private sector cost of funding (which itself puts a value on risk) better value than the public sector cost which does not? How do you break each of the individual risks down? If you can do that, how do you then value them and what probability do you attach to each of them occurring, and if they do, at what cost to the client? The process is very complicated and has dogged the progress of individual transactions and the PFI as a whole in its early years.

Today, there are literally hundreds of potential PFI projects coming forward where people have been wrestling with these issues for months getting into years. Now a fresh challenge has begun to emerge—we have a contract between the public sector and the private where there appears to be value for money and risk transfer—but is it financeable? Many projects have reached, or are reaching, preferred bidder and their sponsors are now beginning to talk to financiers to understand their requirements, only to find that not only are financiers imposing conditions that have not been anticipated, and that they will not accept some of the risks that are being transferred. In other words, the deal is not financeable and therefore there cannot be a deal.

But the picture worsens—there is not just one set of requirements for private sector funding. Providers of debt, providers of sub-debt and providers of equity all have different requirements. They all have their own lawyers and they all have an interest and a say in the way in which risks can be structured, the returns or costs of finance they require, and need to be party to the way in which a transaction is structured.

Providers of debt are relatively straightforward in their requirements. They will need some form of completion, performance, or financial guarantee during the construction period and some form of revenue guarantee thereafter. Where a number of parties is involved, they often require joint and several guarantees. As lenders into project finance transactions, PFI is a similar proposition and many of the financial ratios that they insist upon are well known and well established in the market. But it is not just a question of cost; lenders will need to be able to sell or syndicate their debt and will therefore want to be satisfied that they have a structure that will be attractive in the debt market. Most, if not all, institutions will therefore approve investments on a 'credit' (i.e. acceptable risks), as well as 'liquidity' (i.e. can we sell it given the structure and interest rate?) basis.

Debt providers take limited risk and consequently lower returns. Investors of equity take higher risk and, of course, demand higher returns. Debt providers will wish to see their investment returned ahead of all other investors; not so for equity providers who will be the first to lose their money in the event that things go badly. Why, then, is it that equity providers are often involved so late in the definition and structuring of a project? Surely, as the investors who stand to lose their money first and who take their money out last, they have the greatest interest in being involved from the outset. They rarely are, and problems ensue when their interest is sought in making an investment into a transaction presented as a *fait accompli*.

It is too often the case that, in structuring transactions, assumptions are made about the cost of debt and some allowance made for equity. When the transaction is tested with potential investors, it quickly becomes apparent that there is too little equity with the debt providers being too close to the front-line—they want to see more equity as a buffer between them and things going wrong. In restructuring the transaction, the need for more equity subsequently increases the cost of the deal—exchanging a, say, 8.5% per annum interest cost of debt for 15% per annum cost of equity. The effect is to make the deal unfinanceable because the cost becomes unaffordable and/or unacceptable.

Where to Now?

PFI is undoubtedly proving itself in areas that have traditionally lent themselves to project finance-type techniques like transport. The shadow toll mechanism, coupled with the availability of surplus assets through which private sector investment can be leveraged, will undoubtedly enable the Private Finance Initiative to expand into areas like local authorities, health and education, if, and only if, projects are scoped properly.

The next wave of challenges to the PFI lie in 'private sector created' obstacles in the form of financiers' requirements and the need for competent resources to process and digest the enormous number of transactions coming forward. It is unlikely that PFI can reach its potential given the limited number of resources (in the form of people) available today. PFI is simply too costly to bid, and too time consuming to close, to yield the sort of results required of it if it is to meet the capital shortfall that exists at the moment. A more efficient means of procuring PFI projects needs to be found to ensure that this Initiative yields its potential over the next decade. That 'means' must lie in the form of a public/ private partnership where the private sector is the dominant owner but the public sector can share in the upside and has sufficient controls and is given sufficient commitments that everybody is happy.

Properly developed and handled, PFI *in its derivative forms*, can indeed provide much of the desperately needed investment in new and existing capital stock in the UK. It is a mistake to say that there is one form of PFI, and only one form, and that it will provide the answer to all our problems. It is time for people to get creative and begin to develop some of the lessons we have learned in trying to apply PFI to the more challenging areas of public service where it is desperately needed. The hope is that the excessive expectations that people have put on the PFI and the immense problems that have dogged its progress, do not stop people from giving it enough of a chance. ■

13 The Euro

Noel Hepworth

Institute of Public Finance (IPF) Ltd, Croydon

The uncertainty about whether or not the UK will join the Single European Currency system and adopt the euro is confusing to organizations. However, this chapter explains why the public bodies should begin making arrangements for the risks and opportunities that a switch to the euro might create. To do otherwise would be to add to risk and that would be very unwise in the competitive environment in which all public organizations are expected to manage.

From 1 January 1999, companies will be able to choose whether to manage their financial affairs in euro, in both euro and the national currency or in the national currency alone. There will be no compulsion and no prohibition; figure 1 gives the EU's timetable for the Single European Currency system. There is considerable evidence that many companies will choose to either operate in euros, or in dual currencies, as soon as possible and for a number this will mean starting on 1 January 1999. Invoices will therefore be issued in euro, payments made in euro

Figure 1. Euro timetable.

From 1 January 1999
•Exchange rates of participating countries are 'locked'.
•The ecu is replaced by the euro.
•Non-monetary transactions can occur in either euros or the national currency.
•New government debt is issued in euro.
•Corporate debt can be issued in either euro or national currency.

From 1 January 2002
•Euro notes and coins will be issued.

From 1 July 2002
•National currencies will cease to be legal tender.

through the banking system, debt issued in euro and financial management systems converted to operate in euros.

At the retail end of the transaction chain, it is unlikely that such transactions will shift to the euro until cash becomes available on 1 January 2002, although it is feasible that the necessary preparations will allow for retail payments in euros using electronic systems to occur before then.

Whether a company decides to switch into the use of euros or to run using dual currency systems sooner rather than later will depend upon its circumstances. Many of the major companies operating in several countries of the European Union (i.e. multinationals) have already decided to switch to using the euro from 1 January 1999—Volvo, Philips and Siemens are examples. They propose to make the switch whether the countries in which their head offices are located decide to join the Eurozone or not. Similarly, companies with many transactions in countries likely to join the Eurozone will find it in their interest to switch sooner rather than later and many other companies will be influenced by the attitudes of their suppliers, purchasers of their products and investors, by the strategic opportunities they see as emerging and by the decisions of their competitors. For example considerable operational savings can be achieved through recognizing that subsidiaries can be managed in future as if they were part of a domestic market; a reduction in foreign currency transactions reduces the costs of currency risk and that can lead to a relocation of manufacturing and purchasing arrangements, as well as affecting decisions about investment. Companies will also be able to reorganize their financial management processes and achieve economies because they will be able to run, for example, one financial management control system, and one purchasing and invoicing system. They will also be able to amalgamate different treasury and banking arrangements.

However, there will be some increased costs in preparation for the euro. New software will probably be required although probably not for internal financial management purposes. New vending machines, money exchange mechanisms and till systems will be needed. The changes which will be required will need careful planning and that will divert resources from other activities. IT costs may be high because of the coincidence of the software/hardware changes required for the introduction of the euro and the changes needed to solve the 'year 2000' problem.

For industry and commerce to fail to take steps to prepare for the introduction of the euro has potentially serious consequences:

- They may be made more vulnerable to competitive threat as competitors make the change.
- They may be unable to respond to the changing market conditions which the creation of the Eurozone will bring about.
- The longer the process is left, the more it is likely to be rushed, with the possibility of mistake, inadequate planning, higher cost and hence risk.

The Uncertainty in the United Kingdom

We do not know when the UK will adopt the euro. Therefore many organizations in the UK, including public service bodies, have not even begun to make preparations. Is this a wise position to adopt?

An argument is that if the UK is to stay out of the Single European Currency system then the euro will be a foreign currency and will be treated as such by organizations in their accounting, financing and management processes. However, will it really be like that?

First there will remain the prospect that the UK may join at some time in the future. Second, multinationals based in, or operating in, the UK are likely to use the euro in their trading and dividend payments forcing other UK organizations to accept euros for their everyday activities or alternatively requiring banks to make the conversion which may be costly; in other words the euro is unlikely to be confined to the capital markets. Third, those companies with strong links to Eurozone countries are likely to find it in their interest to trade in euros because they will be under considerable competitive pressure from their Eurozone partners risking as a result losses through the strategic reappraisal of purchasing, manufacturing and investment decision which the introduction of the Single European Currency will generate.

Should Public Bodies Prepare for the Euro?

Public service bodies may feel that, even given the arguments that as they operate wholly within the UK (with a few notable trading exceptions) and, as they are largely involved with retail transactions, then these reasons for preparing for the change are very much diluted.

However, there is another set of arguments about why preparation for the introduction of the Single European Currency is desirable:

- Public service bodies are as much affected by the 'millennium problem' as private organizations. If software/hardware has to be changed to cope with that problem, a sensible precaution is to provide at the same time the flexibility to allow the body to accommodate the introduction of the euro at some (unknown) period in the future.
- A regular renewal process of vending and ticket machines (parking ticket machines for example) is always underway and it would be sensible to include in the specification for the new machines the requirement that such machines should work with the new currency.
- Public service bodies handle large amounts of cash. Cash tills and coin-counting machines ought to be able to handle both currencies.
- Failure to plan will result in significantly increased costs with the accompanying risk of an inability to acquire the new software/ hardware and other equipment associated with cash handling on time. Imagine the prospect of not being able to pay social security and housing benefits or to collect council taxes or parking charges because of a failure of preparation.

In summary, preparation reduces risk and, as the essence of the new public management style which now exists is competition, then organizations need to plan and organize to minimize risk wherever risk can be foreseen and the obverse of risk is opportunity. Preparation for the introduction of the euro will allow decisions to be made about new software and equipment and a reorganization of systems and arrangements that might otherwise be delayed. Preparedness will also create commercial opportunities, for example by one local authority making available new systems to another.

Effects of the Euro

Public services bodies are in no different position from private organizations, with the exception that most are not trading across national borders. But they have the same basic management requirement. The main areas of activity that will need review are:

- Financial management systems—including software and hardware.

- Treasury operations, particularly where sophisticated 'hedging' instruments are used.
- Payroll and pension calculation arrangements.
- All charging systems, including private patient charges.
- All cash handling mechanisms and systems.
- Credit card arrangements.
- Ordering and invoicing systems.
- Direct debit systems.
- Banking arrangements.
- Benefits systems.
- Council tax, billing and collection systems.

There may also be accounting (i.e. financial reporting) consequences, particularly over the treatment of the currency gains and losses which will arise when the currencies become locked.

In addition, arrangements will need to be made to train staff in familiarity with the new notes and coins; to help them understand the impact on their pay and similarly with pensioners; and to help them educate and assist clients, customers and citizens. Apart from the impact upon their own activities, most public bodies are also likely to have a public education role to prepare the general public for the change. That process, though, is likely to be some time off and an essential requirement is to manage any public education campaign in a way which prevents it peaking too early.

There is also one other factor which public bodies are particularly vulnerable to and that is fraud on themselves. All change creates opportunities for fraud and a change of the magnitude of the introduction of the euro obviously enhances these opportunities. So an important element in the planning process should be an assessment of the fraud risk.

Some concern has been expressed about the content of contracts—will the introduction of the euro effectively frustrate contracts? The answer to this is almost certainly 'no', although some concerns have been expressed about how financial contracts operating under New York law will be affected. In drafting the European legislation introducing the euro, great care has been taken to ensure that contracts will not be frustrated and the question should not therefore cause much, if any, diversion of effort.

Who is Doing What to Assist Organizations to Change?

The Bank of England has issued a series of publications under the title of *Practical Issues Arising from the Introduction of the Euro*. These are mainly concerned with capital market issues but do contain some information on the issues for business. These publications are freely available from the Bank.

Also the Fédération des Experts Comptables Européen (FEE) has established a major information project with the European Commission designed to use the accountancy profession across Europe as a major source of advice and information. FEE has established a major database of relevant information and this is accessible on the Internet (http://www.euro.fee.be/). Enquirers can search the database by topic, by country, by language and by document origin. Topics include accounting, audit, banking arrangements, billing, bookkeeping, capital market transaction, capital structures, cash, clients, controllership, conversion planning, customers, education, foreign currency, financial management, financial reporting, fraud, invoicing, information technology, insurance, investments, legal issues, marketing, payroll, pensions, pricing, public administration, purchases, sales, software, strategic issues, taxation, training and treasury. As part of the project, FEE will be publishing newsletters, checklists, research into specific problem areas and brochures setting out the effects upon particular types of organization, including public sector bodies. It will also be organizing pan-European conferences and working with national accountancy bodies to provide seminars and to develop local programmes of activity. The distinguishing feature of the FEE project is its concentration on the detail of the decisions that organizations need to make.

Copies of the database will also be published on CD-ROM and the newsletters, checklists, brochures and other outputs also will be available on CD-ROM. These can be obtained from CIPFA or directly from FEE in Brussels, 'phone 00 322 285 4085 or from 00 322 231 1112.

In addition, a number of the major banks have also published useful information and copies can be obtained from their head offices. ■

14 Public Audit

Mary Bowerman
Sheffield University Management School

This chapter highlights some of the deficiencies of the current arrangements for the external audit of public services. Solutions proposed by the Cabinet Office, the Treasury and the Nolan Committee have concentrated on the margins and some of their proposals could trigger a domino effect with an unpredictable outcome. By tinkering, we risk damaging the audit 'eco culture'. Public audit needs to be reviewed by the incoming government on a much more strategic level.

Public audit is currently enjoying a high public and political profile; it has been the subject of a series of reviews by the Nolan Committee and the government; it also forms part of the Labour Party's plans for promoting the accountability of local bodies. A number of political scandals in the early 1990s contributed to an erosion of public confidence in the holders of public office. Issues of probity, fraud and corruption have rarely had a higher profile. Searches for ways to improve probity and accountability, such as the Nolan inquiries, have reinforced the view that the public has a right to expect high levels of accountability from its public services.

Britain's auditing regime has, for some time, strained to keep pace with an increasingly fragmented structure of government. The most recent audit acts (the Local Government Finance Act 1982 and the National Audit Act 1983) were the first attempts in over 100 years to address the constitutional role of public sector audit. However, they were far from a thorough reappraisal of the role of state audit within the modern state structures and were essentially a clarification and reinforcement of existing understandings. The way in which public services are delivered has changed dramatically in recent years; audit legislation has tried to match these changes in an *ad hoc* and, at times, ill-conceived manner. The full impact of the acts and the practice of audit under their provision have not yet been fully assessed.

The effects of 'new public management' on the structure and management of the public sector and the growth of non-departmental public bodies (NDPBs) have reinforced doubts about the adequacy of the 1983 Act. The environment within which public sector audit is operating is undergoing significant changes and the precise role of audit in the changing public sector is far from clear. In the meantime, increasing emphasis is being placed on audit as a means delivering accountability, but it is not clear that audit can meet these expectations. It is therefore timely for the role and practice of public sector audit to be reassessed.

Recent Reviews of Public Audit

The Nolan Committee was established to examine the conduct and standards of individuals in public life. However, a number of witnesses—including CIPFA, the Audit Commission and the National Audit Office (NAO)—placed these issues in the wider context of corporate governance and the role of audit in providing assurance on standards of probity and propriety in public services (Evans and Thornton, 1997). The first report of the Nolan Committee (1995) touched upon audit arrangements and recommended that the Government should undertake a review aimed at bringing all audit bodies up to the standard of the best (see figure 1).

Figure 1. The first Nolan Committee's main recommendations regarding public audit.

Review of arrangements for external audit
'The Treasury should review the arrangements for external audit of public bodies, with a view to adopting the best practices to all'.

NHS public interest reports
'The Audit Commission should be authorized to publish public interest reports on NHS bodies at its own discretion'.

NAO inspection rights
'We believe, in principle, that the propriety of all public expenditure should be capable of review by the appropriate public auditing body. We see much merit in the Comptroller and Auditor General being granted inspection rights over all public expenditure. Where such rights do not already exist, this could be achieved through contract terms or grant conditions attached to public funding'.

This review was conducted by the Cabinet Office and Treasury within a broad remit of examining the legal framework and the audit of public bodies, including 'local spending bodies'. Despite the scale of the task, the team comprised just two people and in March 1996 the findings of the review were published in a white paper on *Spending Public Money: Governance and Audit Issues*. The review suggested only incremental, mainly technical, changes. Its proposals were fairly unambitious, the most significant finding was that funding bodies should be responsible for over-viewing the audit process (see figure 2).

The second Nolan report on local spending bodies (1996) reiterates the views expressed in the first report, and suggests that audit after the event should be tougher (see figure 3). Significantly, and somewhat at odds with the Cabinet Office/Treasury review, Nolan suggests the full application of the public audit model to bodies such as training and enterprise councils (TECs).

It is disappointing that the two reviews appear to conflict over the central issue of whether there should be common audit requirements for the expenditure of public money and also that they leave so many issues unresolved—for example the question of who should appoint external auditors.

Therefore, despite reviews and considerable attention from the media and politicians, it is by no means clear what the precise future role of audit is likely to be. There is, however, a recognition that public audit can potentially play an important role in securing higher standards of conduct in public life and that it will remain relatively high on the policy agenda for the foreseeable future.

While is apparent that much is expected of audit, it is not clear what audit is intended to do. Evans and Thornton (1997) suggest that the Government has made: 'no attempt to define a coherent framework of public audit' and that there is a need for a common code of audit practice for local public spending bodies, underpinned by a common set of principles of public audit.

Arguments about the scope and application of public audit revolve around the issue of whether one believes that all public money should, potentially, be subject to the same level of audit scrutiny, regardless of whether it is spent by a government department or a private company. There are two polarized positions on this. It has been argued that the expanded scope public sector

Figure 2. The Government's proposals for audit in *Sending Public Money.*

NAO access

The NAO should have inspection rights to all executive NDPBs and to companies which such NDPBs wholly or mainly owned—but stress should be targeted at key areas and shouldn't create an unnecessary burden. NAO should also have access to contractors' records if they are necessary for the audit.

Strategic oversight by sponsoring department/funding body

The sponsoring department/funding body 'must ensure that those receiving [funds] have adequate financial control arrangements, including appropriate internal and external audit...they are in a good position to ensure that the audit framework is satisfactory and that quality is maintained'. The external auditor should send copies of audit reports to the sponsor department.

More NAO comparative studies

The NAO's Comptroller and Auditor General (C&AG) 'may also be able to extend value for money studies by developing more systematic work on comparative performance, both overtime and between NDPBs, in areas where similarities in their activities make such analysis useful'.

Public interest reports (National Health Service)

The Audit Commission should be able to publish public interest reports on NHS at its own discretion.

NAO/Audit Commission review of co-operation

'To help strengthen the effectiveness of public audit, the Government believes that it would be useful for an independent reviewer to look at the interface between the national audit agencies where more than one has capacity to act. The review would appraise the merits of different working methods where a large number of bodies deliver similar services at local level and consider the scope for possible rationalization and joint working, taking into account the collaboration that already exists'.

Market testing public audit

NAO should make more use of private sector firms—competition and market testing.

audit imposes an unnecessary burden on organizations in a market-driven public sector. Alternatively, there is the view that all expenditure of public money needs to be subject to the same high standards of regularity, probity and value for money audit; and there is concern that an audit/accountability gap is emerging in areas which receive only a rudimentary audit. An increasingly entrepreneurial public sector requires a balance to be struck between innovative measures to improve efficiency (which may entail risk) and the scrutiny required by audit (which may stifle innovation).

Furthermore, analysis of audit in practice shows there is a lack of clarity about the purpose of audits and that there are some fundamental tensions and anomalies within current audit arrangements. For example is the role of the auditor to help management or to blame them? There is confusion about who is the client for the audit, and whether the public should have access to audit reports. There is considerable variation in the audit approach between different sets of auditors; whether they conduct an audit or a review; how much access they have; and in arrangements for their co-operation. On the

Figure 3. The second Nolan Committee's main recommendations regarding public audit.

Effective post event auditing
As far as possible, control should be limited to setting policy guidelines and operating boundaries, complemented by an effective audit framework and sanctions.

Full application of the public audit model
'The relevant departments should ensure that TECs and LECs are subject to the full weight of public sector audit...where a citizen receives a service which is paid for wholly or in part by the taxpayer, then the Government or local authorities must retain appropriate responsibility for safeguarding the interests of both the user and the taxpayer regardless of the status of the service provider'.

A single auditor
'As far as possible, a single external auditor should be responsible for all aspects of public audit. The framework to achieve this should be devised in consultation with the national auditing agencies and other relevant bodies [it] should address requirements of various statutes and funding bodies'.

question of policy, there are some restrictions on how far auditors can examine policy but, conversely, it appears that in some instances auditors can, and do, set the agenda and influence policy.

Until these questions and uncertainties are addressed we will continue to build our public audit edifices on weak foundations. The most recent government review has been described as a 'missed opportunity' (Evans and Thornton, 1997), it therefore lies with the incoming government to undertake a fundamental review of public audit and its role in relation to public accountability.

The first stage of such a review, before getting involved in the detail of audit techniques and institutions, should involve asking four basic questions:

- Whom do we want to hold to account?
- What do we want them to be accountable for?
- Whom do we want to make them accountable to?
- How do we want to use the accountability information?

Whom Do We Want to Hold to Account?

There is much confusion over who should be accountable and to whom. The quest for increased public accountability is portrayed as ways of making public bodies (officials and politicians) accountable to the public. This can be distinguished from *political accountability* whereby politicians are accountable to the public (usually via the ballot-box) and *managerial accountability* whereby officers are accountable to their superiors through the hierarchy up to politicians. The political accountability model appears increasingly inadequate due to loss of trust in politicians, low turnout in elections and extended periods of one party government. It is further weakened through the separation of policy from operations (as in executive agencies) and, at the extreme, the location of power and authority in un-elected bodies (for example TECs). Such developments fall outside of the traditional accountability models as accountability for many NDPBs and the NHS is via Ministers with no automatic link to Parliament. This, combined with an increasing proportion of local authority finance being provided by central government, means there is arguably an accountability gap to the national taxpayer for spending at local level. A further gap, frequently overlooked, is the restriction on audit in playing a constitutional role in illuminating the accountability of politicians to the public. As Jackson (1993) commented: 'while political leaders are keen to introduce systems which will ensure operational performance is measured and evaluated, they do little to enable the evaluation of the strategic performance of public services. To do so would be to evaluate the effectiveness of policies and, therefore, to put into the political domain politically sensitive information that would be used to judge, in the political arena, the efficiency and effectiveness of the policy-making process'.

Conversely, Walker (1996) believes that auditors are perceived as 'constitutional actors', in that they have a remit to check and balance the operations of legislators and executives. He argues that this role may be welcomed by politicians as audit can provide a set of rules which relieves them of the need to exercise (and take the blame for) their discretionary powers. Nevertheless, our public audit bodies cannot question the merits of policy and therefore do not hold politicians to account.

What Do We Want 'Them' to be Accountable For?

There is still some ambivalence as to whether society is happy to rely on accountability for outputs, which is the type of accountability in keeping with an entrepreneurial culture, or whether there is still an expectation that there should also be accountability over the processes. There is an inherent conflict here as bodies have been encouraged to operate independently and on business lines and so control over processes appears as excessive interference. These issues were not adequately addressed by the Cabinet Office/Treasury review; although Nolan appears to favour the accountability for outputs model; however, at present features of both approaches are apparent and there appears is little thought to which is appropriate or desired by the taxpaying public.

Whom do We Want to Make 'Them' Accountable To?

Public auditors are expected to be both watchdogs for the public and catalysts for change, helping those responsible for services to improve them. The central issue is whether we want accountability to remain internal within the hierarchy of providers, funding agencies, sponsoring departments and Ministers (managerial) or external to the public. The helpful nature of much of the auditors' work emphasises the internal aspects of accountability but in doing so it has neglected the elements of public debate and sanctions which were features of traditional public accountability.

Tensions emerge because the auditor is not only the neutral certifier of management's account but also a consultant to management, as well as a commentator on or judge of management's performance. The auditor must attempt to strike a balance between apportioning retribution and blame with coaxing and encouraging management towards better performance. Butler (1995) acknowledges the conflict caused by the roles of 'watchdog' which should be conducted in public and the role of 'consultant' which should be conducted in private. If the findings from the auditor's consultant role (i.e. value for money reports) are made public then this could jeopardize trust and could cause authorities to be defensive about the auditor's findings. At the same time, keeping these reports private denies the public (and possibly elected members) the information which they need to make a comprehensive judgement of the performance of the authority. Clearly the auditor has a difficult task of attempting to satisfy several stakeholder groups; it is unclear which, if any, group should take priority if there is a conflict of interest. The rhetoric surrounding public audit suggests that the public watchdog role is the most important, in practice it is acknowledged that the two must be balanced. However, the Cabinet Office/Treasury review introduces a third main client for the audit: the sponsoring department. This may further marginalize the public watchdog role.

The tendency to view management as the main client for the audit is likely to be reinforced by the market testing of audit services in health and local authorities. The impression is created that organizations are responsible for selecting the auditors and in negotiating fees levels, number of days of audit work etc. Some NHS bodies are already lobbying strongly for the right to appoint their own auditors. These trends need careful monitoring to ensure that they do not undermine independence. Increasingly, too, the audit bodies are required to compete for central government audits. The risk here is that the auditor is encouraged to regard the audited body, rather than the citizen, as the customer. As has happened in the private sector, this could lead to an unwillingness to upset the 'customer' for fear of losing the audit.

How Do We Want to Use the Accountability Information?

The next dilemma is whether we should use audit as a control mechanism (there to give assurance that taxpayers' money has been well spent, that citizens receive adequate levels of service, to provide information to enable us to complain and to censure those who wasted public money), or whether we develop audit as a way to help organizations learn how to manage better?

In the *control* role the auditor acts as a watchdog on behalf of the taxpayer/citizen. This is the role which the Labour Party envisions for the Audit Commission in its proposal that the Commission should intervene in a council's management where 'one or more services were failing or costing far more than could be justified' (Labour Party, 1995). The proposals suggest that the Audit Commission should set up an advisory team to help the council and should monitor a recovery plan; if the Commission is still dissatisfied it should have the power to recommend to the Department of the Environment (DoE) that a management team be sent in to run the service. The risk with this approach is that the auditor may be perceived as intrusive and may exacerbate distrust, so that the auditors advice may go unheeded.

Conversely, in the *learning* role where the auditor acts as a consultant on behalf of the organization, there is a risk that the auditor may lack independence, may identify with the management rather than the public and that the audit findings may remain confidential to the organization

An Audit Framework—the Prerequisites

Some consensus about these four issues is necessary before we can tackle the question of the audit framework because the accountability process is the prerequisite to the system of audit. A change in one will affect the other. It is also possible to think of them in terms of compensating for each other—for example if the accountability model is rigorous and demanding, then there may be scope for making the audit model a more flexible, consultancy-style role; however, if the accountability model is based on delivered outputs then this may allow for more of a watchdog/whistle-blowing role for the auditor. Because many important questions have gone unanswered for some time, we are beginning to see the consequences in terms of gaps and inconsistencies in the accountability process, but also in terms of the development of audit services. The following section discusses some of the symptoms of disequilibrium caused by the audit system and the accountability system running separately and suggests some options which may have a place within a new, more radical, audit framework.

Audit Independence

The Cabinet Office/Treasury review contends that Parliament has made funding bodies responsible for ensuring that public money is properly spent—'their routine monitoring and value for money work can be considered as part of public audit'. This statement has serious implications for audit independence: essentially it requires the internal audit sections of the funding bodies to act as quasi-external auditors responsible for overseeing its purchasing decisions but without an effective outlet for their findings to the public or Parliament.

In addition, audited bodies are increasingly expected to meet the audit fees for both financial and value for money audits, apparently with little thought as to how to encourage bodies to follow up fraud issues. Furthermore, if organizations are to continue to appoint their own auditors and to have some discretion over the scope of the audit, how are they to be encouraged to set appropriate standards? The potential dangers are obvious—that public bodies will select the audit option which will cause them least embarrassment and expense. Private sector auditing has recently experienced a crisis of confidence, if we want avoid similar problems in the public sector then we need to build in additional safeguards.

Is it reasonable to expect the organizations to pay for their own monitoring? If the cost of a fraud enquiry must be met from an already stretched budget, then will it be followed up and exposed or swept under the carpet? If public audit is to be considered a public good, then there is a strong case for arguing that it should be funded by the public and should report to them. The NAO charges fees for financial audit work only, the Audit Commission's auditors and the firms charge for all audit work—this tends to reinforce the view that the organization is the client and has implications for independence as well as accountability.

Rationalizing Audit

Problems of co-ordination exist in two main areas:

•The number of auditors with rights of access to some public bodies (for example Nolan cites the situation for TECs where seven different sets of auditors may visit). This situation imposes additional burdens on the audited bodies in responding to the auditors' enquires.

- The potential overlaps between the two main audit bodies: the National Audit Office and the Audit Commission regarding the value for money auditing of local government and the NHS, and for value for money auditing in relation to housing and education.

The obvious option here is to merge the national audit agencies into one body with a wide remit. I have previously argued against this (Bowerman, 1994), suggesting that the individual cultures are a strength; however it seems that more recently the potential for overlap has increased. Both bodies have responsibilities in the fields of health, education, housing and local authorities and are increasingly funded through central government.

A less radical alternative would be to rationalize the auditors' duties in accordance with the purchaser/provider divide of their clients; with, for example, the NAO auditing the funders and the Audit Commission responsible for the audit of schools, hospital trusts, housing associations etc.

Another option would be to keep two audit agencies, but differentiate by function rather than by the bodies which they audit. Both agencies could audit the same organizations but one could specialize on audit for public accountability and the other on the consultancy/advice/support performance measurement aspects. Existing specialisms of the national audit bodies would suggest NAO for the former and the Audit Commission for the latter. This arrangement would have the merit of having a clear unambiguous audience for the audits.

A further obstacle to rationalization is the considerable divergence between audit frameworks in the UK in terms of audit scope, appointment of auditors and audit techniques. If the Cabinet Office/Treasury review is implemented, a series of different audit frameworks will be developed by the different funding bodies. An alternative, and neater, approach would be to have a set of guiding principles and audit standards intended to apply to all public audits. There is already broad agreement over what this should involve, the international supreme audit bodies have a similar publication as do the USA. The US has a set of government auditing standards for all auditors of federal, state or local government organizations, programmes, activities and functions. The guidelines apply to financial and performance audits and consider general standards (for example independence and quality control), field work standards (planning, evidence etc.) and reporting standards. The standards put considerable emphasis the comprehensive nature of government audit and on co-operation between different sets of auditors and encourages them to rely on each others' work to satisfy some of their requirements.

If the UK were to produce a similar set of standards and guidelines, this need not necessarily tie us into a uniform public audit model, we could for example require funding bodies to justify why they think their providers should be allowed to opt out of some aspects of the requirements. If all public auditors were operating to the same rule book it would be easier to operate reliance arrangements.

Involving the Public

It seems almost a truism to say that the findings of public audit should be public, yet despite the breadth of scope of public audit, its findings are surprisingly invisible to the public. For example the majority of audit findings in local authorities, except where serious problems are discovered, are not as of right in the public domain. The public are not entitled to see the audit management letter which summarizes the audit, although in practice these are often placed in the public domain. Local value for money reports are primarily targeted at the chief officers of the authority and may not even be copied to all elected members.

Public visibility is particularly poor in the case of audit findings in the NHS. The auditors' reports go to non-elected boards and in some cases to the Secretary of State. The involvement of the Secretary of State should, theoretically, provide a link between the auditor and Parliament but in practice the process is not open: Parliament has no automatic access to such reports. The publication of NHS public interest reports will go just a short way towards remedying this. Trust boards can still decide not to make the management letters a public document

For the remainder of public money, access to the auditors' findings varies considerably, in many cases the auditors' report comes to rest with the sponsoring/governing bodies. It is not clear whether the public will ever find out if, for example the Further Education Funding Council has concerns about a college, whereas under local authority control the auditors would have looked at financial controls and systems probably each year, and conducted regular value for money reviews, it is likely that the findings would have been in the public domain giving the local public a chance to exert pressure.

Change is needed on two fronts; first, making published audit reports more accessible and, second, by developing arrangements whereby the auditor is encouraged to see the public as a major stakeholder.

Why should it be so difficult and expensive to obtain published audit reports? For example if a citizen wanted to obtain the Audit Commission's Citizen's Charter indicators for local government they would have to pay about £50 for the various volumes covering the range of services. In other countries, for example the USA, citizens are entitled to free copies and the reports are frequently available on the Internet. OFSTED reports are now on the Internet—why not audit reports and PAC reports?

Options for involving the public in the audit process might include using 'citizen auditors' who could be consulted as part of the audit process and where appropriate could even participate in an audit. This approach builds upon the principles of corporate governance but introduces elements from 'citizen juries'. Instead of acting as non-executive directors of the organization, the citizens in this instance would be more independent with allegiance to the general public rather than to the organization. As a further extension of the concept, independent citizens could be members of the audit committees of public bodies, to observe, and to influence through feedback, the audit process and its findings, but also to act as catalyst to the organization in responding positively to audit findings.

Such mechanisms are not a panacea, there would be problems over the choice of citizen representatives and the legitimacy of their opinions, there is also a danger of dominance by particular interest groups; however, such initiatives would allow for a more deliberative response to the audit and could help reassert the public as the ultimate client of the audit.

Maximizing the Impact of Public Audit

As far as public accountability is concerned it is not helpful merely to make available quantities of information (for example the local government Citizen's Charter indicators). This puts the burden of evaluation onto the public. The indicators tend to concentrate on managerial performance rather than enabling the evaluation of policy-making and are therefore of little use to the public in holding anyone to account. Unless the responsibilities of politicians for the performance of public service organizations is adequately recognized then public service managers are likely to be held to account for decisions over which they have no input or control. Attitudes on this issue are changing, for example the Labour Party (1995) has proposed a greater interpretative role for the Audit Commission: 'We believe that the Commission should be refocused to incorporate a standards inspectorate, which would present a professional report to local councils and local people on a council's record in reaching, exceeding or falling short of the targets it has set itself. The Audit Commission could also assess against comparable councils the stringency of targets a council set in the first place. This external professional input would help councillors and local people make a more informed judgement about their council'.

This takes us back to the question of how useful is the work of the auditor if it does not embrace evaluation, particularly of policies, as this effectively lets politicians off the audit/accountability hook. However, the audit agencies do occasionally stray very close towards policy evaluation, and, despite the restrictions imposed by legislation, appear to have more discretion than they currently exercise to undertake more probing studies. More consideration should be given as to how the auditor can add value by reporting issues which are of greatest concern to the public, for example on the effects of internal market changes on the health service (which despite numerous requests for an investigation has never been reviewed by the Audit Commission or the NAO). In particular, NAO reports are sometimes accused of being too guarded. For example a recent NAO report on regulation of the utilities consisted of 290 pages of facts, figures, descriptions and questions but does not have either conclusions or recommendations. The NAO has the constitutional responsibility and possibility to conduct hard-hitting reviews; it has reporting channels to Parliament and the public and is frequently identified by the press as the guardian of the public interest; yet on the important question of regulation of the utilities it stops short of providing a rigorous assessment of the process and its implications.

At the other extreme, some of the work currently undertaken by the external auditors could more usefully be carried out within the organizations concerned. The external auditors do considerable amounts of data collection and assessment which arguably could and should be undertaken by the audited bodies, individually or collectively; for example the comparative data produced by the Audit Commission—including the Citizen's Charter indicators. Ideally, management should now take over quality exchange or bench-marking clubs and thereby take responsibility for their own performance. This could release external audit effort to examine probity and accountability issues and would allow audited bodies to take responsibility for the integrity of their own internal control and corporate governance systems.

Conclusions

The public is encouraged by the Government, the national audit agencies and the media to see the auditors as strong, powerful, independent, and hard-hitting. There has never been any suggestion in the public sector of an expectations gap between what the auditor does and what the public think they do, as there has been in the private sector. But perhaps there is a previously undiscovered gap which is just beginning to show up. Do people assume that all of the auditors finding are reported, at least to their elected representatives? Do they assume that the auditor is working on their behalf and that they have a right to know the auditors' findings? Do they realize that there are large amounts of public money which are not subject to the full rigours of public audit?

If public accountability is the primary objective of public auditing, then the process may benefit from being adversarial as opposed to helping management. This may require auditors to report directly on their evaluation of an organization's performance rather than simple giving a bland opinion.

This chapter has pointed to some of the deficiencies of the current arrangements for the external audit of public services. Both the Cabinet Office/Treasury review and Nolan have raised some important issues and made suggestions that could help bring audit into line with development in the public sector; but they have concentrated on the margins and some of their proposals could trigger a domino effect with an unpredictable outcome. By tinkering we risk damaging the audit 'eco culture'. We need to open out the review of public audit on to a much more strategic level. The fundamental questions we need to address are what are, or should be, the accountability relationships? This requires open and full consultation with the public, politicians, managers and auditors. Anything less risks divorcing the audit arrangements from the public's requirements and expectations. ■

References

Bowerman, M. (1994), The National Audit Office and the Audit Commission: co-operation in areas where their value for money responsibilities interface. *Financial Accountability and Management, 10*, 1.

Butler, P. J. (1995), *Review of the Audit Commission* (Audit Commission, London).

Cabinet Office/HM Treasury (1996), *Spending Public Money: Governance and Audit Issues*, Cm 3179 (HMSO, London).

Evans, M. and Thornton, S. (1997), *What is the Proper Scope of Public Audit?* (CIPFA, London).

Jackson, P. M. (1993), Public service performance evaluation: a strategic perspective. *Public Money & Management, 13*, 4.

Labour Party (1995), *Building Local Communities.*

Nolan Committee (1995), *Standards in Public Life*, Vol. 1, Cm 2850-1 (HMSO, London).

Nolan Committee (1996), *Standards In Public Life—Local Spending Bodies*, Cm 3270-I (HMSO, London).

Stewart, J. D. (1984), The role of information in public accountability. In *Issues in Public Sector Accounting* (Phillip Allan Publishers, Oxford).

Walker, D. (1996), The rise of public audit. In *Adding Value? Audit and Accountability in the Public Services* (CIPFA, London).

15 The Voluntary Sector

Jenny Harrow

South Bank University Business School, London

The twin themes of governmental responsibility to the voluntary sector and the sector's own responsibilities for sustaining its identity and independence recurred throughout 1996. Co-ordinating responsibility at central government level for the sector moved from the Home Office to the Department of National Heritage. The effectiveness of departmental (Home Office) funding of voluntary organizations was the focus for a critical National Audit Office report, with subsequent response by the Public Accounts Committee. An independent 'commission' on the sector's future in England sought government action in 'raising the voltage' in its relations with the sector; and the Government's response was muted. In local government, impending changes in structures were likely to affect those relations. Charities' support from and attitudes towards National Lottery funding continued to be a central concern.

The Size and Nature of the Voluntary Sector

The voluntary sector is, in the phraseology of the *UK Voluntary Sector Statistical Almanac, 1996,* a 'moving target' (Hems and Passey, 1996). Including charities (in the sense of registered, legal entities) and private non-profit making bodies, much of the sector is characterized by the voluntary effort of its workers and supporters, yet many such organizations are funded extensively by statutory bodies. Government sources present the sector as 'large' but indeterminate, 'perhaps 400,000 to 700,000 voluntary organizations in the United Kingdom' (Sproat, 1996). More analytically, drawing on the Office for National Statistics' *Survey of Charitable Organizations*, Hems and Passey (1996) provide a comprehensive and authoritative picture of the sector. They describe one in which 120,000 'general charities' had in 1994-95 'almost £12 billion in income, operating costs of almost £11 billion, net assets of £35 billion, and contributed 0.6% to Gross Domestic Product'.

Almost half the sector's income is voluntary, that is grants and donations, primarily from the general public (36%), from government (28%), and from within the sector (9%). Hems and Passey note that 'the level of direct financial support from business is very low (4%)'.

Partnerships

Despite providing players of increasing importance economically, the sector's identity is blurred; making problematic much public policy debate on the sector's status, role and future. Predominantly, discussion describing voluntary/statutory relations as those of 'partnership', does little more than ascribe a quality of relationship without clarifying what either party means by this phrase. The Labour Party's March 1996 Consultative Document on the sector, for example, called opaquely for the relationship between government and the sector to be 'renewed' (Labour Party, 1996). While the numbers of registered charities in England and Wales is rising (181,467 in 1995), the intertwining between 'public' and 'charitable' bodies is a growing feature, with the former in some cases seeing translation into the latter as a form of salvation. For example, Hounslow local authority was reported in October 1996 as seeking to convert its leisure services department into a charitable trust, which 'a study by KPMG suggested could save £700,000 a year'; this creation of a 'quasi-charity' being a move already made by other local authorities (NCVO, 1996).

At central government level, inter-sector relationships relate primarily either to policy-making, or to individual departments' own funding of particular organizations. That funding (for which the 1995 breakdown had yet to be published by December 1996) reflects departments' own priorities (which may not necessarily be fully in line with each other), and emphasises the extent to which the sector is being supported where its work coincides with or reflects departmental objectives. In support of those objectives, some departments are increasing their use of sector 'umbrella' or 'intermediary' bodies, as the distributors of funds. In Wales, from April 1997, local bodies' funding from the Welsh Office will be channelled via the Welsh Council for Voluntary Action. In October 1996, a press release from DNH announced two new grants programmes within the Government's 'Make a Difference (Volunteering) Initiative' are to be 'administered by the Community Development Foundation on behalf of the Department of National Heritage'. The press release noted that: 'The Community Development Foundation is both a charity and a non-departmental public body', raising intriguing questions of visibility and accountability.

Changes in Government Departmental Responsibilities

The Home Office's long-standing responsibility for policy co-ordination for the voluntary sector moved to the DNH in May (Bottomley, 1996a). A new grouping, with the interlocking tasks of responsibility for work on the voluntary sector, volunteering, charities and community development, the Voluntary and Community Division (VCD), incorporated the Home Office's Voluntary Services Unit. The rationale for this move (subject to Opposition criticism as occurring without the slightest discussion or consultation with the sector) was hard to understand. Harrow and Vincent (1996) suggest that the move will prove problematic for the sector's interests, not least because of 'the impression...gained in Whitehall that DNH is stretched and short-staffed'.

The nature of the structures make them difficult to describe as part of the 'machinery' of government, in part because important variations in these mediating structures occur with the nations of the United Kingdom, so making them, properly, 'machineries' in the plural. They may be better seen as a series of 'networks', where complex series of relationships exist, to respond to changing situations (following Mintzberg, 1996*). Such networks are in themselves 'moving targets' and their operations may mean that some voluntary organizations find it easier than others to gain entry. Harrow and Vincent (1996) suggest that this points towards some government/voluntary organization

---

*Mintzberg (1996) identified five models for organizing government's controlling authority or *superstructure* and the activities of its agencies, or *microstructure*. These are the Government-as-Machine model, the Government-as-Network model, the Performance Control model, the Virtual Government model and the Normative-Control model.

relationships as akin to mentoring. They also tease out the critical differences in governmental structures, as between England and Wales, Scotland and Northern Ireland, in outline maps, which are published in *The Voluntary Sector and the 'Machinery' of Central Government*, which is available free to Public Finance Foundation members (tel. 0171 543 5701).

The 'Commission into the Future of the Voluntary Sector'

An independent inquiry, aiming to provide 'a clear vision for the role of the voluntary sector in England', set up by the National Council for Voluntary Organizations (NCVO) and chaired by Professor Nicholas Deakin, reported in July. Its quasi-government title—'a commission'—emphasises the closeness of at least some elements of the voluntary sector to the public sector, as well as the importance which is intended to be attached to its deliberations. The Commission's report stressed the need for the sector to retain its independence and diversity, while detecting a 'decline 'in the policy influence of the sector, albeit 'along with many other bodies outside government' (Deakin, 1996). Acknowledging how crucial it was for the sector to 'continue to be judged favourably in the 'court of public opinion' (*ibid.*), and emphasising its own 'agenda for action', the Commission made recommendations across a vast canvas—including regulation, fiscal support, contracting, managerial strategy and practice, performance evaluation and sector probity.

Central to its raft of recommendations is that proposing the drawing up of a 'concordat between the government and representatives of the sector, as a code of good practice, for future relations' (*ibid.*, p. 123). The content of the 'concordat', its purposes and relevance to public relationships that seem mostly in flux make this recommendation, and doubt over who the signatories might be, makes this, as a Government Minister acknowledged, a 'very important' but also 'very difficult recommendation' (Sproat, 1996). The Government's response, in November 1996, was predominantly a reiteration of the value of existing approaches, processes and structures. Bluntly, given the sector's diverse nature, 'the Government does not believe that a formal concordat is a sensible or usefully achievable objective' (DNH, 1996).

Recommending a review of the VCD/DNH effectiveness, 'preferably within one year', the 'Commission's preferred solution is its transference to a central position in the Cabinet Office...equivalent to the Citizen's Charter Unit'. This is a solution to a problem more identified within the sector than within government; that is, its low profile. An example of this view is the evidence from the Association of Chief Executives of National Voluntary Organizations, calling for a 'Ministry for the voluntary sector', to offset the situation in which 'the third [i.e. the voluntary] sector is more often...invisible' (*Third Sector*, 1996). Arguing that the DNH transfer was motivated by a desire to strengthen this co-ordinating role, the Government felt that 'the Deakin report...does not make the case [for] a further move' (DNH, 1996). The Commission's case for a Parliamentary Select Committee specifically for the sector was also rejected.

The extent of internal differentiation in the regulations and structure of the sector in the UK as a whole is highlighted by this Commission's applicability in England. A separate Scottish 'Commission' is due to report in Autumn 1997. It is expected to press in some areas for parity with England and Wales, with the Scottish Council for Voluntary Organizations' noting that 'the absence of a Charity Commission in Scotland [means that] all charities suffer from the lack of a well resourced body to give them advice' (SCVO, 1995). While the Charity Commission itself in its most recent annual report (Charity Commission, 1996), stresses its sector-supportive and developmental functions, emphasising that it 'is not a simple regulatory body', it is ironic that the English 'Commission' does not see scope for its role to be enhanced or further highlighted. The 'Commission', in fact, argued for the establishment of a formal advisory group drawn from user charities—presumably to help regulate the regulator. The Government response, in turn, is equivocal—'the Charity Commission is already seeking and acting on feedback from its users'—as it is on recommendations for 'creating an independent Charity Appeal Tribunal', and on the development of a 'single definition of charity, based on a new concept of public benefit' (DNH, 1996).

The National Lottery

The shift of responsibility for the sector from the Home Office to the

DNH finally brought the five distribution arms of the National Lottery, (for charities, the arts, sports, 'heritage' and the millennium), within one departmental remit. By July 1996, the National Lotteries Charities Board (NLCB) had 'awarded £318M to more than 4,000 organizations involved in a wide variety of worthy causes', with more than half the awards made by the remaining boards to voluntary organizations working in sport, the arts and heritage; it is estimated that 'more than £800M from the first full year of lottery sales will go to charities and voluntary organizations' (Sproat, 1996). The complexities and uncertainties of charitable giving complicated attempts to assess the Lottery's impact on the sector's fund-raising; with some charities claiming major losses, and others reporting increased donations. A government-funded research programme, looking at charity income before and after the Lottery's establishment, is expected to produce its final results in 1998. Meanwhile, voluntary sector based analyses err on the side of pessimism, the Institute of Charity Fund Raising Managers' survey, showing that more than two-thirds of charities 'blame falls in street collections on the National Lottery' (Debenham, 1996). A VSO 'Youth Poll', showing that 89% of young people would prefer to buy a lottery ticket than give charity a spare pound, led VSO to ask 'has the National Lottery wiped out the next generation of charity givers in just 18 months?' (Watts, 1996)

House of Commons questions on this topic bore witness predominantly to demands for constituency equality in receiving allocations of Lottery cash, rather than in challenging its workings (for example, its handling of unsuccessful applications) or indeed the definition of what counts as a 'worthy cause'. In the previous year, approximately 13,000 of the 15,000 applications received by the NLCB were rejected and in March 'all the distributing bodies' were described as 'trying to set in hand...schemes' to advise and assist those organizations whose first applications were unsuccessful (Bottomley, 1996b). Wider concerns that NLCB funding will effectively replace funding from other government sources have also been voiced; as have those regarding its allocative decisions, thus far towards 'less' as well as the 'more' popular 'good causes'. A strong defence of the Lottery activity, of the proper operation of the additionality principle—'there is no evidence that Lottery funds are being used as a substitute for public funds'—and the choice of a private sector operator are all found in the government response to the Deakin commission (DNH, 1996).

Performance Measurement: the National Audit Office (NAO) Report and its Aftermath

Where government funding of voluntary organizations occurs in pursuit of meeting the funding department's own objectives, it is important not only for those organizations to demonstrate their successful working, but for the funding departments to monitor and report on those achievements (Mintzberg's 'Performance Control' model of government management). In March 1966, an NAO report on 'Home Office Support to Voluntary Organizations' examined 18 grants made by the Voluntary Services Unit, and 24 grants made by six other Home Office divisions, assessing funding strategies, monitoring procedures and the extent of evaluation to ensure that planned outcomes were achieved. A patchy approach to monitoring was found, with 'not all...organizations producing meaningful performance indicators...and some said that the Home Office generally accepted the performance information given without comment' (NAO, 1996). Variable progress from the 1990 Efficiency Scrutiny Report on Government on Government Funding of the Voluntary Sector (Home Office, 1990) had occurred; not all divisions had publicised their grant schemes, and not all grants had agreed terms and conditions attached. Sharing knowledge within the department was sought, so that good practice in performance measurement was made known as was proactivity. Given that 'the organizations funded and the relative size of their grants have changed little from year to year', the Home Office was recommended to 'actively assess alternative...providers and the scope for new and innovative projects' (*ibid.*).

In April 1996, the Committee of Public Accounts took evidence, its report concurring strongly with the NAO's report, seeking the development of 'more challenging and meaningful' indicators of performance, faster action by the department once reviews have shown need for change, and moves from core towards programme and project funding (PAC, 1996). The potential for 'complacency' among the too-regularly-funded existed; as did the appearance of some 'closed shops': in one area '53 applications received and 53 turned down' (*ibid.*). At the crux of the discussion was the balancing act required in working with funded organizations and measuring performance. For one organization, where the Home Office was 'dealing with an organization based on voluntary effort, we are not dealing with a non-departmental public body', the retort from the Committee was clear—'Yes, but you are dealing with a body that has over £6M in public money' (*ibid.*). In further reply, and emphasising the VSU move to DNH, a Treasury minute asserted importantly that 'core funding remains an efficient means for furthering DNH's objectives and building long-term relations with established providers' (Treasury, 1996).

Local Government Relations

The developing pattern of local government reorganization in England looks set to change relationships between local authorities and the voluntary sector. The rolling programme of structure reviews by the Local Government Commission in England is complete, with no national blueprint for change but decisions made according to the needs of each area. New unitary authorities have been coming into being into being over a period of time. Thus in many areas, new relationships with the voluntary sector, after some very long-standing joint working will need to be developed; while in 14 counties, the *status quo* is maintained. Here there are inevitable concerns about the unitary authorities' funding and working plans, and the new Local Government Association is expected to make an important contribution here.

In Scotland, where unitary authorities are also coming into existence over a period of time, one report suggested that the 1997 moves 'could affect more than 5,000 projects which have been receiving around £100M a year from local government' (*Third Sector*, 1996). Forward planning uncertainties were highlighted in the report gave the example of 'the new Glasgow unitary authority [which] has guaranteed funds to voluntary and community organizations for just six months of the 1996 to 1997 tax year'. A differing source of uncertainty over continuing funding was reported from Northern Ireland in the wake of the breakdown of the cease-fire (*Third Sector*, 1996). European Community funding of approximately £250M had been allocated via a number of voluntary sector intermediary bodies to a range of community programmes, and the Northern Ireland Council for Voluntary Action was reported as concerned that this five-year grant would not be renewed after 1997. While it might have been expected that the sector as a whole was increasingly looking to the EC as a funding and policy-making source, it seems more likely that this is the case only for a relatively small number of organizations, and then only some of the larger charitable groupings. The Deakin commission, surprisingly, 'received little evidence about the implications of developments in Europe' (*op. cit.*, 76).

Openness in the Sector—the Nolan Committee

In early 1996, the Nolan Committee's Second Report, *Local Public Spending Bodies*, included housing associations within its remit. Recognizing that housing associations had themselves examined their governance structures and produced new codes of practice, they were seen as needing to pay particular attention to securing genuine tenant involvement and improving accountability, through membership schemes. Its third inquiry, 'looking at aspects of local government', and 'where local government fits in to the Committee's overall ethical framework and its seven principles of public life', started taking evidence in October 1996. With initial questions ranging across the roles of councillors and officers, and relationships with contractors, it is likely to highlight the relations between service-providing charities and local authorities. The NCVO's written evidence to Nolan recommends setting up a 'national protocol' on the status and duties of councillors with their own voluntary sector interests; and increased openness, with authorities publishing lists of all organizations they fund, and for what purpose.

The Government/Voluntary Sector Agenda

Public policy-making in relation to this sector runs the perpetual risk of being classed, concurrently, as too radical for some and too conventional for others. In a pre-election period, parties' attitudes have tended towards heaping praise rather than criticism on the sector. Yet the difficulties of being policy-specific for a sector where most definitions are partial, and where competition between voluntary organizations has always existed in some forms, albeit often disguised and restrained, is also clear. The perpetual use of the term 'partnership' to describe a whole shifting pattern of liaisons and alliances, some temporary, some permanent, some uncertain in their intent, would appear to suit everyone; and no-one. The argument by some public policy figures that there are 'too many' voluntary bodies and 'overlap' misses the point. It is the individual choices of people to set up and sustain such organizations. Moves towards sector rationalization would always run the risk of dissipating that sense of choice, a perpetual motivating factor.

It is also a mistake to see the voluntary sector as a higher-quality, cheaper-cost service providing replacements for public services over a wider scale. Not only will many organizations have no inclination or capacity for this route, but this is to downgrade the innovative capacities of public services. Voluntary organizations have their imperfections and it is not the role of governments to persist in trying to iron these out for them, producing quasi-governmental monolithic bodies, what are becoming cheerfully described as GoNGOs—'Government-Owned NGOs'.

The Deakin commission, wisely and realistically, avoided a blueprint approach in its deliberations; leading to inevitable (and inappropriate) criticisms of 'fence-sitting'. It is, however, possible to see many of its proposals for public policy change as being of interest predominantly to the larger voluntary bodies. In a sector which is highly segmented, with greatest numbers clustered at the small operational end, it is possible that government policy will increasingly need to make more clear to which elements of the sector they are addressing their concerns. Tidying up the varying governmental structures and shifting responsibility apparently nearer to the decision-making heart makes less sense than increasing the openness about what those structures look like, 'who fits in where', and in turn being clear about access to the governmental system, both for funding and lobbying purposes. On the contrary, why not allow for some *more* untidiness, and experimentation in models of governmental regulation and support, as a means of *recognizing* the value of diversity and divergence which the sector exemplifies? Following Harrow and

Palmer (1995), differing models of voluntary organization governance, and of regulation, perhaps drawing on a charities' inspectorate for support, guidance and regulation, as an additional arm of the unique Charity Commission, should be possible. If alternative structural models, identified on the basis of local appropriateness and need, are 'good enough' for local government, surely this is the case for the voluntary sector as a whole? ■

References

Bottomley, V. (1996a), Commons *Hansard* (1 May), column 528.

Bottomley, V. (1996b), Commons *Hansard* (4 March), column 13.

Charity Commission for England and Wales (1996), *Report* 1995 (HMSO, London).

Deakin Commission (1996), *Meeting the Challenge of Change: Voluntary Action into the 21st Century* (NCVO Publications, London).

Debenham, C. (1996), Lottery to blame for fall in spontaneous donations. *Third Sector* (July), 3.

DNH (1996), *Raising the Voltage: The Government's Response to the Deakin Commission Report* (November).

Harrow, J. and Palmer, P. (1995), Some alternatives for charity governance. Paper presented to the Association of Chief Executives of National Voluntary Organizations' national conference (June).

Harrow, J. and Vincent, J. (1996), *The Voluntary Sector and the 'Machinery' of Central Government* (CIPFA, London).

Hems, L. and Passey, A. (1996), *The UK Voluntary Sector Statistical Almanac* (NCVO Publications, London).

Home Office (1990), *Government Funding of the Voluntary Sector: Profiting From Partnership* (HMSO, London).

Labour Party (1966), *Labour and the Voluntary Sector: Setting the Agenda for Partnership in Government* (London).

Mintzberg, H. (1996), Managing government, governing management. *Harvard Business Review* (May–June).

NAO (1996), *Home Office Support to Voluntary Organisations*, HC 315 (HMSO, London).

PAC (1996), *Thirty Seventh Report, Home Office: Support for Voluntary Organizations*, House of Commons Session 1995-96, 15 July (HMSO, London).

SCVO (1995), *What Future for the Scottish Voluntary Sector?* (SCVO, Edinburgh).

Sproat, I. (1996), Commons *Hansard* (23 July), column 214–222.

Third Sector (1996), Chief executives call for charity ministry (22 February).

Treasury (1996), *Minute on the Thirty Seventh Report for the Committee of Public Accounts, 1995-96*, Cm 3384 (HMSO, London).

Watts, S. (1996), Giving to charity. *NCVO News* (July).

Williamson, A. P. (1992), The voluntary sector's role in managing societal instability in Northern Ireland. In Gidron, B., Kramer, R. M. and Salamon, L. M., *Government and the Third Sector: Emerging Relationships in the Welfare State* (Jossey-Bass, San Francisco).

16 Social Security and Personal Social Services

Geoffrey Hulme

Public Finance Foundation, CIPFA, London

In 1996, the Government brought forward further measures to help implement its strategy of containing the growth of social security by targeting it more narrowly on those considered to be in greatest need. The cumulative effect of the measures taken in recent years is expected to reduce the real-terms growth of non-cyclical expenditure to 3.2% in 1996-97 and to 1.7% in 1997-98, compared with an average of 4.5% a year over the four years to 1995-96.

This chapter outlines the developments during the year in social security and personal social services, and discusses the issues that are likely to be on the agenda in the next Parliament.

Social Security Under the Conservatives

Social security is by far the Government's largest spending programme. In 1995-96, it cost £93.3 billion (including £3.4 billion for administration, and around £3 billion for spending in Northern Ireland not included in the Department of Social Security [DSS] budget). It thus constituted 34.7% of government spending on services. It has also been the fastest growing programme, increasing by 84% in real terms (i.e. after taking out the effect of general inflation) over the period from 1978-79 to 1995-96. This was more than double the growth in spending on services generally (37%), and only the much smaller law and order and personal social services programmes had higher growth rates.

Since 1979, the Government has been looking for politically acceptable ways of limiting the growth of expenditure by cutting back on lower-priority features of the system, as well as by detecting and deterring fraud and abuse. Current strategic objectives are similar to those in earlier years—to focus benefits on the most needy; to minimize disincentives to work; to simplify systems and adapt them to people's needs; to bear down on fraud and abuse—in short, to increase the efficiency of the system.

The Social Justice Commission established by the Labour Party to contribute to its thinking (but not to determine its policy) put more emphasis on the positive role of social security:

- To prevent poverty where possible and relieve it where necessary.
- To protect people against risks, especially in the labour market and arising from family change.
- To redistribute wealth from richer to poorer people.
- To redistribute resources over people's life-cycles.
- To encourage personal independence.
- To help promote social cohesion (Social Justice Commission, 1995).

Strategies that the Government has adopted to try to achieve its objectives of increasing the efficiency of the system include:

- Cutting, with varying degrees of severity, the benefits paid as of right to people who meet qualifying conditions, so that people have to rely more heavily on benefits that are means-tested (i.e. depend on coming below defined levels of income and capital). The cuts include revaluation of benefits in line with inflation rather than earnings, and reducing the scope of the earnings-related part of the state pension scheme (SERPS).
- Replacing parts of the statutory system by regulated private provision (for example replacement of sickness benefit for most people by employer-run statutory sick pay and incentives to opt-out of SERPS).
- Replacing parts of the open-ended social security system by budget-controlled public provision (for example transfer to local authorities of support for people in nursing homes).
- Tightening the rules for and reducing benefit levels under means-tested and other conditional schemes (for example replacement of payments for individual special needs by standard benefits for defined broad groups and by loans under the budget-controlled Social Fund; reducing the entitlement of young people to income support and housing benefit).
- Anti-fraud measures.
- Restructuring benefits to reduce disincentives and increase incentives to

take paid work (for example family credit for people in work; experimentation with subsidies for employers who take on long-term unemployed).

The most significant of the new measures announced in 1996 were:

- The benefits paid of right to lone-parent families and the premium rates of other benefits paid to lone parents are to be phased out—from April 1998 lone parents making new claims will be paid the same levels of benefit as couples with children.
- Housing benefit is to be brought closer to the average of housing cost, by paying to people whose rents are above the average for the area a figure that is only half the difference between their rent and the average. For single people under pension age, the calculation will be based on the average area rent for a single room in shared accommodation. (This extends a restriction announced in 1996 and due to apply in 1997 to single people under 25.)
- Council tax relief (through Council Tax Benefit) will apply only to people in the lowest-value property (above Band E).
- An additional £0.5 billion is to be spent on additional measures to combat fraud and evasion, including increased checks before benefits are awarded, new visits to claimants, targeted reviews of high-risk groups (i.e. those where evasion is known to be common), local anti-fraud drives encouraging the public to use a free telephone number to report, in confidence, people thought to be cheating on social security. Additional savings of £2.1 billion are expected (unlike similar measures in the past, an attempt has been made at even-handedness between social security and tax evasion, counter-measures on both being presented as part of a 'Spend to Save' initiative).
- Introduction of pilot schemes to test the costs and incentive effects of paying new or additional in-work benefits to unemployed people who take up low-paid work.

Recent Trends in Expenditure and Current Prospects

Table 1 shows the totals of social security benefit expenditure in Great Britain (excluding Northern Ireland and cost of administration) over the four-year periods in 1992 and 1996 and tables 2 and 3 show percentage growth in cash and real terms. The figures are analysed by group of beneficiary:

- *Elderly* people, who receive retirement pensions (based on the weekly national insurance contributions which they and their employers have paid, and supplemented by income support and housing benefit for those whose income and capital fall below defined low levels).
- *Sick and disabled* people, many of whom suffer loss of income and incur additional costs because of their disability and who may be entitled to certain benefits based on insurance contributions (notably Invalidity Benefit), to other allowances related to the degree of disability (for example Mobility Allowance and Attendance Allowance) and to yet others related to income
- *Families* who receive child benefit irrespective of their income and may be entitled to family credits (if parents are in work but have low incomes) and to one-parent benefits (if they bring up children alone).
- *Unemployed* people who for six months receive a Job Seeker's Allowance (formerly unemployment benefit) based on insurance contributions and then, or later, may receive means-tested income support and housing benefit if income and capital fall below the defined levels.

For each group, expenditure has increased well above the rate of growth in national output and income. Over the past 16 years, the total has risen by an average of 3.8% a year, while GDP rose by only 2.3% a year, thus increasing the ratio of social security expenditure to GDP from 9.7% to 12.3%.

Table 1. Expenditure totals (£M).

Financial year	*1992*	*1996*
Elderly	34,150	40,150
Sick and disabled	16,130	23,110
Family	13,840	17,830
Unemployed	9,360	8,620
Widows etc.	1,810	1,930
Total	75,340	91,650

Table 2. Cash growth in expenditure (percentage over periods shown).

Financial year	*80-84*	*84-88*	*88-92*	*92-96*	*80-96*
Elderly	54.9	25.9	46.0	17.6	230.7
Sick and disabled	57.2	72.0	88.6	43.3	626.7
Family	63.7	36.7	57.1	28.4	359.5
Unemployed	151.0	-17.5	72.5	28.4	240.7
Widows etc.	35.8	-10.9	49.6	-7.9	103.2
Total	66.6	25.2	58.8	21.6	304.1
Inflation	29.0	22.1	28.0	10.0	121.9

The highest rate of growth has been in benefits for *sick and disabled* people (a real-terms average of 7.7% a year, increasing the share of social security spending from 14% to 25%). It is accounted for to a small extent by improvements in benefits, but mainly by an increase in take-up of benefit, which is probably due to a combination of more people knowing what they are entitled to and more people dropping out of an increasingly competitive labour market on health grounds (in effect, substituting retirement on health grounds for unemployment).

The highest proportion of benefits goes to the *elderly* (44% of the social security total), but the average growth rate has been lower (around 2.5%) and has fallen—reflecting current demographic trends. People are living longer, but the pensioner population levelled off in the 1990s because relatively low birth rates in the 1920s and 1930s mean that fewer people are currently reaching retirement age (the situation will change over the next 30 years as the post-war baby boom reaches pension age). Factors for growth have been the maturing of SERPS, as people build up the contribution record that entitles them to higher pensions, and the growth in housing costs which affects all groups and reflects a change in policy away from subsidized rents in favour of market rents and means-tested support for individuals.

Family benefits have also grown by well over the rate of growth in the economy (an average of 4.7% over 16 years). This reflects some improvement in benefits for low-income families in work through the family

Table 3. Real-terms growth in expenditure (average percentage a year).

Financial year	*80-84*	*84-88*	*88-92*	*92-96*	*80-96*
Elderly	4.6	0.8	4.4	4.1	2.5
Sick and disabled	5.0	9.0	11.3	9.4	7.7
Family	6.1	2.9	6.3	6.4	4.7
Unemployed	18.1	-9.3	8.9	-2.0	2.7
Widows etc.	1.3	·0.6	5.1	1.6	0.5
Total	6.6	-4.9	6.6	5.0	3.8

credit scheme, but mainly increasing take-up of benefit by the growing number of one-parent families. Cost-containment measures have included not always increasing child benefit in line with inflation and, more recently, reducing the additional payments made to single parents.

Agenda for Next Parliament

The *Yearbook* is being written before the manifestos appear, which will seek to set the agenda for the next Parliament. But the main sets of issues are fairly clear. They fall into two broad groups: retirement pensions and other benefits for the elderly (which accounts for 44% of total cost); and social security for people of working age (which accounts for the rest if family benefits are included).

Retirement Pensions

The Government's strategy on pensions has been to index the basic state pension in line with prices; to encourage people to opt out of SERPS (the state scheme, which supplements the basic pension) into private schemes; and to leave people who have inadequate total pensions to claim means-tested income support. They stress the growth in private pension fund investment (over £600 billion), growing participation in private schemes (from 43% to 62%) and growth in average pensioner earnings (by over 50 % in real-terms).

Problems that are highlighted by Opposition parties, for example *Getting Welfare to Work* (Labour Party, 1996) and by several independent reports, for example *Social Justice* (Commission on Social Justice, 1995) and *Pensions: 2000 and Beyond* (Retirement Income Inquiry, 1996) include:

- The continuing fall in the value of the basic pension as a proportion of what people earn in work (from 20% of male average earnings in 1977, to 15% in the early 1990s, to around 10% in the 2020s, when the children of the post-war baby boom reach pension age).
- The disadvantages of means-testing (high administrative costs and residual stigma so that over half a million people do not receive the benefits they are entitled to).
- Inadequacy for many people of SERPS, the state top-up pension.
- The high administration costs of low-level private pensions and the over-selling of these by many companies, which took advantage of the incentives offered by the Government.

In previous elections, the Labour Party proposed to restore the link between the basic pension and earnings but the public expenditure effects led them into proposals for taxation, which probably lost them votes and contributed to electoral defeat. New Labour's caution on taxation is reflected in avoidance of any commitment to improve the basic pension, though, if elected, it is likely to come under pressure to do so. A possible compromise would be to review the basic pension towards the end of the Parliament and take stock of what improvements there have been in the living standards of the working population, and of whether and how the retired population should share in that improvement.

Decisions on the future shape of state pensions have to take into account the effects of longer term demographic trends on their financing. State pensions are financed by the contributions of people currently in work (the 'pay-as-you-go' principle, as distinct from an invested fund), but the ratio of people in work to pensioners will fall when the children of the post-war baby boom reach retirement age (from 2010 onwards), so that fewer workers will be paying for more pensions, and either pensions will need to fall or contributions rise (certainly in real-terms and probably as a proportion of earnings); as a result pensioners' interests will be at greater political risk.

The *Social Justice* report proposed a twin-pronged approach:

- •A guaranteed *first-tier pension* to be achieved by topping up from taxation the basic pensions of those whose total pension and other regular income does not come up to a guaranteed (or assured) minimum level.
- •In order to reduce the need for topping up from taxation, people in work would be required to make a minimum contribution to a *second-tier pension*, for which they would be able to choose between private provision and a state scheme. The latter would be either be either a modified version of the present SERPS (with improved coverage for self-employed, carers and people on low incomes), or a new state-sponsored (but not necessarily state-run) funded scheme. The latter would cost an extra 0.5 to 0.7% in the transition from pay-as-you-go to a funded scheme, and the final pension would depend on the success with which the fund was invested, but it would give greater ownership rights to the pensioners and would reduce (but not eliminate) the risk of adverse political interference.

The Retirement Income Inquiry (chaired by Sir John Anson, a retired Treasury permanent secretary and former chairman of the Public Finance Foundation) reached similar conclusions after a more detailed exploration of the options. The Inquiry came down in favour of replacing SERPS by a new nationally-funded scheme set up by government but sufficiently independent for its income and expenditure not to count as taxation and public spending. The levels of the assured pension and of the minimum contributions could be varied from time to time according to public preference as judged by the government of the day. But the Anson Inquiry suggests starting the assured pension at 20% of gross average earnings (currently £73.50 a week, compared with the present basic pension of £58.85), and starting the minimum contributions at 4.8% of earnings shared between employers and employees.

The Labour Party is examining variants of these approaches:

- •A 'pension entitlement' which would provide automatic assistance to the poorest pensioners, using a simplified, pensioner-friendly system of assessing their resources.
- •New forms of 'second pension', which would be provided mainly by various kinds of funded pension schemes, including the present type of single-

employer occupational schemes, new multi-employer schemes and personal pension schemes with lower administrative costs than those currently on offer; SERPS would remain for those who want to remain in it and it might be developed to provide a 'citizenship pension' for people such as carers and low-paid workers who would not otherwise be able to afford a second pension.

Some within the Labour Party are arguing for an improved SERPS, financed by additional contributions (for example see Lynes, 1996), but the leadership has so far ruled out raising the current level of employee contributions, and has put the emphasis on encouraging voluntary saving (for example through individual savings accounts, which people could use for contingencies during their working life but, as they approach retirement, could be used to enhance their pension).

The Conservatives, on the other hand, are proposing to take their present strategy a stage further to phase in, over the long term, a fully-funded, privately-based scheme on the lines of that developed in Chile and adopted elsewhere in South America. People entering the labour market towards the end of the decade would receive rebates on their national insurance contributions which they would be required to invest in individual schemes which would form the individual's pension pot, the value of which would be realized on retirement. It would thus resemble some of the other proposals for second pensions, except that there would be no reserve state scheme for those who preferred it and there would not be a separate basic pension, though the state would guarantee that the pensions paid by the compulsory private pension plans do not fall below the level of the basic pension (which would continue on the present basis for the present working population). The present pattern of tax relief would be reversed for the new workers, so that their contributions would be taxed but their pensions would be tax free.

Benefits for People of Working Age

Reviews of social security for people of working age include the reports of an enquiry by the Joseph Rowntree Foundation (1995) and the Dahrendorf Enquiry (*Wealth Creation and Social Cohesion*, 1995) initiated by the Liberal Democrats. Common themes have been:

- Concern about the disincentive effects of the Government's emphasis on means-testing through the poverty and employment traps (earnings wholly or largely eroded by the effects of withdrawing benefit on return to work).
- The need for social security policies to combine with other government policies for education, training and promotion of employment-rich growth, in order to respond to the structural problems of a global economy in which a combination of trade and technology have reduced the demand for and return to low-skill labour and have produced wastefully high levels of unemployment and what the Dahrendorf Report calls the 'dynamic of decline of low-income communities'.
- Forms of social insurance which increase incentives to work including bigger disregards of earnings for people in work, changes in the tests of availability for work to allow for training and voluntary work and start-up grants for people starting work. They support the Government's experiments with subsidies to employers to take on long-term unemployed.

All parties accept the principle of getting people off benefit and back to work using pilot schemes drawing on experience in other countries (for example the JET scheme in Australia and the GAIN programme in California, which tailor benefits, employment and training services to help benefit claimants back to work). Opposition parties argue that they will pursue positive measures with more vigour than the present Government.

The Labour Party has made a specific commitment to use the proceeds of a windfall tax on the profits of the privatized utilities to finance an new deal for the 18–25 age group, which will offer four options as alternatives to benefit: full-time education option (those without basic educational qualifications to be able to retain benefit for six months, or longer with satisfactory progress); employer option (tax rebates for employers who take on long-term unemployed and provide minimum training); voluntary sector option (enabling voluntary organizations to take on extra young people on a weekly wage equivalent to benefit plus a fixed sum for six months and with training opportunities); and environmental task forces, organized locally and co-ordinated nationally, offering opportunities for work and training.

If Labour is elected, key issues will be the yield of the windfall tax, how quickly it can be introduced and whether, in the interim before new positive measures can take effect, the Government should reverse any the proposed tightening of the rules on housing benefit and benefits for lone parents.

For the longer term, there is need for extensive consultation to find out which developments command greatest support among the people they are intended to help, as well as among the public which pays the bill through taxation. There will be difficult priority choices and, initially, the emphasis may need to be on pilot schemes and monitored local initiatives to find out which approaches give the greatest added value in terms of return to useful activity, of increase in individual self-respect and of reduction in marginalization.

On social security and public expenditure choices generally, there is a need for improved political market research to find out what people's priorities are as and when national economic growth makes resources available for higher spending or tax reduction and, if sufficient growth is not forthcoming, whether and how people are ready to put a bigger proportion of income aside for their own pensions or to help the less fortunate.

Personal Social Services

Expenditure on Personal Social Services (PSS) has more than doubled under the present Government. In the 14 years to 1992-93, it grew in real-terms by an average of 3.6% a year and over the next three years annual growth accelerated to over 8% due to the phased transfer from social security of responsibility for meeting the care costs of elderly and disabled people without means (under the community care arrangements introduced in 1993-94).

In 1996-97, local authorities in England were budgeting to spend around £8 billion, compared with £7.3 billion in the previous year. The Government's figure for what it regards as appropriate (the Total Standard Spending [TSS] taken into account in calculating Revenue Support Grant) was £7.5 billion in 1996-97 (after adjustment for transfer of functions) and has been set at £7.8 billion for 1997-98. The latter figure is thus below the budgeted figure for the current year and authorities will have to meet the cost of a further phase of transfer from social security. It seems likely that, as in previous years, they will use such freedom of manoeuvre as they have under the Government's limits on their budgets (capping) to spend above TSS, but they are under pressure to increase spending on schools and it seems likely that PSS growth will reduce.

By the time of publication the Government will probably have published a White Paper on plans for the next Parliament, which may include proposals for a greater shift of responsibility from local authorities, at least for delivery of services. The record and prospective performance of local authorities is likely to be on the agenda, as is the financing of residential and nursing home care.

A report from the Joseph Rowntree Foundation has proposed a new social insurance scheme to replace present arrangements under which residents have to contribute from their capital (including the value of their house) above defined limits (see *Public Services Yearbook 1996-97*). Arrangements of this kind have been introduced, or are under consideration, in other countries (for example Germany and Japan). The Government's view has been that this is an appropriate subject for private insurance and it has been consulting on possible incentives to private insurance, including protection of an increased amount of capital for people who buy insurance of this kind. Opposition parties may be inclined to go down the Rowntree route but will have to consider it against other social priorities, which may have greater weight than enabling people who need care in their final years to bequeath more capital to their heirs. ■

References

Commission on Social Justice (1995), *Social Justice: Strategies for National Renewal* (Vintage).

Joseph Rowntree Foundation (996), *Income and Wealth*, Report of the Joseph Rowntree Foundation Inquiry chaired by Sir Peter Barclay (Joseph Rowntree Foundation, York).

Labour Party (1996), *Getting Welfare to Work*.

Tony Lynes (1996), *Our Pensions: a Policy for a Labour Government* (Eunomia).

Retirement Income Inquiry (1996), *Pensions: 2000 and Beyond* (Shellwing, Folkestone).

17 Health

Anthony Harrison and Bill New

King's Fund Policy Institute, London

1996 was another tough year for the National Health Service as it struggled to reconcile growing demands for emergency care and expensive new forms of treatment within its limited budget. The Government reasserted its commitment to a tax-funded NHS and continued programme of reform, outlining measures which could lead to new ways of providing primary care. Nevertheless, a long list of difficult issues remained for the incoming government to tackle.

1996 ended as it had begun, with hospitals closing their doors to patients. So the impression remained that the National Health Service (NHS), after five years of continuous reform and large increases in the volume of resources available to it, was unable to cope with the pressures created by demographic change, new technology and rising patients' expectations for better quality care.

The pressure on hospital emergency facilities was highlighted during the first quarter of 1996 by a series of cases involving patients being ferried from one hospital to another, including a boy from Stockport who died on the way to Leeds Royal Infirmary after three hospitals closer to his home had been unable to provide the facilities that his condition required. His case, like that of Jaymee Bowen in the previous year, to whom Cambridgeshire Health Authority had denied publicly funded treatment for her rare leukaemia, appeared to epitomise the state of the NHS in 1996, a service unable to cope.

Underfunding?

Not surprisingly, there were voices raised during the year suggesting that the NHS could not survive solely on the combination of public funds and patient contributions by which it is currently financed. In the words of Healthcare 2000 (1995), an *ad hoc* group established with the support of the pharmaceutical industry:

While there may be no conclusive evidence that the NHS is presently underfunded, international comparisons, the explicit rationing of some health services and public opinion lead us to conclude that there is a gap between resources and demand which shows signs of increasing as we move into the next century.

Their report goes on: 'we believe it is not possible to expect the continuing gap between resources and demand to be closed through increased tax funding alone'.

As we have argued elsewhere, there are strong grounds for arguing that Healthcare 2000's conclusions are ill-founded, particularly the implication that identifying a 'gap' automatically requires that it be 'closed' (Dixon *et al.*, 1997). Nevertheless, there was evidence that many health authorities and trusts were in serious financial trouble. In May 1996, a small number were bailed out with *ad hoc* injections of cash; this happened again November 1996. According to figures released by the Healthcare Financial Management Association (1996) in December 1996, district health authorities revealed a net deficit of £87M at the end of 1995-96. In a pre-election year the Government was particularly vulnerable to the charge that the NHS was not 'safe in its hands'. It reacted in two ways.

First, during spring and summer, measures were announced and a series of advisory documents published which were designed to improve the capacity of the NHS to deal with the next peak in demand for emergency care: the winter of 1996-97. Health authorities were required to demonstrate to the regional executives that their providers were well prepared. But, as the National Executive could offer them no advice as to the levels of emergency demand they were likely to have to deal with, any such assurance was of only limited value (Harrison, 1996).

Second, in November 1996 it published a white paper *The National Health Service: A Service with Ambitions* (Secretary of State for Health, 1996) which set out its reasons for believing that the NHS could continue to survive as a tax-funded service. It also reaffirmed a commitment, made during the previous election campaign, to increasing funding for the NHS in real terms on a year-on-year basis. This pledge has been honoured—but only just, and not beyond 1999. The 1996-97 settlement favoured primary care and provided for an increase in Hospital and Community Health Services current net expenditure of only 0.1%, adjusted for general inflation (direct communication from the NHS Executive, March 1996). The final outturn figure may be different, depending as it does on actual levels of general inflation and other adjustments, but it was nevertheless an extremely low settlement in comparison to the 3.1% yearly average increase between 1978 and 1995. Furthermore, the NHS Executive estimate for volume expenditure, adjusted for the generally higher level of health care inflation, actually indicated a *reduction* in net NHS resource availability. So it was quite predictable that NHS hospitals would be under severe pressure in the winter of 1996-97. In addition, changes to the methods used to allocate the national total to individual health authorities meant that some received much smaller increases than the national average. In these circumstances, it is scarcely surprising that some authorities found it hard to balance their books.

Financial crises in the NHS are nothing new—they first emerged in the early 1950s (Guillebaud Committee, 1956) and have recurred regularly thereafter. There have been individual years in the recent past, 1977-78 and 1985-86 for example, where real resource growth has been below or near to zero but these years have always been followed by a period in which expenditure increases were higher than average (see table 1). Health spending thereby 'caught up' with the long-term trend. However, the 1996 Budget indicated little respite from fiscal rectitude up to the new millennium. The settlement for 1997-98 is rather more generous than for the current year—a 1.5% real increase in the NHS control total. But less widely publicised have been the indicative figures for the *following* two financial years up to 2000. These show that real growth is predicted to be 0.3% for 1998-99 and zero for 1999-2000 (HM Treasury, 1996). The suspicion is that these figures represent pure political expediency, designed to portray future PSBR estimates in the best possible light. In practice, an incoming government will need to revise spending upwards if history is any guide. The alternative would be a truly unprecedented period of low NHS expenditure growth which would go a long way towards confirming the Healthcare 2000 analysis.

Drug Costs

The tension between financial constraints and technological advance is

Table 1. NHS total net expenditure growth (1974–1996), England.

Financial year ending	*Real growth adjusted for general inflation (% change on previous year)*	*Volume growth adjusted for health service inflation (% change on previous year)*
1974	2.9	0.3
1975	11.2	0.1
1976	5.4	2.7
1977	0.5	0.8
1978	-2.8	1.4
1979	1.6	2.2
1980	1.7	-1.1
1981	10.1	2.8
1982	2.0	3.1
1983	1.7	2.1
1984	1.0	0.8
1985	2.2	1.1
1986	0.2	0.5
1987	3.9	0.7
1988	4.3	1.7
1989	3.5	0.4
1990	0.8	1.6
1991	4.1	3.7
1992	6.9	3.9
1993	6.0	4.4
1994	0.6	0.8
1995	3.7	3.2
1996	2.4	2.2

Source: NHS Executive (March 1996).

well illustrated in the field of pharmaceuticals. Drug expenditure is growing faster than other sectors of the NHS, chiefly because of the higher inflation in drug prices compared to general inflation. Spending on pharmaceuticals has grown from 6.6% of the NHS total in 1975 to 10.1% in 1994 (Bloor *et al.*, 1996). Some new drugs—for example a clot-dissolving agent for acute myocardial infarction—can cost up to £816 for a single dose. Similarly, beta-interferon, a drug used for the treatment of multiple sclerosis, may only reduce hospital admissions by one day every three years while costing about £10,000 per patient per year (Ferner, 1996). And statins, which treat those with high cholesterol levels, have been estimated to cost £361,000 per life year saved for certain categories of patient (Smith, 1996).

The high cost of drugs like these is leading to new conflicts over who should undertake their rationing. In the past, with open-ended drug budgets, GPs would generally be happy to take on prescribing responsibilities for patients previously under consultant supervision. Both fundholders (who must meet drug expenditure out of their budgets) and non-fundholders (who are set indicative prescribing budgets) are increasingly reluctant to absorb the cost of new drugs. Anecdotal evidence indicates that some GPs are resisting the prescription of highly specialized drugs because (they claim) they lack clinical expertise; hospital consultants suspect that it is because they do not wish to bear the financial consequences. Hospital consultants themselves are under pressure from health authorities only to prescribe a certain number of courses of expensive drugs, like beta-interferon, or perhaps not to prescribe at all. The Government, on the other hand, issued an Executive Letter which asked purchasing authorities and providers 'to develop and implement a prescribing approach for beta-interferon through hospitals' (NHS Executive, 1995), implying that the Government was not expecting that these drugs would be withheld from consultants by health authorities.

New Policy Proposals

A Service with Ambitions did not address these tensions. Instead, it set out a number of broad objectives for the future of the NHS none of which bore directly on them:

- A well-informed public.
- A seamless service, working across boundaries.
- Knowledge-based decision-making.
- A highly trained and skilled workforce.
- A responsive service, sensitive to differing needs.

These objectives are not new—they have appeared in the annual NHS

Planning and Priorities Guidance over recent years. But it is what the white paper does not say that is more interesting than what it does. The conspicuous absence is any mention of further institutional reform. After five years of continuous revolution, the Government, it would seem, had settled for the non-contentious: improvements to the quality of care through professional development and informed decision-making. Markets, competition and the rest of the rhetoric of the 1990 Act are not mentioned. Instead, the white paper's concluding statement includes the sentence: 'We have asked the management team of each health authority, NHS Trust and those in primary care, to plan their own contribution to achieving our ambitions'. It is as if the 1990 Act had never been passed, never mind implemented.

There is an exception to this silence on institutional reform: a brief and low key reference to another white paper on primary care *Choice and Opportunity* (Secretaries of State for Health, Scotland and Wales, 1996a) published a few weeks previously, and a further paper *Primary Care: Delivering the Future* (Secretaries of State for Health, Scotland and Wales, 1996b) which was published in December. *A Service with Ambitions* describes these as means for taking forward the kind of improvements to primary care which fundholders and others had already been making. In fact, the two primary care white papers effectively 'deregulate' primary care and open the way for major changes in the way it is provided.

Primary Care Reform

Throughout the 1990s, the implementation of the 1990 NHS and Community Care Act has dominated the political debate over the NHS. As far as primary care is concerned, however, it is arguable that the 1990 Contract was a more significant event. For the first time, the Government set out a range of activities—cervical cytology, childhood immunization and health checks for the elderly—which GPs were encouraged to carry out by financial incentives. These target payments appear to have had a significant impact on GP behaviour, even if the response has been poorer in deprived areas—the so-called 'inverse care law' (Silcock and Radcliffe, 1996). In the years since, with the development of fundholding, the Government has aimed to give GPs leverage over the way that other services, particularly hospital care, are provided by giving them varying degrees of control over purchasing decisions.

These two white papers turn the focus on primary care itself, including not only general practice but also a range of other professionals such as nurses, pharmacists and therapists working in the community. The first, *Choice and Opportunity,* acknowledges that the way that GPs are funded and their typical form of organization, the independent professional practice with self-employed status, has proved in many ways an obstacle to change. Even under fundholding, finance for family health services, which pay for GPs, dentists, and eye and pharmaceutical services, remained separate from finance for hospital and community health services. This has proved an increasing anachronism in a world in which the divisions between the two forms of service are becoming blurred. The Government itself has encouraged the transfer of care from hospital to general practice, but it has not created the financial framework for it. Instead, GPs have been expected to absorb the extra workload within their existing, very broadly specified, terms of contract. With the exceptions listed above, they are not paid more if they absorb work previously done by hospital or other NHS staff.

A second anachronism has been the sharp division between the position of GPs and that of other professionals. To many, general practice and primary care are synonymous terms, but, increasingly, the contribution of the other professions is being recognized, for example in primary care teams. As things stand, however, the leader of the team has to be a GP and none of the other professions is able to be a practice partner.

To remove these and other obstacles the white paper proposes:

- A salaried option for GPs which would make it possible for trusts to employ them.
- Practice-based contracts which would embrace non-medical professionals.
- A single budget for general medical and hospital and community health services.

These changes require primary legislation which the Government has committed itself to introducing in 1997. If this is passed, it will open the way for new forms of service which will both strengthen primary care where it is weakest, in the inner cities, and provide some degree of competition for established practices. The white paper indicated an intention to proceed, as had the dental white paper in its field, by piloting these measures in particular areas—a cautious approach which belies the potentially revolutionary nature of the reforms.

Agenda for the Next Government

Much of what a new government must aim to do is uncontentious: the broad objectives quoted earlier find general approval, as have the primary care white papers and other specific initiatives such as improvements in the availability of information both to patients and practitioners. But other issues will be more controversial.

Service Reconfiguration

For almost all of their time in office, the Conservatives have ignored the hospital sector. More precisely, the Government has taken a wide range of initiatives which have affected hospitals—for example, reduction in junior doctors' hours and changes in post-graduate training—which have made it hard for many hospitals, particularly smaller ones, to maintain medical cover. But it has not had a hospital policy as such, leaving health authorities and trusts to tackle the awkward task of responding to both staffing difficulties and financial pressures. In many parts of the country, both urban and rural, these are combining to make it hard to maintain the existing pattern of services, yet closure proposals have typically been fiercely resisted. The nettle of closures in urban areas, and possibly subsidies or other measures of protection in rural ones, will have to be grasped before long.

Capital Finance

Closely linked is the issue of capital finance. By the end of 1996, no *substantial* scheme had actually been agreed through the Private Finance Initiative (PFI). A number of schemes had been approved but were, in effect, stalled because agreement could not be reached with private sector interests. In London, the rationalization of hospitals proposed in the report of the committee of inquiry chaired by Sir Bernard Tomlinson, turns almost entirely on projects such as the rebuilding of the Royal London Hospital making effective use of the PFI. In one case, the trust concerned—the combined Guy's and St Thomas' Hospital Trust—announced in December 1996 that it could not do so. The November 1996 Budget settlement, however, announced further cuts in publicly provided capital which, even if some PFI schemes did begin, would mean a fall in real capital spending in the coming years (Ward, 1996). Some way out of this impasse must be found.

Mental Health

In February 1996 (NHS Executive, 1996), the Government published proposals for nurse-run units to act as alternatives to acute in-patient units, the latest in a series of initiatives designed to improve mental health services. It is hard to detect any signs of the previous ones being effective: a report prepared for the London Commission (Johnson *et al.*, 1997) revealed intense pressure on in-patient facilities, poorly developed community alternatives and a low level of management capacity. A white paper is promised for early 1997. Whatever it says and however accurate its analysis, serious doubts will remain unless it shows convincingly that it has identified ways of actually improving services on the ground.

Rationing

With purchasing as a separate activity, it was widely predicted that this would lead to implicit rationing becoming explicit. Gradually it has done so but the Government has refused to get drawn on the issue. In January 1996, for example, the Secretary of State issued a statement affirming that no clinically effective treatment should be ruled out of NHS provision (Department of Health, 1996). It is hard to see how this stance can be maintained much longer. In the case of long-term care, after criticism from the Health Service Commissioner, the Government accepted that there had to be explicit criteria for continuing care support so as to clarify where the responsibility of the NHS ended and those of local authorities began. However, it decided that these should be determined locally, within central guidelines. There is now a good case for the political centre taking a clearer position on where the boundary of

NHS care lies in all sectors, including dentistry, cosmetic procedures, infertility treatment, gender reassignment, and long-term nursing. The question of which agency should provide these services is ultimately political and should be a matter for the Government, not individual, unelected health authorities.

More generally, the issue of rationing should be publicly acknowledged by the Government and a lead taken in developing a national debate about the need to ration, the principles on which it should be based and the necessary democratic mechanisms to hold decision-makers to account. The alternative is for evidence of rationing to continue to emerge in highly publicised individual cases in apparent contradiction to official pronouncements. The danger is that the public will lose confidence in the NHS and become less willing to support the levels of taxation necessary to sustain it.

Accountability

One way of sustaining confidence in the NHS among the public at large is to encourage decision-making in *partnership* with lay people, as a means of improving the legitimacy of those decisions. In particular, the way that health authorities and individual clinicians make decisions about how to use resources remains opaque to most members of the public. In the face of evidence that individual patients are having treatment withheld, this may breed mistrust—faceless bureaucrats, it may be thought, saving money and making life easy for themselves.

For a number of years the Government has encouraged an improved dialogue between health authorities and their local communities, but there is little evidence that this has significantly altered the relationship between those who make the decisions and those who are affected by them. A new government should support experimentation with more formal and deliberative forums where lay people can directly contribute to decision-making in certain circumstances. In particular, a number of citizens' juries have been piloted during 1996 as one way of achieving improvements in democratic participation and legitimacy (Lenaghan *et al.*, 1996).

Management

During the past five years the number of managers has grown rapidly, leaving the Government vulnerable to the charge that its reforms have led to more bureaucracy rather than better care. Accordingly, it took a series of measures to reduce management costs both within the central department and NHS Executive, as well as health authorities and trusts. But as the discussion of emergency care and mental health above suggest, the NHS requires much better management than it now has, in all parts of the Service. It is faced with a large number of issues such as hospital reconfiguration, provision of a reliable system of emergency care, and an effective mental health service, where all the skills on which a health service relies must combine to produce better quality of care. This is a management task of the highest order which demands contributions from both the centre and localities to get right. It may well mean that the centre will have to cease pretending that planning is dead and reassert the role of regional health authorities in guiding capital and service planning.

Conclusion

The final item is the survival of the NHS itself. This will require an increase in the real resources available to it and hence almost certainly a growing tax burden. If the new Government is unwilling to finance that and if it continues to call for notional increases in productivity via the annual targets for the purchaser efficiency index, then there is a serious risk that Healthcare 2000's analysis will prove correct. To prove it wrong will require both technical improvements in service design and management, and political innovation.

A *Service with Ambitions* states that: 'Throughout its history the NHS has found ways of accommodating the pressures on it, and there is no reason to doubt its ability to do so'. Quoting the report of the Guillebaud Committee, established in the 1950s by a Treasury worried about the rising cost of the NHS, it points out that the question of whether the NHS could cope with the pressures upon it is almost as old as the NHS itself. Whatever Government takes office during 1997, it will find itself an heir to a well-established tradition. But while the question may be the same, there will still be a need to devise new answers. ■

References

Bloor, K., Freemantle, N. and Maynard, A. (1996), Can expenditure on drugs be contained efficiently? In Harrison, A. (Ed), *Health Care UK 1995/96* (King's Fund, London).

Department of Health (1996), Looking after health in the new millennium, press release (8 January).

Dixon, J., Harrison, A. and New, B. (1997), Is the NHS underfunded? *British Medical Journal, 314*, pp. 58–61.

Ferner, R. E. (1996), Newly licensed drugs. *British Medical Journal, 313*, pp. 1157–1158.

Guillebaud Committee (1956), *Enquiry into the Cost of the National Health Service*, Cmd 9663 (HMSO, London).

Harrison, A. (1996), Winter warning. *Guardian* (16 October).

Healthcare 2000 (1995), *UK Health and Healthcare Services: Challenges and Policy Options* (Healthcare 2000, London).

Healthcare Financial Management Association (1996), NHS trust accounts database for 1995-96 published. Press release (20 December).

HM Treasury (1996), *Financial Statement and Budget Report* (Internet).

Johnson, S. *et al.* (1997), *London's Mental Health: The Report to the King's Fund London Commission* (King's Fund, London).

Lenaghan, J., New, B. and Mitchell, E. (1996), Setting priorities: is there a role for citizens' juries? *British Medical Journal, 312*, pp. 1591–1593.

NHS Executive (1995), New drugs for multiple sclerosis. EL (95)97 (15 November).

NHS Executive (1996), The spectrum of care—a summary of comprehensive local services for people with mental health problems. HSG (96) 6 (19 February).

Secretary of State for Health (1996), *The National Health Service: A Service with Ambitions,* Cm 3425 (HMSO, London).

Secretaries of State for Health, Scotland and Wales (1996a), *Choice and Opportunity. Primary Care: The Future.* Cm 3390 (HMSO, London).

Secretaries of State for Health, Scotland and Wales (1996b) *Primary Care: Delivering the Future.* Cm 3512 (HMSO, London).

Silcock, J. and Radcliffe, J. (1996), The 1990 GP contract—meeting needs? *Health Policy, 36*, pp. 199–207.

Smith, R. (1996), Rationing health care: moving the debate forward. *British Medical Journal, 312*, pp. 1553–1554.

Ward, S. (1996), Road to recovery? *Public Finance* (29 November), p. 12.

18 Education

John Graystone

Association of Colleges in the Eastern Region, Cambridge

At the Labour Party conference in September 1996, Tony Blair emphasized that his three priorities in government would be—'education, education and education'. In fact his comments could have been made by any of the political party leaders and underlined the fact that education is a key priority.

The breakdown in discipline at the Ridings School and confusion over who exactly was at fault; increases in the number of expulsions from schools; the improvement in examination results (it must be a result of falling standards); poor teacher morale; problems over school security; reductions in expenditure on further education; some universities considering whether to charge top-up fees as a way of solving their financial crisis—these all continued to dominate newspaper column inches and draw attention away from the successes of the sector. And successes there have been. Examination passes at GCSE and A level have never been higher. There is now much more information about schools and colleges and there is greater choice. The delegation of budgets to schools has general approval and parents have the opportunity to be more involved in their children's schooling. Participation in post-16 education has reached levels undreamt of a few years ago. And the quality and volume of research in higher education (HE) institutions have risen.

The Conservatives' approach has been to bring the market-place into education by increasing competition and choice, thereby improving standards and quality. Indeed, an underlying theme of the 1996 Budget was the quality of delivery of public service, particularly education. Customer focus has replaced producer centredness.

But a key plank of the Conservative Government's policy—the establishment of grant-maintained (GM) schools (schools which have opted out of local education authority control) and city technology colleges (schools funded by industry)—has remained disappointing. By December 1996—

eight years after the Education Reform Act 1988—there were only 1,149 grant-maintained schools in operation, about 4.5% of the 24,000 state schools in England (AMA, 1996a) and an increase of only 65 in the previous 12 months. If the move towards GM status in schools has not been the success envisaged by the Government, then hopes are pinned on the reintroduction of selection. John Major's dream is of a grammar school in every town. Perhaps selection, rather than freedom of choice, is the clarion call of late 20th-century conservatism.

If local education authorities (LEAs) have successfully clung to their schools, the incorporation of further and higher education institutions has resulted in a significant reduction in the influence of LEAs in post-school education. Further education (FE) colleges and the universities are now run by business-led corporations and funded primarily by national funding councils.

Expenditure

Expenditure on education remains a critical factor. The public expenditure survey (PES) settlement set Total Standard Spending (the Government's view of the total revenue spending which local authorities should incur) for 1997-98 at £45,665M, an increase of £738M or 1.6% over 1996-97. The Education Standard Spending—the amount spent primarily on schools—was set at £18,088M, as against the adjusted figure of £17,455M for 1996-97, an increase of £633M or 3.6% (Ernst and Young and CIPFA, 1996). The Service Working Group Education (SWGE)—a local authority officer group which meets with Department for Education and Employment officials—estimated that net revenue expenditure for education in 1996-97 was in fact £18,432M (AMA, 1996b)—much higher than the ESS figures. Local authorities indeed claimed a shortfall of 2% following the 1996 Budget. CIPFA has predicted that more than 10,000 jobs could be at risk. The School Teachers' Review Body (1996) gave teachers a phased award of 3.3%, placing increased strains on local authority finances (Rafferty, 1996b).

In further education (FE), the 1996 PES settlement showed a reduction in funds made payable to the Further Education Funding Council (FEFC) in England from £3,070M in 1996-97 to £3,011M in 1999-2000. This 2% reduction over three years needs to be set against a projected increase in student numbers of 8% over the same period. Efficiency gains of 5% per year over the three-year period are expected. The settlement was better, however, than many expected—income was boosted by a gross increase in funds of £80M over two years, over and above that set out in the 1995 PES settlement. However, the sector was stunned by the announcement in early 1997 that the Government was to cease payments for demand-led funding for colleges that exceed their targets—estimated to be up to £100M in a full year.

In higher education (HE), the gross increase in the PES settlement was £200M over the two years from 1997, not enough to reverse the cuts of £270M announced in 1995. The Higher Education Funding Council for England (HEFCE) will receive £3,448M in 1997-98 reducing to £3.37 billion in 1999-2000. As in FE, this money has strings attached. £20M for research equipment has to be matched by private funding. Efficiency gains of 0.5% in 1997-98, rising to 4.5% in 1999-2000, mean an estimated 6% reduction in real terms (Ernst Young and CIPFA, 1996).

Current Legislation

The 1996 Education Bill, intended to gain Royal Assent by Easter 1997, proposed that schools should have the right to appeal to the Secretary of State over the heads of local authorities if they wanted to become grammar schools. GM schools were to be given new freedoms to add nursery or sixth-form provision without formal notice. County and voluntary schools would have been able to select up to 20% of their pupils by ability or aptitude; GM schools up to 50%. The Funding Agency for Schools (FAS), which funds GM schools, would have been able to set up a GM school anywhere. These provisions were dropped from the Bill after the announcement of the general election on 17 March 1997. What remained in the depleted Act was least controversial.

All governing bodies will have to ensure that good discipline and behaviour are promoted in the school. This includes a written statement of general principles which the headteacher must use in drawing up rules for enforcing good behaviour. Pupils can be excluded from a school on fixed-term exclusions up to 45 days a year. The Qualifications and National Curriculum Authority (QNCA) will be formed from the School Curriculum and Assessment Authority (SCAA) and the National Council for Vocational Qualifications (NCVQ).

In July 1996, the Nursery Education and Grant Maintained Schools Act 1996 received Royal Assent. The nursery voucher scheme, piloted in four local authorities in 1995-96, will become a national scheme from 1997. Nursery education has been removed from local authority control and is being financed through the issuing of vouchers—each worth £1,100 per year—which can be cashed at institutions providing nursery education. The scheme was criticised by the all-party House of Commons select committee on education for doing the opposite of what it was intended to do—reducing rather than widening choice. The viability of many voluntary and private providers has been threatened by schools taking on more four-year olds while lacking the teachers with the skills to work with this age group (MacAskill, 1997)

Educational Issues

Schools

During 1996, the state of Britain's schools received much publicity. The tragic events at Dunblane Primary School, the murder of Philip Lawrence, a highly respected London headteacher, and the horrifying machete attack on pupils at a Wolverhampton primary school focused attention as never before on dangers facing teachers and pupils. A DfEE working group on school security recommended that guidance be issued on improving school security and identifying good practice on effective co-operation between schools and the police. The erection of security cameras and wire fences was in sad contrast to the trend towards widening public access to schools. Much debate focused on moral decline and led to a SCAA consultative paper setting out values and principles for action covering society, relationships, the self and the environment. Its publication led to a predictable row over what should, or should not, be included (SCAA, 1996). Consideration of core values will continue to be an important theme in 1997.

The media circus that swarmed around the Ridings School in Calderdale painted a picture of an education system in disarray. What emerged was a lack of clarity over responsibility for maintained schools—was it the DfEE, the LEA, the governors or the headteacher who stood to take the blame? Or was it the teachers or the parents? There was one important bonus for LEAs. The Government, backtracking on its 1980s policies, saw LEAs as playing a key role in the running of their schools. Indeed, Gillian Shephard's criticism of Calderdale Education Authority underlined the fact that it had a definite role to play. The anti-LEA rhetoric that dominated the late 1980s and early 1990s had all but disappeared as Ministers and civil servants realized that the running of schools was no easy matter.

A survey commissioned by the *Times Educational Supplement* concluded that 'teachers are fed up with having to teach children in even larger classes, and working in schools which are dilapidated, underfunded and overstretched'. Teachers felt they were being made scapegoats for many of society's ills (Sutcliffe, 1997).

Their morale was not helped by a seemingly innocuous consultative paper from the DfEE in October 1996. From 1 September 1997 (the original intention was 1 April 1997), teachers seeking early retirement would have to have part of their pension paid for the rest of their life by the employer—the LEA in the case of maintained schools, the governing body of the GM school, the corporation of the FE sector college or higher education institution. Under the previous arrangements, teachers over the age of 50 who were made redundant or wanted to retire early (with the agreement of their employer) had ready access to their pension administered by Teachers' Pension Agency. The prediction is that few educational institutions would be willing in future to grant early retirement.

This controversial shift in policy has taken place because of the high cost of the number of qualified teachers retiring early—only one in five teachers continue working till 60—and the lack of sufficient numbers of new teachers to replace them. The teaching force will become older, promotion opportunities will be blocked, and there is a risk of many staff staying on reluctantly. The DfEE issued a draft circular seeking to address these problems by the introduction of actuarially reduced pensions and a 'stepping down' arrangement by which teachers with responsibilities nearing retirement could take a less responsible post without adversely affecting their pension (DfEE, 1997).

The approach used in school inspections by the Office for Standards in Education (OFSTED) has been controversial. A day rarely seemed to pass by without the chief inspector, Chris Woodhead, appearing on some conference platform or in a TV/radio studio, or writing in the national press, pointing to weaknesses in schools or defending OFSTED's approach. Sir Bryan Nicholson, previously chair of the National Council for Vocational

Qualifications, addressing the North of England conference, called for a reform of the school inspection service. He criticized it for the lack of support for failing schools and stated that it was 'an Anneka Rice kind of service—OFSTED dives in, shakes everything up and helicopters off' (Nicholson, 1997). Whatever its critics might say, OFSTED has focused attention on standards in schools.

The June 1996 White Paper, *Self-Government for Schools,* set out proposals for schools to identify performance targets to enable comparisons to be made with other schools and to build these into school development plans. The new inspections arrangements from September 1997 will lead to the more regular inspection of 'weaker' schools and to identify 'serious weaknesses' in inspection reports. The inspection cycle will move from four to six years (OFSTED, 1996).

Whereas OFSTED has attracted much attention, the inspectorate of FE colleges was due to complete the inspection of every FE college in 1997 with little public criticism as to its approach. A consultation paper on proposed new inspection arrangements was generally welcomed in the sector and implemented with some modifications. An underlying theme in school and college inspections is the move towards self-assessment. In FE, a long-term aim of the inspectorate is to monitor colleges' quality systems and restrict full inspection to colleges where there are difficulties.

1996 saw the publication of the long-awaited report of the Committee on the Review of Qualifications for 16–19 year olds chaired by Sir Ron Dearing. It recommended a national framework of qualifications which would be allocated to four levels—advanced, intermediate, foundation and entry. A national certificate should be introduced to recognize achievement at the intermediate and advanced levels. The term 'applied A level' should replace General National Vocational Qualification (GNVQ) (advanced level). GNVQs are a broadly based vocational alternative to the General Certificate of Secondary Education (GCSE) and GCE A level at three levels. The Government's intention is that 50% of 16 and 17 year olds will take GNVQs in the longer term. Dearing supported retaining the A level—the 'gold standard' of the education system.

Further Education

The Further Education Funding Council in England (FEFC) funds 453 self-governing further education, sixth-form and designated colleges, as well as other institutions where courses are franchised or sponsored for the purpose by FE sector colleges.

The funding methods devised by the funding councils encourage colleges to increase student numbers and take account of the costs of the initial assessment and guidance of students, student retention and student achievement, especially that related to the national training and education targets (NTETs). By the end of 1996-97, most colleges' average level of funding (ALF) will be within +/- 10% of the median. This is in marked contrast to the very wide levels of funding inherited from the days when colleges were funded by LEAs. The funding methodology is currently being reviewed and changes are likely to be in place from 1998.

The overall number of students in England in FE sector colleges increased by 17% from 3,006,000 in 1994-95 to 3,519,200 in 1995-96. The number of students in colleges funded by the English FEFC increased by 27% from 2,168,000 to 2,745,100. This increase was primarily focused on part-time students (up 37%), whereas full-time students increased by only 4%. Seventy-nine per cent of FEFC-funded students were adults, i.e. aged over 19, and 75% studied part-time (FEFC, 1996b).

Recruitment of students is a priority for all colleges, yet colleges continue to receive uncapped demand-led funding—albeit at a lower level—for units above the core. Retaining students once they are enrolled has become an increasing priority. The cost of courses taken by students not achieving their intended qualification has been estimated at £500M a year (OFSTED/Audit Commission, 1993). Under the FEFC funding methodology, colleges lose income if students drop out of courses.

The FEFC reported that only 47% of colleges had sound finances and that 34% could face financial difficulties if they encountered adverse circumstances. Nearly a fifth were described in *FE Now* as in a 'weak financial position'. The projected operating deficit for the sector for 1995-96 was £119M (FEFC, 1996c). The next few years are likely to see an increase in college mergers, often driven by financial concerns and further reductions in staff. And colleges will compete strongly with schools for the 16–19 market.

Accountability was a major focus of the deliberations of the Nolan Committee which investigated the work of FE and HE corporations (governing bodies). The sectors emerged relatively unscathed from his report—standards of conduct were generally 'very good'—especially when compared with Nolan's comments on Members of Parliament (Committee on Standards in Public Life, 1995 and 1996). However, a number of important recommendations were made such as the need for each institution to adopt a 'whistle-blower's charter' to ensure that staff were protected if raising concerns about academic standards or misuse of public funds.

The importance of the working relationship between the governing body and college management was emphasized when the principal and other senior manager at Britain's second largest college (City of Stoke College) were dismissed after it was found that the college was facing an unexpected £8M deficit, much of it a result of overstating student numbers. An easing of the regulation of colleges by the FEFC became less likely as a result.

Higher Education

The 1991 White Paper, *Higher Education: A New Framework,* set an ambitious target of around one-third of all eligible young people to enter higher education by 2000. This target had been virtually achieved by 1993-94. Numbers had increased by 50.4% from 654,000 full-time equivalent students in 1989-90 to 984,000 in 1993-94. The age participation index rose from 17% to 30%. Since then the numbers and participation rates have been frozen by the Government, which while seeking to control public expenditure had to fund the costs of increased participation. The current funding methodology provides a strong incentive to HE institutions to hit exactly their agreed targets—exceeding or falling short brings financial penalties.

The Government introduced a mixed system of grants and loans from 1992-93. The main rates of grant and loan will be broadly equal in 1996-97. The combined grant, loan and parental contribution will rise by 2.5% for 1997-98.

There has been a funding crisis in HE. In 1996-97 the *Times Higher Education Supplement* estimated that 3,000 posts were lost through voluntary and compulsory redundancy and early retirement. The maximum tuition fees reimbursed through mandatory awards are fixed by the Government. As a means of raising additional income and assisting in funding expansion, a number of HE institutions have considered charging students top-up tuition fees of £1,000 per student per year from 1998. However, a decision by vice chancellors has been postponed until the report of a committee of enquiry, chaired by Sir Ron Dearing, set up to review funding for HE. The establishment of the committee has neatly helped diffuse HE funding as a political issue as the report is not due until after the general election. The Committee of Vice Chancellors and Principals, in their evidence to Dearing, called for a complete reform of the funding system of HE.

The 1995 Budget reduced capital funding for further and higher education by one third. The Private Finance Initiative (PFI) was intended to substitute for and make up the reduction in 'publicly funded' capital expenditure. But colleges and universities have proved reluctant to take advantage of PFI. Commercial funding of FHE is around £2 billion. The 1996 Budget predicted an additional £1.1 billion in the three years from 1997-98 to 1997-2000.

The 1996 Research Assessment Exercise showed that average ratings for universities have increased. The conclusion drawn was that this was clear evidence of an improvement in the quality and volume of research. But this success led to concerns that HE institutions were concentrating on research at the expense of teaching.

Educational Policies: The Political Parties

Education was a key policy area in the general election. The Conservatives want to consolidate their reforms and attract private finance into education. Quality, standards, choice and, now, selection are at the heart of their policy. 'Charter schools' are being considered under which parents and teachers could set up self-governing schools with basic state funding, topped up with finance from local businesses and voluntary organizations. This idea has been tried and developed in the USA (Carvel, 1996). The Conservative Party supports the right of schools to select pupils by ability and the publication of primary school league tables for 11 year olds, both of which are opposed by the Labour Party. A new Conservative Government would reintroduce those measures dropped from the Education Act 1997.

The reforms set out in the Further and Higher Education Act 1992 would continue at a slower pace. The Government is placing emphasis on lifelong learning, with proposals for career development loans for older students and tax concessions to companies who invest in the continuing education and training of their staff. In the longer term, there may be a move towards vouchers or credits for post-compulsory education, though these have been ruled out in the short term. Some on the right of the Party would want the privatization of the funding councils—possibly passing on their funding responsibilities to banks.

The Labour Party's policy documents published in 1995—*Diversity and Excellence: A New Partnership for Schools*, and *Excellence for Everyone: Labour's Crusade to Raise Standards*, formed the cornerstone of their education policy. In early 1997, Tony Blair, in a television interview, reiterated his commitment to education—'an Education Bill will be the first Bill in the first Queen's Speech' (Blair, 1997). He promised that an incoming Labour government would pass educational legislation to reduce primary school class sizes, encourage home-school contracts between schools and parents, and set national minimum homework requirements. Interestingly, the response by Gillian Shephard, Education and Employment Secretary, was not to rubbish the proposals but to say that much had already been done.

The Labour Party is committed to phasing out the assisted places scheme, opposing the reintroduction of grammar schools (parental ballots will decide the future of exiting schools) and winding up the nursery voucher scheme. The role of the LEA would be strengthened, with each LEA setting out an agreed admissions policy for its area and overall three year strategic educational development plans detailing how standards would be raised.

A new national qualification for headteachers would, in time, become compulsory and rigorous appraisal of all teachers emphasized.

Under life-long learning, the Labour Party is committed to four principles—quality, access, equity and accountability. Their proposals include a unified qualification route for 14–19 year olds, and a merging of the funding councils and TECs at regional level. The independence of FE colleges would be maintained, while business-led governing bodies would be reformed to include local authority, staff and student members. In higher education, the party now supports the principle of student loans as the only way of paying for expansion and access, but will wait for the recommendations of the Dearing Committee of enquiry before coming to a firm policy.

The Liberal Democrats' policy views were summarized in *Excellence for All* (published in 1994), and *Investing in Our Future* (published in 1996). The party echoes the views of the other parties by emphasizing the importance of improving standards, and seeking to maintain diversity in schools. The creation of further GM schools is opposed in favour of enhancing the role of fully democratic 'local education departments'. GM schools would be brought under 'light touch' local control, with local education departments being given an important strategic role. The assisted places scheme would be abolished. The key policy which distinguishes the party from the others is its commitment to increase spending on education by 'an additional £2 billion, paid for if necessary by putting an additional penny on income tax'.

Conclusions

Education has had a high political profile in the general election. The key differences between the parties is the overall funding of education, the role of GM schools, selection of pupils by ability and the assisted places scheme. All parties now support attempts to improve literacy levels, the publication of examination results, although the Labour Party and Liberal Democrats prefer value-added rather than raw scores. The Liberal Democrats have argued strongly for tax increases to fund expansion, the Conservatives have pushed for efficiency, and the Labour Party are looking to fund increases in expenditure from economic growth, a windfall tax on privatized industries, and savings arising from a reduction in employment.

All three parties therefore agree on the key importance of improving standards of education, although the means of achieving this varies. However, the wide differences in educational policy that existed in the 1980s and early 1990s have all but disappeared. ■

References

Association of Metropolitan Authorities (1996a), *Education Information Circular 12/96.*

Association of Metropolitan Authorities (1996b), *The Budget and Local Government Financial Settlement* (Education Committee).

Blair, Tony (1997), *Breakfast with Frost* (12 January).

Carvel, J. (1996), Tories plan to boost opt-outs. *Guardian* (31 December).

Committee on Standards in Public Life (1995), *Standards in Public Life* (chairman Lord Nolan), First report, Vol. 1, Cm 2850-1.

Committee on Standards in Public Life (1996), *Local Public Spending Bodies* (chairman Lord Nolan), Second report, Vol. 1, Cm 3270-1.

Dearing, Sir Ron (1996), *Review of Qualifications for 16–19 Year Olds* (School Curriculum and Assessment Authority, London).

Department for Education (1991), *Higher Education: A New Framework,* Cm 1541 (HMSO, London).

Department for Education and Employment (1996), *Self-Government for Schools,* Cm 3315 (HMSO, London).

Department for Education and Employment (1997), *Early Retirement for Teachers,* Draft Circular (17 March).

Ernst and Young and CIPFA (1996), *Corporate Strategy 97* (CIPFA, London).

Further Education Funding Council (1996a), Public expenditure survey settlement 1997/98 to 1999/2000. Circular 96/30.

Further Education Funding Council (1996b), Student numbers at colleges in the further education sector and external institutions in England in 1995-96 (Press release, 17 December).

Further Education Funding Council (1996c), *Council News No 35.*

MacAskill, E. (1997), Nursery voucher scheme condemned by MPs. *Guardian* (13 March).

Nicholson, Sir Bryan (1997), Address to the North of England Conference, January.

Office for Standards in Education/Audit Commission (1993), *Unfinished Business: Full-Time Educational Courses for 16–19 Year Olds* (HMSO, London).

Office for Standards in Education (1996), *Report on the Consultation Arrangements for the Inspection of Maintained Schools from September 1997* (OFSTED, London).

Rafferty, F. (1996), Massive job losses may follow deal. *Times Educational Supplement* (6 December).

School Curriculum and Assessment Authority (1996), Consultation on values in education and the community (SCAA, London).

School Teachers' Review Body (1997), *Report* (HMSO, London).

Sutcliffe, J. (1997), Enter the feel-bad factor. *Times Educational Supplement* (10 January).

19 Criminal Justice

Barry Loveday
University of Portsmouth

Criminal justice policy was dominated, in 1996, by the White Paper 'Protecting the Public' (Cm 3190). In a wide-ranging set of proposals, the White Paper represented the culmination of a programme on crime identified by the Home Secretary at the 1993 Conservative Party Conference. A series of Parliamentary bills following on from the White Paper could fundamentally change sentencing practices by the introduction of mandatory sentences for a range of offences. This, and the provision of wider surveillance powers for the police and new rules of disclosure of evidence, are a product of the public commitment made by Home Secretary Michael Howard to adopt a more aggressive law and order stance and to 'take the fight against crime to the criminal'.

Election Blues

One consequence of the 1996 White Paper, *Protecting the Public,* has been a flurry of Parliamentary bills along with legislation controlling the sale of knives and guns; the Home Secretary tried to push through some 13 bills designed to improve the Government's standing on law and order before the General Election. In addition to Michael Howard's Crime Sentences Bill, the Police Bill, the Fire Arms Bill and the Sex Offenders Bill, private member's bills will include a Public Entertainment Licence Bill, giving the courts new powers to close clubs where police have found evidence of drugs. The Under-Age Drinks Bills will give police powers to seize alcohol from those under 18. New prison policy is reflected in a bill which will introduce testing of prisoners for alcohol and the DNA Profiling of Prisoners Bill, which will give the police powers to take genetic fingerprints of prisoners convicted of violent or sexual crime.

If successful, this legislation will effect the most comprehensive and significant change to criminal justice policy during John Major's leadership of the Conservative Government. There has been some unexpected posturing from the Labour Party: Labour has criticized the Government for not including enough measures against child abuse and stalkers. During the course of the Crimes (Sentences) Bill and Police Bill, the Labour opposition abstained on crucial clauses restricting judicial discretion and the protection of civil rights. The policy of compliance adopted by Labour, reflected the fact that law and order had become not just a major election issue, but also a test of Labour's credibility as a possible future governing party. Being at least as tough on crime as the Conservatives is New Labour's way of burying any residual public image of a party which was soft on crime. The crime control nostrums of the Home Secretary have, therefore, been rather faithfully reflected in the position taken by Labour. If a new consensus on law and order has been established, it appears to be far to the right of anything postulated by the Labour Party in either the 1980s or early 1990s. Both the shadow home secretary, Jack Straw, and the Labour Leader, Tony Blair, have condemned street beggars and 'squeegee' merchants, while applauding zero tolerance policing (MacAskill, 1997).

Moving into election mode has, therefore, shifted parties very much to the right. Labour strategy, which appears to be to outflank the Government on a policy area which it has traditionally monopolized, means that on a number of issues it is now difficult to distinguish in terms of the policy between the two major parties.

Crime Control

In its Crime (Sentences) Bill, the Government intends to introduce major changes to sentencing practices in England and Wales. The most significant of these would end the discretionary powers of the judiciary in sentencing for a number of serious offences. Under the legislation, for repeat offenders, mandatory sentences will be imposed. Unless there are genuinely exceptional circumstances, the courts could be required to impose a minimum sentence of three years on offenders over 18 years, who are convicted of domestic burglary and have two or more previous convictions for similar offences. As research has shown that most burglars are persistent offenders, the Government argues that the penalties imposed on those convicted are not a sufficient deterrent and that 'a short spell in prison has become an acceptable risk' (Cm 3190).

In addition, mandatory minimum prison sentences are planned for drug dealers convicted of drug trafficking offences involving Class A drugs and who have two or more previous convictions for similar offences. Where the offender is liable to a mandatory sentence, the court will be required to impose a minimum sentence of seven years. The Government is determined that those who trade in 'human misery and ruined lives should get the punishment they richly deserve: a very long prison sentence'.

Repeats of violent offences and sexual offences will automatically attract a life sentence. Where an offender is convicted of murder, the court will also be required to impose a mandatory sentence of life imprisonment. In these cases it will remain the Home Secretary's responsibility to set the tariff which the offenders must serve. In introducing automatic life sentences, the Government argues that these are better described as 'automatic indeterminate sentences', which provide greater discretion to hold those offenders where it is believed that he/she will reoffend if released (Cm 3192).

The trial judge will specify the tariff to be served for retribution and deterrence and, at the end of that period, the Parole Board will determine whether it is safe to release the offender. Furthermore, if released, an offender who has served and automatic, indeterminate sentence, will remain on licence and subject to recall: 'for the rest or his or her life'. The Government argues that the public should receive proper protection from persistent violent and sex offenders, which means that the courts must be required to impose such automatic sentences while releasing the offender if, and only if, it is safe to do so (Cm 3190).

In the Crime (Sentences) Bill, the Government also intends to introduce 'honesty in sentencing'. In future, offenders sentenced to custody will serve the full term order by the court. Automatic early release and parole will be abolished. In future, prisoners will have to earn early release by co-operation and 'positive good behaviour', which will be assessed throughout their sentence; the maximum remission will be 20% of the term of imprisonment originally imposed. The Government expects that judges will take into account the changes to early release, and does not expect a general increase in the period of time offenders serve in prison.

Fighting Crime—Howard's Way

The Government has responded to a Home Affairs Select Committee Report on organized crime published in 1995 with the introduction of a new Police Bill. The report stated that while organized crime was in the UK, not on a scale found in many other countries, it remained a cause for concern. Within the Police Bill, a series of clauses significantly enhance the ability of law enforcement agencies to gather intelligence, while also ensuring that they are 'properly structured' to tackle serious and organized crime more effectively. The intelligence gathering capability provided by the Police Bill, follows on from the Security Service Act 1996, which has mobilized MI5 in support of the police when they combat criminal gangs, drug traffickers, money launderers and other organized criminals. Under the Police Bill, chief constables and their deputies were originally planned to be given power to issue warrants to bug and enter property, homes and offices, whenever they believed it was necessary to do so to 'combat serious crime'. Serious crime is very broadly defined within the Police Bill and includes offences which involve use of violence or substantial financial gain. It also includes any offence where an offender could expect a prison sentence of three years or more, and any offence 'involving a large number of persons in pursuit of a common purpose' (Travis, 1997).

The original Police Bill did not offer any exemptions to police electronic surveillance or search, for example by journalists, doctors or lawyers. In the original proposals, a warrant for surveillance or entry would have been authorized 'when it was thought likely to be of substantial value and the police were satisfied that what the action sort to achieve, could not be reasonably achieved by other means'. The police would have been able to 'search any property, inspect any file and scrutinize any personal documents which they considered relevant'. This surveillance would have been monitored by a single commissioner (a former judge) who would review retrospectively what the police had already done. The Government suffered a major defeat in the House of Lords, when peers overturned a key element of the Police Bill pertaining to the issue of warrants for electronic surveillance. Amendments by Labour and the Liberal Democrats required that the police should seek, other than in emergencies, authorization from a judge before entering and bugging homes. An alliance of senior judges and lawyers persuaded the Lords that it was an essential civil liberty for the police to get prior authorization before bugging private property rather than after. It is now likely that the Government will have to accept the principle of prior authorization before a warrant is issued. Although Mr Howard claimed, that, as a result of the vote, 'criminals would be clapping their hands', it was always unlikely that his proposal would survive its critics in the House of Lords who have regularly struck down government legislation. The Police Bill will also establish a National Crime Squad (NCS). The co-ordinator of the NCS will have executive powers to direct IT resources from a national to an international perspective to combat organized crime. The Police Bill will also place the National Criminal Intelligence Service (NCIS) on a firmer statutory footing by giving it a separate identity: NCIS will become a separate body removed from the Home Office and accountable to a National Police Committee.

Protecting the Public

Michael Howard's crime and police legislation has generated a strong reaction among senior members of the judiciary and most practitioners in the criminal justice field. In a damning indictment of the Government's crime plans, the then Lord Chief Justice, Lord Taylor, claimed that: 'Never in the history of criminal law have such far-reaching proposals been put forward on the strength of such flimsy and dubious evidence' (Travis, 1996a).

In the course of a House of Lords debate, the Lord Chief Justice was to question why all the central features of government policy, so recently propounded on criminal justice, were being jettisoned and replaced by 'their exact opposite'. Challenging the concept of mandatory sentences, The Lord Chief Justice argued that it could not be right for sentences to be passed without regard to the gravity, consequences or other circumstances of the offending. It was reported he found support from every corner of the House of Lords, with the former Master of the Rolls arguing that Mr Howard's White Paper *Protecting the Public* demonstrated an unprecedented and deplorable message from the government to the public, 'not to trust the judges' (Travis, 1996a).

Elsewhere, senior law lords were to highlight the extraordinary contradiction which *Protecting the Public* represented in terms of the Government's own crime strategy. Lord Ackner said that, as recently as 1990, the Government's White Paper on *Crime, Justice and Protecting the Public*, did not suggest that prison worked, apart from its 'warehousing' function. Indeed, the Government's view then was that prison could not be seen as an effective means of reform for most prisoners, but, rather, was 'an expensive way of making bad people worse'. In the 1990 White Paper, the

Government had specifically argued against the imposition of minimum sentences or interfering with judicial discretion. The same White Paper had stated 'no government should try to influence the decision of the courts in individual cases. The independence of the judiciary is rightly regarded as a corner stone of our liberties' (*Times*, 20 May 1996).

Lord Ackner also said that mandatory sentences could prove to be counterproductive as defendants might contest a case which would, if they were found guilty, result in life imprisonment. And juries confronted with such mandatory penalties imposed by the courts might refuse to convict even when there was reason to believe the defendant was guilty. Concern about the increased acquittal rate by juries had strengthened the argument in the 1990 White Paper against the introduction of minimum sentences. These, it said, could, as a result, lead unjustly to more guilty men and women going free (*Times*, 20 May 1996).

Subsequently, Lord Chief Justice Bingham argued against the imposition of mandatory sentences and for the retention of judicial discretion. He claimed that there was a case for abolishing the mandatory sentence of life sentence for murder as there was a need to tailor a sentence to the facts and circumstances of the particular case (Dyer, 1996). In a subsequent debate, two former home secretaries challenged Michael Howard over his crime programme. They argued that the Home Secretary was treating law and order issues as 'a race for votes' and that mandatory sentences would only succeed in turning out more accomplished criminals (Travis, 1996a).

Prison Policy

In the 1996 White Paper, the Government committed itself to prison expansion. The Government believes that 'prison works'. Using prison as a means of reducing crime is based on American claims that incarceration will reduce the offence rate as prisoners are denied the opportunity to commit crime. The Home Secretary's penal policy is driven very largely by American experience rather than official advice from his own department. Home Office research suggests that an increase of 25% in the prison population is required to reduce crime by 1%. Michael Howard believes that to argue that imprisoning people has not worked 'simply flies in the face of the facts' (Travis, 1996b). Maximizing incarceration is based on the apparent success of this policy in the USA. Many policies, indeed, pursued by the Home

Secretary do now appear to have their origin there. These include such US imports as boot camps and electronic tagging, the interest in automatic life sentences and a commitment to prison expansion. Michael Howard who, in a candid demonstration of acquiescence to everything American, came close to renaming the probation service the 'Corrections Agency' has also actively encourage American private prison companies to expand their operations in Britain (Travis, 1996b).

If the Home Secretary is aware that getting tough on crime has proved to be extremely popular among the electorate, he may have overlooked the consequences of mandatory sentences in America. One consequence of these has been an explosion in jury trials where defendants are aware that admission of guilt means life imprisonment. In California, where a 'three strikes' policy has operated for the longest time, 47 of the state's 125 civil courts have now been pressed into hearing criminal cases. The chief of the Los Angeles Police Department has also suggested that an increase in shootings of police officers reflected an increased determination among potential 'three strikes' defendants to avoid arrest. With a total of 1.5M prison inmates, sustaining such a massive prison programme can only be achieved by cutting expenditure in other public services. California is now spending more on prisons than higher education. There also appears to be no clear evidence that imprisonment has been a primary factor in reducing crime rates in America: no clear correlation has been found between those states with a substantial prison population and those with low prison numbers and the crime rate (Katz, 1996).

Despite the American problems, the Home Secretary intends to pursue a similar programme. On the Crime Sentences Bill, he argued that an extra 12 prisons would be needed to accommodate the 11,000 extra criminals who would be incarcerated under the new law. This, he argued, would be the biggest change in the fight against crime this century. Private companies would be invited to build the new prisons which would be repaid by way of an annual fee over 25 years at an expected cost of around 3 billion. An additional 900 prison staff would be needed, although these might be employed by private companies.

Go to Jail

The projected 11,000 increase in the prison population will be in addition to the recent increases in prison numbers. The prison population has risen by 25% over the last three years, and at the beginning of 1997 was around 58,000. A *Times* editorial congratulated the Home Secretary for reversing years of Home Office orthodoxy which, it alleged, saw the main index of success at being not crime figures dropping, but the prison population declining (*Times*, 9 October 1996). Yet it was apparent that this policy had generated a crisis, to which the Director General of the prison service, Richard Tilt, found it difficult to respond. Following a series of successful local protests against the construction of prisons, a desperate search for possible prison sites became necessary. A new prison warehouse is planned for Lancashire, utilizing a former Pontin's holiday camp, which will house 700 inmates. The extra capacity will also be provided by using a floating prison moored in Portland Harbour near Weymouth. This 'floating maritime facility', the *Resolution*, was formally used as a prison ship in New York harbour and has a capacity for 400 inmates. The former holiday camp and floating structure are necessary to deal with the current rises in the total prison population. Prison numbers were officially predicted to reach, for 1996, an end of year total of 53,200. By December 1996, it had already reached 58,500 with an extra 600–700 defenders being imprisoned through the year, an average on a monthly basis of 500 more prisoners than the 150 originally planned for by the prison service.

Increased numbers of prisoners must be accommodated despite a 13% cut in the Prison Service budget over three years, which has been demanded by the Treasury. Treasury-driven cuts make it likely that, in future private prison companies will shoulder the burden of prison expansion. An official study said that the 10-15% difference in operating costs between public and private prisons was largely explained by low wages and worse conditions of service offered in the private sector (Travis, 1996c).

New Labour's Plans for Criminal Justice

'Tough on crime' has proved to be one of the most effective sound bites in the history of the Labour Party. Labour has supported zero tolerance policing, and denounced street beggars and the homeless. Labour also abstained on significant clauses during the passage of the Crime Sentences Bill. It has supported the Government's decision to restrict disclosure of evidence to defence counsel now enshrined in the Criminal Procedure and

Investigation Act 1996, even though a senior member of the Bar Council argued that the legal profession could have no confidence in a system where the defence were dependent upon the Crown and the police for what they could see. Defence counsel will now be dependent on ethical policing where police will be expected to disclose only material evidence which might undermine the prosecution case. The President of ACPO said that they had set up a working party to consider how the new disclosure rules would be implemented (White, 1996). Subsequently it was discovered that the Crown Prosecution Service were organizing a major training exercise to implement the new Disclosure provisions 'fairly and effectively' (Mills, 1996). Labour also supported the Government's proposals for restricting legal aid and has promised to implement any reform of legal aid it might inherit after the general election from the Major Government. Labour has, nevertheless, developed a policy programme which demonstrates clear water between it and the crime control strategy pursued by the current Home Secretary.

Reforming Youth Justice

Arguing that the central issue confronting society remains the increasing problem of youth crime, a Labour Government will direct immediate attention to a major overhaul of youth justice. Basing its strategy on local evidence of a hard core of persistent young offenders and the failure of existing machinery to deal effectively with repeat offenders, Labour intends to streamline youth justice. After 25 years, responsibility for children will return to the Home Office which will set up a National Youth Board. Using the Board, a Labour Government intends to exercise more authoritative national leadership in tackling youth crime. Local authorities will be given a key role in dealing with youth crime. To emphasize this new role, a statutory duty will be placed on local authorities to develop crime prevention partnerships with the police and place this activity at the centre of all local authority activity (*Tackling Youth Crime*, 1996).

Being tough on crime and the causes of crime will end any confusion over welfare and punishment. This will be dealt with by concentrating on sanctions aimed to change the behaviour of young offenders. Formal cautions will be replaced by a final warning, which will trigger community intervention with both young offenders and their families. Youth courts will take a more informal inquisitorial approach. And, under legal aid, defence counsels will only be provided in cases where the facts surrounding guilt or innocence have been contested. For persistent young offenders, a fast track system will be established to ensure that these are dealt with more speedily than currently by magistrate's courts.

Reparation

Greater emphasis will be placed on changing the behaviour of young offenders by way of reparation in sentencing. More emphasis will also be placed on monitoring and feedback so the courts have information on the outcomes for those they sentence. This would be encouraged by a change in the orientation of youth courts, away from a preoccupation with legal processes to one of confronting young offenders with their behaviour and providing practical solutions for changing it.

Labour believes that the community must be protected from a hard core of young offenders who can be expected to continue offending while on bail. It will be tougher about controlling young offenders on bail by the use of local authority secure accommodation for remanded youngsters who are 'too out of control for bail in the community or an ordinary children's home'. Local authorities will be allowed to develop intermediate facilities where supervision and security is greater than in a children's home but less rigorous (and costly) than secure accommodation, to protect the community from repeat young offenders. Labour also takes the view that young people aged 10–13 years are capable of differentiating between right and wrong, especially in offences involving theft or damage to property and they intend reforming the *doli incapax* rule.

Audit Commission

The proposals outlined by Labour appear to be in line with the findings of research conducted by the Audit Commission in its report on *Misspent Youth—Young People and Crime* (Audit Commission, 1996). The Audit Commission argued that the youth justice system was not helping to reduce offending behaviour. The Commission's report noted that a quarter of known offenders were under 18 and that while three out of five offenders aged between 10 and 17 years, identified by the police, were cautioned, little was done to deal with their behaviour. For those prosecuted, half of the proceedings against young people were discontinued, dismissed or ended in discharge. The report argued it was necessary to speed up court processes to end delays, introduce more intensive supervision of persistent offenders, and evaluate the effectiveness of sentences in reducing reoffending.

Because no one agency could deal with the long-term issues, which would include pre-school education for under fives, the Audit Commission recommended that local authorities should take the lead in developing a multi-agency approach to identify areas of high risk, consult residents about crime problems and identify ways to solve them. Help should be provided with parenting, employment and training opportunities developed while youth services should encourage positive leisure opportunities for the young in areas of high deprivation (Audit Commission, 1996).

Council Estates

Areas of high deprivation were highlighted in a report published by the Institute of Fiscal Studies in 1996. It found that council estates had become the dumping grounds for the poor, unemployed and the benefit dependent. On these estates, around half of all adult males could be expected to be unemployed while, of those who worked, half earned less than £6.00 an hour. The average income of council tenants in 1993 was found to be 20% lower than in 1973. Being tough on the causes of crime would, therefore, require positive intervention by the Government by seeking to break the cycle of decline experienced by Britain's poorest families. It was for this reason, presumably, that the Home Office's Report on *Young People and Crime* recommended that every effort should be made to reduce unemployment among the young by educating and training every young person to a level where they were able to perform useful jobs 'including caring and looking after the vulnerable' (Home Office, 1996).

New Labour and Crime Prevention

Labour are committed to a preventative policy, which it believes will have a greater impact on the crime rate than incarceration in the long term. In its most recent policy statement, Labour emphasized the impact of community decline on the relationship between parents and children, particularly when whole communities were affected by large-scale unemployment and the loss of hope. Family relationships can, a Home Office Study suggests, determine whether a young person commits crime or does not (Home Office, 1996).

Labour have argued that little or no support is provided to parents who may experience problems arising from poverty and the stress and marital discord which often results from this. This problem, Labour believes, is compounded by the absence of work opportunities for young people leaving school. Unemployment rates for young white males, stands at 20% and are much higher than for males from ethnic minorities, particularly Afro-Caribbeans (*Social Trends, 1995*). Related to the absence of employment, is the explosion of drug abuse among the young. A study conducted by the Institute for the Study of Drug Dependence estimated that up to £1.3 billion of property was stolen in the UK to fund heroin use (*Tackling the Cause of Crime*, October 1996). Labour intends to hit drug dealers hard, while providing a more effective range of treatment for drug addicts.

To break the spiral of crime and drug abuse, Labour will finance a programme of youth training by introducing a 'windfall' tax on public utilities. Labour intends that every young person who has been out of work for more than six months will be offered employment with guaranteed training opportunities, full-time study with no loss of benefit, or a place on Labour's planned Environmental Task Force. It intends to reverse the worst excesses of care in the community, by providing comprehensive care for the mentally ill, with access to acute beds and longer term nursing care provision, supported housing and social support in the community. Crisis centres will be established to offer sanctuary for those in immediate need. Labour argues that it intends to end 'life on the street as the primary form of community care'.

Tough on Crime

Labour's plans encompass the effects of 17 years of urban decline, where deprivation and loss of hope have created levels of lawlessness which need an immediate response. Labour believes that bye-laws should be available for local authorities to deal with children aged 10 or under who are out, unsupervised, on the street, late in the evening. Labour also intends to introduce community safety orders to enable local authorities to deal with the problem of anti-social criminal behaviour by neighbours. The orders will take the form of injunctions to restrain the behaviour of named individuals. Application for a community safety order will be made jointly by the police and local authority, to deal with 'problem families' whose behaviour was seriously affecting the lives of those living near them (*Tackling the Causes of Crime*, 1996).

Summary of Labour's Approach

Labour policy at the macro level, involves a commitment to neighbourhood policing with an expansion of targeted patrols. At a local level, local authorities will 'come in from the cold' as Labour implements the proposals identified in the 1991 Morgan Report on Community Safety. Local authorities will become, with the police, the primary motors in developing multi-agency crime prevention strategies for which they will be statutorily responsible. In what is likely to be seen as a welcome reversal of the inexorable centralization of power to the centre, much greater emphasis will be placed on local delivery of services. Additionally the chaotic absence of common boundaries between criminal justice agencies, will be confronted. As far as possible, court, probation, prison, CPS, and police boundaries will, in future, be coterminous (Straw, 1996). It is also expected that the highly centralized Crown Prosecution Service (CPS) will be subject to major reorganization. CPS boundaries will conform in future, to police force boundaries, which may improve the overall effectiveness of the CPS, while also improving staff morale within it (Dyer, 1996a).

Labour intends, through a national crime prevention agency, to make crime prevention a top priority in any future criminal justice policy. Prevention always being better (and cheaper) than cure, a Labour Government intends to give a crime prevention agency a range of responsibilities for co-ordinating the work of government departments, local authorities, voluntary and independent bodies such as Crime Concern and NACRO. The Agency's job would be to frame and implement a national strategy using a variety of initiatives to prevent crime and disorder. Labour's crime prevention strategy is likely to prove even more attractive as the huge costs of the Conservative Government's prison strategy becomes ever more apparent. As in 1992, however, it will ultimately be for the electorate to decide whether crime control or crime prevention are implemented to deal with Britain's evident crime crisis. ■

References

Audit Commission (1996), *Misspent Youth: Young People and Crime* (Audit Commission, London).

Dyer, C. (1996), CPU's staff demoralised by red tape. *Guardian* (10 May 1996).

Home Office (1996), *Young People and Crime* (Home Office, London).

Institute for Fiscal Studies (1996), *Living with the State* (IFS, London).

Kate, I. (1996), Bull market in prison and knee jerk politics. *Guardian* (10 May 1996).

Labour Party (1996), *Tackling the Causes of Crime—Labour's Proposals to Prevent Crime and Criminality* (Labour Party, London).

Labour Party, (1996), *Reforming Youth Justice—A Consultation Paper on an Agenda for Change* (Labour Party, London).

MacAskill, E. (1997), Blair opts for zero tolerance. *Guardian* (15 January).

Mills, B. (1996), Disclosure evidence. *Guardian* (18 January).

Travis, A. (1997), Licence to bug and burgle. *Guardian* (13 January).

Travis, A. (1996a), Perversion of justice. *Guardian* (24 August).

Travis, A. (1996b), Is this the way we want it? *Guardian* (25 May 1996).

Travis, A. (1996c), Private prison benefits from lower pay structure. *Guardian* (15 September).

Straw, J. (1996), LSE conference: Law and order at the crossroads (December).

White, R. (1996), ACPO chairman LSE conference (December).

20 Defence

Keith Hartley

University of York

Defence policy-makers have to create armed forces able to protect the UK and its national interests both currently and into the future. Often new defence equipment, particularly if it is expensive, remains in service for 20 to 30 years or more: hence today's equipment might be used for conflicts around the year 2020 and beyond. Uncertainty means that the future is unknown and unknowable so that defence policy-makers and the armed forces have to create flexible general-purpose forces able to operate in a variety of conflict situations in the UK, Europe and the rest of the world.

The need to maintain some armed forces today reflects the probability (risk) that the UK might be involved in a future conflict. The 1990s illustrate this point dramatically with the end of the Cold War and the superpower arms race, the Gulf Conflict and various UN peace-keeping missions (for example in Africa and Bosnia). While this analysis suggests the continued need for modern, well-equipped armed forces as an insurance policy, it does not necessarily justify the current levels of UK defence spending, nor the size of its armed forces, nor the current balance of air, land and sea forces.

Defence Budgets and Choices

No government can avoid the need for difficult defence choices. Decisions are needed on how much to spend on UK defence (the classic guns versus education and the National Health Service debate); how to allocate a limited defence budget between personnel and equipment, between air, land and sea forces and between forces based in the UK, in Germany and in the rest of the world. The results of these choices are reflected in the annual UK defence budget. Table 1 shows trends in the level and composition of UK defence spending over the past 20 years. Since the end of the Cold War in 1990, the level of UK defence spending has declined by about 25%, the number of Service personnel by almost 30%, and the number of Service personnel based overseas by 45%.

Table 1. UK defence budgets.

Items	*75-76*	*85-86*	*90-91*	*96-97*
Total defence expenditure (£M, current prices)	5,346	17,943	22,298	21,425
Total defence expenditure (£M, 94/95 prices)	25,129	28,856	26,956	20,129
Share of defence expenditure on				
Personnel	47.3%	35.6%	39.5%	39.8%
Equipment	33.5%	45.7%	39.6%	39.4%
Other (works, buildings etc.)	19.2%	18.8%	20.9%	20.8%
Number of Service personnel (000s)	347.7	336.4	314.7	227.3
of which Service personnel overseas (000s)	102.4	93.2	87.6	48.1
Average expenditure per Service person (£, 1994-95 prices)	72,272	85,779	85,656	88,557
Defence as share of GDP	4.8%	5.1%	4.0%	2.8%

Source: MoD (1996).

Defence as a share of national output has also declined from some 5% in the mid 1980s, to 4% in 1990-91 and 2.8% in 1996-97. The November 1996 Budget announced further cuts in planned defence expenditure in cash terms of about £800M in 1997-98 and almost £400M in 1998-99 (cuts of some 4% and 2%, respectively).

The Peace Dividend

The reductions in defence spending and Service personnel since the end of the Cold War provide a broad indication of the scale of resources released by the Ministry of Defence (MoD) and the armed forces as their contribution to the Peace Dividend. Further resources have been released from the military-industrial complex through reductions in the number of civilians employed by MoD, the closure of military bases and downsizing in the UK defence industries (job losses and plant closures). However, accurate estimates of the Peace Dividend require assumptions about the level and composition of UK defence spending which would have occurred without the end of the Cold War. Nor does it follow that all the resources released by the UK military-industrial complex have been successfully reallocated and re-employed in the civilian sector of the economy. But what are the prospects of further reductions in UK defence spending?

An Unfinished Agenda

UK defence policy and spending will always be vulnerable to major changes reflecting uncertainty about both external and internal factors. Externally, the threats to the UK's national interests can change suddenly and unexpectedly (for example the end of the Cold War). Nations can become aggressive and technical progress can render obsolescent a whole generation of defence equipment and forces. Examples include the impact of nuclear weapons on armed forces and of the jet engine on military air power. More countries are also acquiring modern weapons either through importing or by creating their own national defence industrial base (for example Iraq).

Internal factors affecting UK defence spending include the performance of the economy which affects the UK's *ability* to pay for defence and the preferences of the electorate which determines society's *willingness* to pay for defence. However, elections are fought on a range of issues, with defence as only one element in the total package. As a result, elected governments have opportunities for interpreting society's preferences and interest groups in the military-industrial-political complex will seek to influence defence policy in their favour.

From 1997 onwards, UK defence policy and the budget will be subject to two pressures:

- First, the continued search for a further Peace Dividend to finance social welfare spending (for example education and health), or to fund public sector investment or lower income taxes.
- Second, the increasing costs of defence equipment. Not only is defence equipment expensive but, in real terms, equipment costs are rising at a rate of some 10% per annum. This increase reflects the technical arms race (technical leapfrogging) and the demands of the armed forces for superior equipment. As a result, weapons costs double about every seven years, resulting in fewer units being bought.

Indeed, some experts forecast that by the year 2025, the UK will be unable to afford a viable force of combat aircraft to replace Eurofighter 2000 (due in RAF service around 2002)! Currently, the four nation collaborative EF 2000 combat aircraft is MoD's largest single equipment programme at an estimated cost to the UK of over £15 billion.

UK Defence Policy to 2000 and Beyond

There are three standard solutions to the choice dilemma. First, the *defence review option*, where a government would reassess the threats to the UK and its commitments. Second, the *'fudge it' option*, reflected in equal misery, salami slicing and a defence review by stealth. Third, the *efficiency option*, where further efforts could be made to improve the efficiency with which resources are used in the military industrial complex. At the same time, a UK government could make a long-run commitment to create a new world order based on the UN offering genuine collective security guarantees to all nations; major multilateral disarmament; international agreements to restrict arms exports; and tying aid to developing countries to reductions in their defence spending.

A *defence review* needs to reconsider whether the UK wishes to maintain its world power aspirations. The UK's continued pursuit of leading nation status (number 2 in NATO) is reflected in overseas bases, nuclear forces, a balanced range of air, land and sea forces with modern equipment capable of world-wide operations and a substantial national defence industrial base with a major arms export business. An indication of the military costs of leading nation status can be obtained by comparing UK defence burdens with those of other European nations not seeking leading nation status. Table 2 suggests that, compared with the median for NATO Europe, the UK has consistently incurred a higher defence burden equivalent to some 1% of its Gross Domestic Product (GDP) in 1995. Of course, nations differ in their perceptions of the threat and their willingness to pay for defence, including the use of conscript forces which under-estimate the true costs of defence. Also, UK citizens might regard the extra military burdens of leading nation status as worthwhile (good value for money).

A defence review which concluded that the UK should abandon its

Table 2. Defence costs as share of GDP (%).

Country	*1986*	*1990*	*1995*
UK	4.8	4.0	3.1
Belgium	3.0	2.4	1.7
France	3.9	3.6	3.1
Germany	3.1	2.8	1.7
Italy	2.2	2.1	1.9
Netherlands	3.0	2.6	2.1
Sweden	2.6	2.6	2.5*
NATO Europe: median	3.1	2.8	2.1
USA	6.6	5.5	3.9

Note: Sweden: 1994 data.
Source: SIPRI (1996).

leading nation status would involve a major shift in UK defence policy. It would require further reductions in UK defence spending of the order of 30%, including a complete withdrawal from overseas military bases and no further need to maintain a balanced range of air, land and sea forces capable of world-wide power projection. There would be major adverse impacts on the new equipment programme and on the UK defence industrial base. Inevitably, such drastic changes in defence policy would be opposed by interest groups in each of the armed forces and in the defence industries likely to suffer from the loss of leading nation status. Such interest groups will stress the need to protect the UK's 'vital interests' from future unknown and unknowable threats and the economic contribution of the UK's defence industries to jobs, technology and exports.

Even if the UK maintains its leading nation status, there is a need to review again the size of its forces based in Germany. In 1996, there were 27,000 Army personnel based in Germany. The RAF has already announced plans for the complete withdrawal of its forces from Germany by the year 2002. Questions have to be asked about the need for UK forces in Germany and whether a reduced force of, say, 10,000 troops would be adequate to meet whatever threat which is believed to exist. However, since MoD changed its budget from a functional costing to the new management strategy and top level budgeting, it is no longer possible to obtain publicly available information on the costs of maintaining UK forces in Germany. Indeed, the new defence budgeting arrangements mean that Parliament and the electorate cannot obtain information on the annual cost of various forces such as the Trident nuclear deterrent, the Navy's aircraft carriers, air defence, transport aircraft squadrons and army units based in the UK and in various overseas locations.

A government can always avoid or postpone a politically-sensitive defence review by pursuing the *'fudge it' option*. This means the cancellation of some projects, the stretching of programmes, delays in delivery and less training for the forces. The result is that the UK *appears* to meet its defence commitments, but that its forces become less effective as they operate older equipment with less training and become 'overstretched'.

The *efficiency option* is attractive since, if successful, it allows more defence to be purchased from a given budget. This option has been pursued vigorously since 1983 reflected in MoD's competitive procurement policy for equipment and its market testing of activities traditionally undertaken 'in-house' by the armed forces (contractorization). To achieve further efficiency savings would require continued pursuit of these policies with a greater willingness to buy foreign defence equipment 'off-the-shelf' and a more radical approach to market testing and contractorization. There are, however, two other policy approaches which offer efficiency savings:

- The economic principle of *substitution*.
- The *European* solution.

Substitution

There are alternative ways of achieving protection. For example equipment might replace manpower; nuclear forces can replace conventional forces; ground-based missiles can replace manned fighter aircraft; attack helicopters can be used instead of tanks; air forces based in the UK could replace ground troops based in Germany; reserves and civilians might replace regular Service personnel (for example police in

Northern Ireland). Some of these substitution possibilities have implications for the traditional monopoly property rights of each of the Services. Attack helicopters operated by the Army could take over the close air support role undertaken by the RAF, while maritime patrol aircraft operated by the RAF could replace the Navy's anti-submarine frigates. Faced with such threats to their traditional monopoly property rights, each of the Services will claim that their role is 'vital' and that a joint Service approach is 'essential' to provide an adequate defence. In which case if, say, the Navy and the RAF believe that both maritime patrol aircraft and frigates are needed for the anti-submarine threat (where is this threat coming from?), then they must be prepared to sacrifice other items from their budgets or from the Army budget (there are no free lunches—something has to go).

As the unit costs of equipment rise faster than defence budgets, a nation will find that it can no longer afford to equip a viable force of next-generation fighting units. Here, one solution would be to choose between the three Services, cutting back on one of the fighting services (not necessarily the one most affected by rising unit costs) to release funds for the others. For example, a preference for retaining a modern air force and the associated UK aerospace industry might be at the expense of a considerably reduced Army or Navy.

A Single European Market for Defence Equipment

A Single European Market for civil goods and services is regarded as worthwhile; but defence is different. Article 223 of the Treaty of Rome means that the rules which apply to public procurement in the Single Market do not apply to defence equipment; the results are costly. Europe is characterized by inefficient defence markets. Within the European Union (EU), support for national defence industries has resulted in:

- Duplication of expensive research and development programmes. For example Europe is developing three types of advanced combat aircraft, namely, the Gripen (Sweden), the Rafale (France) and the Eurofighter (EF) 2000 (Britain, Germany, Italy and Spain). Total development costs on EF 2000 are estimated at over £12 billion, with the UK paying a 33% share.

- Relatively short production runs reflecting small national orders so that there is a failure to obtain economies of scale and learning. For example, production orders are estimated at some 300 units each for the Gripen and Rafale and about 600 units for the EF 2000. An order for over 1,200 units of one type would offer savings in unit costs of 10%–20%: a substantial saving on unit production costs of over £30M per aircraft!
- Domestic defence markets in some EU nations characterized by national monopolies (for example aerospace, tanks, warships), government protection and preferential purchasing, cost-based contracts, subsidies and state ownership of defence companies.

Extending the Single European Market to defence equipment is expected to result in three major economic benefits. First, greater competition following the 'opening-up' of national defence markets. Second, savings in costly R&D resulting from less duplication of similar types of equipment. Third, savings in production costs due to the economies of longer production runs.

Table 3 shows three possible scenarios for creating a Single European Market for defence equipment. Each scenario assumes a liberalized competitive market either restricted to member states of the EU or open to the world. A European Armaments Agency could have a possible role in creating a Single Market, with each scenario offering potential efficiency savings. Scenario II offers the greatest cost savings reflecting both competition and longer production runs; but this scenario is likely to be the most difficult policy to implement: hence scenario III is the 'second-best' solution.

Creating a Single European Market for defence equipment is not without its problems and costs. There are problems of creating a 'level playing-field', some firms, towns and regions will be losers; there is the potential for collusive tendering and pressure to create Fortress Europe for defence procurement resulting in protectionism, cartels and inefficiency. Furthermore, to maintain competition in the Single European Market is likely to require the Market to be opened-up to the world, particularly to US firms which would be a major threat to the

Table 3. Single market scenarios.

Scenario	*Liberalized competitive market Estimated % cost saving*	
	EU	*World-wide*
I National procurement by national defence ministries	10+	15+
II A European centralized procurement agency buying standardized equipment and replacing national defence ministries	15+	20+
III A twin-track model with competition for small to medium projects and collaboration for large projects	12+	17+

EU's defence industrial base.

In November 1996, the UK joined a Quadrilateral European Armaments Agency with France, Germany and Italy. The UK is involved on an equal basis in the Agency's formation and development with the aim of achieving a more efficient, effective approach to the management of *collaborative* defence programmes. In joining the Agency, the UK is committed to four policy guidelines for collaborative ventures:

- First, a more commercial approach to future co-operative programmes and their supporting structures.
- Second, procurement from the most efficient supplier.
- Third, programme management vested in a single prime contractor responsible for delivery of the programme to time and cost.
- Fourth, opposition to protectionism and a Fortress Europe policy.

While these policy guidelines are economically attractive, they are politically difficult to implement. Established interest groups in the military-industrial-political complex of some of the European member states will continue to favour collaborative programmes with work allocated on the basis of *juste retour* and support for national champions.

Conclusion

UK defence policy will continue to reflect the needs for difficult choices as the next government seeks to 'stretch' the limited budget over a range of tasks and requirements. A radical defence review is an obvious option but it would not be a permanent solution. Threats change and technical progress creates new and costlier weapons requirements. Defence policy is always evolving and adapting to change in an uncertain world. The pressures on the UK defence budget mean that a more radical application of the substitution principle and pursuit of the European solution cannot be avoided.

Acknowledgement

Parts of this chapter are based on research funded by the ESRC as part of its Single Market Programme. ■

References

MoD (1996), *UK Defence Statistics 1996* (Ministry of Defence, DASA/HMSO, London).

SIPRI (1996), *SIPRI Yearbook 1996* (Oxford University Press, Oxford).

Cmnd 3223 (1996), *Statement on the Defence Estimates 1996* (Ministry of Defence/HMSO, London).

21 Housing

John Perry and Simon Hooton

Chartered Institute of Housing, Coventry

The exceptionally drastic cuts to the housing programme in the 1996 Budget called into question the Government's commitment to maintaining any public sector investment in future. Housing associations, having previously been seen as major providers, were the subject of cuts which will reduce their output below the Government's own, unambitious targets. Local authorities are in most areas now unable to sustain their own housing stock in reasonable condition, much less add to it. Transfer of stock out of the sector seems to be the only route offered by the present government. Labour, as the alternative governing party, has promised release of capital receipts from council house sales as the main plank in its investment strategy.

In the Autumn of 1995, the House of Commons Environment Select Committee conducted an inquiry into housing need. This came on the back of the Government producing a new set of household projection figures to the year 2016. The figures revealed that 4.4M new households are expected to emerge over the next decade. In response, the Department of the Environment (DoE) published its projections of how many social affordable homes need to be built for those emerging households who could not be expected to purchase homes on the open market. The DoE projected that somewhere between 60,000 and 100,000 new homes were needed each year to keep pace with demographic changes. The Chartered Institute of Housing produced its own figures which concur with the upper end of this range, but were concerned to add in the backlog of unmet needs since 1991, which if solved in a decade would push the figure up to 120,000 per annum. Adding in Scotland and Wales, pushes it over the 140,000 mark. These figures were further verified by the research of Alan Holmans, former Chief Economist at the DoE, who conducted a similar exercise on behalf of the Joseph Rowntree Foundation. The all-party Environment Select Committee endorsed the 100,000 per year base line target in its final report (Environment Committee, 1996)

In response, the DoE committed itself to working towards the lower end of its projection—just 60,000 homes. And, instead of focusing on newly constructed affordable properties, they built up their provision of new homes by looking at *new social lettings,* which includes schemes to encourage tenants to purchase existing homes in the private sector. New homes only account for a little over half of the provision target. However, this is still a commitment and these are thin on the ground these days and the Labour Party has implicitly agreed to keep to it.

But was it a commitment? If so, it was not one shared by the Chancellor. His 1996 Budget slashed investment in new social housing. The Housing Corporation budget for 1997-98 will be cut by £344M (cash) on its 1996-97 spending. This 30% cut represents over 16,000 rented homes or, put another way, half of the DoE's paltry target for new affordable rented homes. Even the Chairman of the Housing Corporation was moved to comment that he was 'deeply disappointed' and that the cuts 'will have devastating results for homeless people and those living in poor housing conditions'.

Applying the cut across the full range of Housing Corporation activities indicates that the 60,000 target will be missed by some 15,000 lettings a year. Construction of new rented homes however, even with housing associations making exemplary 6% per annum efficiency savings in construction, is likely to fall to around 20,000 homes per year. This is only one-fifth of what every one else in the social housing lobby calculates is needed.

As well as the problems of building the new homes required, there are enormous problems of disrepair in all tenures. Local authority investment in England on private renovation is nearly one third of its 1984-85 level in real terms. Investment in their own stock has fluctuated up and down, but is now £400M lower than its 1984-85 position (at 1994-95 prices). This year's Budget announcement further exacerbated this downward slide as Basic Credit Approvals to local authorities were cut by £290M (cash), which is £253M more than expected.

Stock surveys conducted in preparation for Large Scale Voluntary

Transfer indicate that the backlog of disrepair in the local authority sector is at least £20 billion and expanding by £1 billion per year. Current provision is not even keeping on top of deterioration in the stock.

What routes are available out of this crisis? The Government offers only one—stock transfer—but the housing lobby has also argued for the release of receipts from council house sales and for a new approach to public investment which would give councils access to private funding in a similar way to housing associations. The first two of these alternatives is already Labour Party policy; the third has been rejected by both main parties (although embraced by the Liberal Democrats). The rest of this chapter briefly examines the three options.

Stock Transfer

By the end of 1995, 51 authorities in England had transferred over 220,000 council homes to housing associations. Nearly all of these authorities had transferred all their stock. No authority in Wales has so far followed this route, and only one authority in Scotland has transferred all of its stock. English councils have used transfers to raise about £3.6 billion of private finance, partly to meet the transfer price but also to invest in improving the transferred stock.

Could transfer be pursued on a much bigger scale? The 1993 report by the Chartered Institute of Housing and the Joseph Rowntree Foundation (Wilcox *et al.*, 1993) had advocated creating local housing companies as vehicles for transfer, rather than following the housing association approach that has been used in all transfers to date.

During 1996 the Government made significant steps to encouraging such new vehicles. Its 1995 Housing White Paper (DoE, 1995) had already accepted the idea in principle. In 1996, a detailed assessment carried out jointly with five local authorities (KPMG, 1996a) was published, and this heralded the announcement of new financial incentives in the form of the Estates Renewal Challenge Fund. During 1997, the first local housing companies are likely to be set up as a result.

Both Wales and Scotland have expressed less interest in the new approach, although Scotland has a well-established practice of smaller scale transfer to community based housing associations. If companies *are* set up in Wales or Scotland, they are likely to have stronger ties with the parent authority and to allow for greater tenant representation. Indeed, it is on this kind of detail that the policy difference between Labour and Conservatives is to be found, rather than on the principle of transferring stock to local housing companies.

Capital Receipts

Selling council houses has proved to be the Government's biggest privatization programme, generating more than £28 billion, or more than the gas, electricity and BT sales put together. But, unlike these other privatizations, the assets sold needed to be replaced.

Since 1989, when legislation put a curb on councils' ability to recycle the proceeds from the right-to-buy scheme, the Chartered Institute of Housing has argued that this money should be put back into rented housing. It is now Labour Party policy to do this—but there has been great uncertainty about the availability of the receipts and the mechanism for recycling them. The report, *Boosting Housing Investment through Capital Receipts* (KPMG, 1996b) addresses these questions. KPMG surveyed English and Welsh authorities to make an estimate of the volume of available receipts. KPMG then looked at the obstacles to their release and how to overcome them.

The survey revealed that about £7.5 billion of housing receipts have been 'set-aside' against debt since April 1990. Of these, some £5 billion have not been used actually to redeem debt. Most of this money is readily accessible. If a government were to 'release' set-aside receipts, and allow full reinvestment of future receipts, housing investment would be significantly increased. Phasing the release over, for example, a four-year period would produce a doubling of councils' housing investment programmes.

However, not all of these receipts are in places where substantial extra investment is needed. For this reason, a means of redistributing the spending power is required so the areas in most need benefit most. The report outlines several ways in which this might be done.

The Labour Party seized on the report as evidence to back up its policy, but has not yet spelt out crucial details of how it would implement the release of receipts. The Conservatives rejected the proposals, even though there are precedents for the release of receipts by the present government.

In Scotland, where until 1996 councils *did* have access to their receipts, policy is now to be changed to be brought in line with England and Wales.

New Approaches to Public Investment

Recently there has been much discussion within the housing field about the merits and demerits of changing public spending rules to allow local authorities to borrow money to invest in housing without losing control of their stock.

The crux of the argument is the need for the government to move away from using the Public Sector Borrowing Requirement (PSBR) as its main financial measure, towards using a broader range of indicators and giving greater prominence to the General Government Financial Deficit (GGFD). Within prudential guidelines, public corporations could then have much greater freedom to decide how to borrow and invest. It would also free local authorities to set up *local housing corporations* to borrow money from banks and building societies to invest in the repair and modernisation of public housing. Unlike local housing companies, these would be wholly owned by the authorities.

The argument that the City would oppose such a move has been challenged by a new report. In *Consensus for Change* (Coopers & Lybrand, 1996), leading City economists recognize the limitations of the PSBR and argue for a broader range of indicators to be put in place to assess and control the government's finances. More than half of those economists interviewed accepted the case for placing greater emphasis on the GGFD, with the caveat that this shift should not be used as a 'smokescreen' for some kind of relaxation of fiscal policy by an incoming government. The change would need to be gradual and be accompanied by a process of education.

Consensus for Change highlighted the fact that the City believe that there would be no problem in raising an extra £1–2 billion per annum for housing should the constraints of the PSBR regime be lifted. This extra investment is vital to council housing and would otherwise be met from the public purse.

Despite scepticism from both main parties, many in the housing world believe that only by giving local authorities equal access to private finance alongside housing associations is there any hope of addressing the crisis of under-investment. ■

References

Coopers & Lybrand (1996), *Consensus for Change: Public Borrowing Rules, Housing Investment and the City* (Chartered Institute of Housing, Coventry).

DoE (1995), *Our Future Homes: Opportunity, Choice, Responsibility* (HMSO, London).

House of Commons Environment Committee (1996), *Housing Need* (HMSO, London).

KPMG (1996a), *Joint Study on Stock Options: Summary Report* (DoE, London).

KPMG (1996b), *Boosting Housing Investment through Capital Receipts* (Chartered Institute of Housing, Coventry).

Wilcox, S. (1996), *Housing Review 1996/7* (Joseph Rowntree Foundation, York).

Wilcox, S. *et al.* (1993), *Local Housing Companies: New Opportunities for Council Housing* (Chartered Institute of Housing and Joseph Rowntree Foundation, York).

22 Transport Policy

Francis Terry

London School of Economics

1996 was a year in which the Government managed at times to inject a stronger sense of purpose into transport policy. A green paper was published—the first for 20 years—and although the proposals were criticized as weak and lacking commitment on funding, there were signs of a change towards a more environmentally-sensitive approach. Some major decisions were reached about new capital projects; though the absence of strategic thinking about a framework for new investment, and the need for effective planning of the nation's transport system in the longer term, stand out. Hopes that the private sector would come forward to share the burden of investment were partially realized, but the launch of new road projects using 'shadow tolls' to contractors began to seem like poor value for money. A number of thorny issues in transport are still scarcely on the policy agenda; what should a new administration do?

In the Department of Transport's annual report, published in March 1996 and setting out public spending plans for the following three years, the Secretary of State, Sir George Young, gave a list of his objectives (Department of Transport, 1996a):

- To promote an efficient market, with prices reflecting the true costs of transport.
- To enable the market to provide greater choice by substantially increasing opportunities for private sector involvement.
- By means of the above, to assist economic growth and to provide greater choice in good quality, safe and accessible services for all transport users.

Many people saw this as reflecting a rather tangential approach, tinged with inappropriate dogma and coy about the real problems. But shortly after, it became apparent that Government was prepared to move towards a more positive stance.

The shift was signalled in a green paper, *Transport: the Way Forward*

(Department of Transport 1996b), published in April 1996. This attempted to summarize and respond to the issues aired in the national debate on transport, which had been launched by the former Secretary of State, Brian Mawhinney and continued by Sir George Young. The green paper also acted as the official response to the *Eighteenth Report* of the Royal Commission on Environmental Pollution (RCEP, 1994), dealing with transport and the environment. It contained some key principles:

- There is a need to 'reduce dependence on the private car'.
- Transport decisions should be taken at the lowest practical level.
- The efficiency of markets needs to be strengthened.
- The link between prices and the wider costs of transport should be strengthened.
- Planning of transport needs to be improved.

Most of these principles reflect the established consensus of professional views about transport policy. The significant point is that, after many years in which Government has positively ignored or undermined the application of them, it has now considerably softened its stance. The almost single-minded pursuit of road construction, coupled with privatization and deregulation as the way forward for public transport, are at last losing favour.

Despite its substantial length and generally sound analysis, the green paper was short on positive proposals for managing transport needs or tackling the environmental implications of transport growth. The most important points are: first, the *trunk road* planning system is proposed for reform, in order to link it more directly to land use planning. At present, regional planning guidance issued by the Department of Transport imposes trunk road plans without discussion, whereas in future, trunk road needs will be considered by local authorities in formulating advice to government. Alternative routes or other options can also be considered ('such as improvements to other forms of transport, or traffic management measures'). A related change is that road schemes will no longer be included in the programme until after consultation has taken place on route options (the reverse of the present situation). The idea of regional road authorities, which was mooted by Sir George Young at the end of 1995, seems have been quashed by his Cabinet colleagues as electorally dangerous.

Second, the tricky question of *road pricing* as an answer to congestion is largely ducked, by suggesting that a permissive power be given to individual local authorities to introduce pricing schemes, while the duty on petrol and diesel is to rise at a rate somewhat above inflation.

In marked contrast to the priorities of the early 1990s, the green paper recognizes the importance of a range of *'alternative' transport* options. It predicts a doubling in the use of bicycles by the year 2002, with an invitation to local authorities to say how they can contribute to the target. Expansion of cycling was followed up by the launch of a National Cycling Strategy, in July 1996. The Government also promised to bring together a group to look at what can be done to make walking a more attractive and safer option, and what role walking can play in reducing car dependence: 'Analysis of the first hundred [experimental 20 m.p.h.] zones has indicated a reduction of 45% in annual accident frequency, and a reduction of 74% in casualties to children and cyclists' (Cm 3234, para. 14.11).

The green paper contains a number of *research* suggestions which may eventually influence policy. There is to be a new study of links between transport investment and economic growth which will analyse the question of whether road building really helps economic growth—hitherto taken as an article of faith by most highway planners. A National Transport Model is to be developed, to allow policy ideas to be tested and scenarios other than traffic forecasts to be explored.

Finally, the green paper reaffirms a number of earlier commitments, for example to reform the system of taxi licensing and to take powers to impound unlicensed lorries.

The Way Forward

The major deficiency identified by critics of the green paper is the lack of commitment to setting targets for restraining traffic levels or emissions from motor vehicles. Without such targets, planning and investment tends to assume that traffic levels will inevitably grow. While the procedural changes in road planning seem sensible, the Government glosses over the inconsistency between its new-found objective of reducing car-dependence and the maintenance of a traditional road-building programme. The green paper reaffirms that by-passes are a good thing and, despite its proposal to examine the issue, that road building helps urban regeneration. The severance of communities by roads and traffic is, in reality, one of the major causes of local campaigns on traffic issues.

A more general criticism of *Transport: the Way Forward* is its absence of a sense of strategic direction. The point is well illustrated by the development of freight terminals. Although Government is committed to getting more freight on rail, and British Rail drew up a master plan some time ago for a series of strategically-placed 'freight villages', low priority was given to it. Financial pressures, planning problems and the onset of privatization meant that only six 'villages' were completed. Now, there is a rush of unco-ordinated private developments, with three terminals in the west midlands either in use or under construction, while London and the south-east has to make do with one congested terminal at Willesden. At least two further terminals are needed in the region, but the mechanisms to promote these seem quite inadequate.

A further criticism of the green paper is that it is environmentally naive. It misinterprets the Royal Commission on Environmental Pollution by treating the Commission's idea of seeking the 'best practicable environmental option' as meaning the best route option for a road, not the best way of solving a traffic problem. Biodiversity is misconstrued: the green paper assumes that more tree planting beside roads will make up for the loss of irreplaceable wildlife habitats. There are strong hints that the Government is looking to increase lorry weights to 44 tonnes for general use, rather than exclusively for journeys to rail terminals, and a consultation paper was subsequently issued (Department of Transport, 1996c). Finally, there seems little effort in the green paper to bring Britain closer to thinking in the rest of Europe. Some of the more imaginative proposals, for example for a 'Citizen's Network' (CEC, 1996a) and on charging for road use (CEC, 1996b) receive little serious attention.

Curbing Car Use

Why is it now so important to reduce our dependence on car travel for an increasing proportion of journeys and for an ever-growing number of trips in absolute terms? Figure 1 shows that car usage relative to other modes has been surging ahead of other modes for the past 40 years. Since 1975, the British drive almost 50% more, walk 20% less and cycle 25% less. Car registrations reached a record high in November 1996 and, if past trends continue, car ownership in the UK will grow from the current total of about 20M to over 35M in 2020; traffic mileage will increase by between 83% and 142%. There is simply no way that the UK could find the resources of money and space to accommodate such growth (Goodwin, 1993).

Nevertheless, the popularity of car ownership has never been greater, as the latest findings from the National Travel Survey reveal, and especially among young people. In 1994, 48% of all 17–20 year olds held a driving licence, and around seven out of ten teenagers expect to own a car by the age of 20. This is as true for those with good prospects as for those who view themselves as having poor prospects: many young people expect to have a car before they have a flat or a job. The members of this age group rely on cars for over 60% of all their journeys, while the proportion actually owning a car has risen from 12% in 1976 to 25% in 1994.

The picture of young drivers has its darker side. Among 17–24 year olds, 26% confessed to 'almost always' exceeding the speed limits when driving. A survey of 18,500 young people between 11 and 16 years reported that over 50% of the boys and 30% of the girls had driven a car, if only for a short

Figure 1. Passenger travel by mode, 1954–1994.

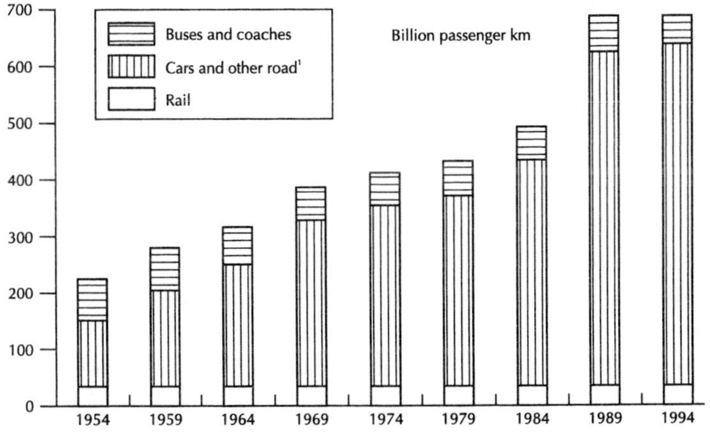

[1] Includes taxis, motor and pedal cycles

distance; and this age group now walks 30% less than 20 years ago. Young people often appear to consider cycling dangerous, public transport is unreliable and expensive and walking a last resort. As the pressure group Transport 2000 recently put it: the 'transport choices' (the Secretary of State's objectives, above) presented to a significant group of the population amount to: 'Risk your life or get a car. Stay at home or get a car. Be forever dependent on Mum and Dad or get your licence and get a car'.

The importance of restraining traffic in towns is well illustrated by recent research in Cambridge. Cambridge has been particularly successful in attracting and retaining employment in the city centre, creating a busy and popular focus for work, study and leisure. Total jobs have increased by 25% since 1981. On the major radial roads leading into the city, traffic crossing the city boundary has risen 50% between 1980 and 1992; while current forecasts expect an increase by 66% over the next ten years.

In contrast with the growth in employment, most housing development has taken place beyond the green belt. The resulting need to travel is very poorly catered for by public transport. Bus services have suffered a decline since deregulation in 1986 to a mere 6% of peak hour journeys, while rail services are targeted on the commercial opportunities for travel to London, rather than local commuting. High car usage is reflected in the highest accident rate per head of population for any English county, with the numbers injured up 65% over the decade 1981-92. In response, Cambridge City Council has promoted park-and-ride schemes and increased cycle use, in a place where there cycling is already the preferred mode for 35% of people going to work. The number using bikes, however, is linked to the high casualty rate. The conclusion seems to be that not only must car use be constrained, but the alternatives have to be much more safe and attractive.

On the wider issue of transport safety, the number of deaths on the roads has fallen for the first time since records began 70 years ago (3,621 fatalities in 1995 compared to 3,650 in 1994). Table 1 gives comparative safety statistics for principal transport modes. The decrease in road deaths is thought to be associated with the reduction in walkers and cyclists, since these are typically more likely to be the victims in road accidents. Despite the prominence given to safety in the Secretary of State's objectives, a look at the approach taken in Sweden shows how a much more determined advance can be made (Swedish National Road Administration, 1995). There, policies co-ordinated between

Table 1. Accident fatality rates for passenger travel in the UK.

Passenger travel by:	*Fatalities per 100M* *hours*	*passenger km*
Bus or coach	0.1	0.04
Rail	4.8	0.1
Water	12	0.6
Air	15	0.03
Car	15	0.4
Foot	20	5.3
Bicycle	60	4.3
Two-wheeled motor vehicle	300	9.7

Source: Transport Statistics Great Britain (HMSO, 1994).

police, local authorities, insurance companies and other agencies are targeted on reducing accidents by young drivers—and raising the standards of proficiency required before a driving licence is issued.

Public Transport

Although *Transport: the Way Forward* was criticized by many as uninspired in its treatment of public transport—relying heavily on rhetoric about bus deregulation and privatization—some worthwhile concessions were made to public transport users. First, and taking a lead from initiatives already tried by local authorities like Nottinghamshire, the Government has decided to promote 'quality partnerships' (with the private sector bus operators), to help re-invigorate bus services. Partnerships are intended to cover such improvements as bus priority schemes on busy roads, better public information, fleet replacement with modern disabled-accessible vehicles and even guided busways. Towards the end of the year, a £31M city-wide information display system at bus-stops was announced for London. These proposals are important for their acceptance of the crucial role which local authorities can play in bringing together transport with other planning strategies, and it was all the more disappointing that the local transport grants announced in December, for 1997-98, would be cut to £746M compared to £830M in 1996-97.

Second, and in a tacit recognition of the inconvenience and confusion caused by rail privatization, the Government announced some palliative measures. On the sensitive question of controlling the fares and services provided by the new private sector train operating companies (TOCs), the Rail Franchising Director is to develop clear criteria for supporting loss-making services, and these will be published. The green paper also made clear that his powers extend to funding rail investment and other upgrading measures, as distinct from merely giving out operating subsidies. A National Train Information Service, using a single telephone number—0345 48 49 50—has been established. The enquiry bureaux linked into the Train Information Service have dramatically speeded up response times, though the information provided is still reported to be unreliable.

For the capital, where public transport accounts for nearly 80% of journeys to work, the Government published a separate *Transport Strategy for London* (DoT/Government Office for London, 1996), a week after the green paper. The strategy was presented partly as a response to the CBI and the business lobby group London First, both concerned about London's future as a business centre, and to London Pride, a partnership of local authorities, business organizations and voluntary groups, which had earlier published an *Action Programme for London* (London Pride, 1995). The strategy has five objectives:

- Maintain and enhance international links.
- Enhance quality of rail and underground commuter services.
- Promote greater use of less polluting modes of transport.
- Facilitate access to central business districts.
- Plug major gaps in the road and rail network.

Among the more detailed proposals are new studies and guidance on traffic management and parking, so as to give more priority to buses, pedestrians and cyclists; funding for a London Cycle Network; new river-bus services on the Thames; and, for the longer term, road pricing—though the strategy declares this to be 'impossible' before 2005.

As with the green paper, the reaction from interested parties was one of general disappointment. The strategy was criticized for its absence of targets or clear transport objectives, and lack of commitments on funding. Indeed,

London Transport's (LT) 1996 allocation was cut by 28%. Nevertheless LT went ahead with publication of its study of a 550-mile regional rail network *Planning London's Transport—To Win as a World City* (LT, 1996). This aims to relieve pressure on the present underground system and provide for known additional demand.

Transport Investment

On the central question of transport investment, matters are in a state of flux. While one can understand the political difficulties about making commitments in the green paper, this was actually the topic on which both public authorities and the private sector would have found it helpful to be given some clearer indications of the Government's expectations. As it is, 1996 was marked by a series of *ad hoc* decisions on major projects—such as the Croydon Tramlink and Midland Metro around Birmingham—with little sense of strategy. The trend at present, as table 2 and figure 2 show, is for public investment to fall rapidly while the Government hopes that new private sector-led schemes will compensate for this under the Private Finance Initiative (PFI) (see Terry, 1996). The privatized bus and rail companies may also raise their direct investment as the businesses develop.

Even so, the volume of new private capital attracted into transport schemes remains modest. The incentives to make the private sector take a substantial burden of the risk associated with new projects may also be very costly. An example is the construction of the Channel Tunnel Rail Link (CTRL), which the Government insisted should be financed and managed by the private sector so far as possible (it threw out an earlier scheme put up by BR as a joint venture). In March, the consortium known as London & Continental Railways won the 999-year concession to build and run the link, but did so after a protracted negotiation in which it has secured a huge portfolio of developable land in inner London, £900M worth of state-of-the-art rolling stock, a brand new terminal at Waterloo, a subsidy of £1.5 billion and a few other incentives as well.

It seems that the CTRL's promoters have been fully seized of the experience of Eurotunnel, which managed to raise all its capital in the markets, and has since found the risks it faced to be almost unmanageable. After more than a year of negotiation with its shareholders, the company achieved a tortuously complex restructuring of its £9.1 billion debt. In

Figure 2. Estimated investment in transport in Great Britain, 1994-95.

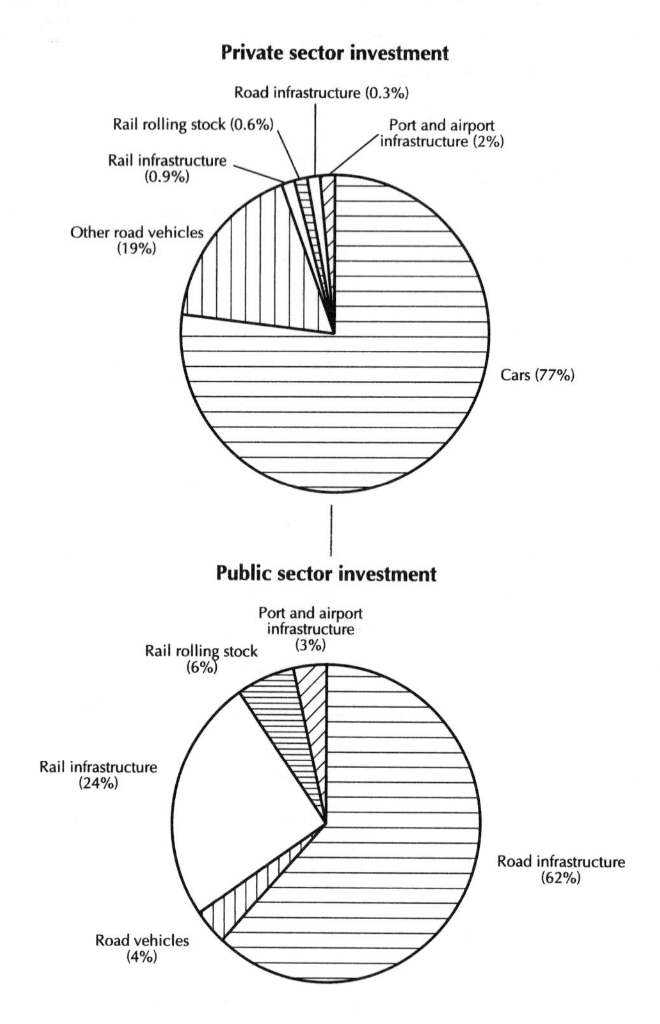

exchange for being rescued from bankruptcy, shareholders are having to accept a lower stake: no dividend is now likely to be paid for another ten years, and share values have fallen from the listing price of 350p in November 1987 to less than 90p (January 1997). Nevertheless, business is brisk, and traffic by the ferry routes has been seriously hit.

Shifting the burden of risk, as a key principle of the PFI, raises special problems in relation to roads, where no charge is made (unlike rail) at the

Table 2. Public sector investment in transport: three year totals, 1990-91 to 1998-99 (£M).

	90-93	*93-96*	*96-99*
Cash			
National Roads, England	5,165	5,344	3,823
Central government support to local authorities[1]	2,691	3,002	2,305
Fixed asset investment in the UK by nationalized industries			
Railway	3,842	3,070[4]	[2]
London Transport	1,697	2,844	2,495
Civil Aviation Authority	281	335	189
Total	*13,676*	*13,712*	*8,812*
Real prices (1994-95)[3]			
National roads, England	5,673	5,335	3,540
Central government support to local authorities	2,943	2,997	2,133
Fixed asset investment in the UK by nationalized industries			
Railway industry	4,200	3,067[4]	[2]
London Transport	1,852	2,830	2,319
Civil Aviation Authority	307	336	175
Total	*14,975*	*13,706*	*8,167*

1. Mostly England only. 2. No three year can be given for forward years since from 1995-96 the privatization process will increasingly pass responsibility to the private sector. 3. Adjusted using the GDP deflator. 4. The definition of investment has been amended, so direct comparisons with earlier years are not possible.

Source: Department of Transport, *Transport Report 1996* (HMSO, London).

point of use. The favoured solution is to use design, build, finance and operate (DBFO) schemes, under which Government sets the specification and obtains planning permissions, but the contractor takes the risk on the cost of construction, including for example overcoming ground conditions which may turn out to be unfavourable. Once the road is open, the contractor continues to meet the cost of maintenance throughout a concession period—usually 30 years. At this point, the Treasury begins paying a 'shadow toll' for each vehicle using the road.

Details of how DBFO contracts work are confidential to the Government and its contractors, but an independent study by Keith Buchan (1996), using information in the public domain, suggested that total costs of a selected scheme (the A36 Salisbury by-pass) would work out between 84% and 131% higher than if conventional public finance were used. The contrast between private capital invested and total 'shadow tolls' received is summarized in table 3. The huge differences are accounted for by the higher borrowing costs in the private sector, the price put upon the risks that forecast numbers of vehicles are not reached, and the higher rate of return on such projects required by contractors. The situation has attracted the interest of the National Audit Office, which is now investigating. It seems likely that, so far as this particular form of 'private finance' is concerned, Ministers are increasingly being put on the back foot. DBFO schemes may also encourage traffic growth, as contractors lobby for developments close to 'their' roads—a move which is surely at odds with the objective of traffic restraint.

By Rail to Victory

1996 was the high watermark for rail privatization, with 38 businesses of the British Railways Board sold off in the 1995-96 financial year and the remainder due to follow by March 1997. A summary is given in table 4. The

Table 3. DBFO road schemes: costs and pay-backs.

Scheme	*Private funding (£M)*	*Projected receipts from shadow tolls*
A19 Dishforth–Tyne Tunnel	25	84
A69 Carlisle–Newcastle	8	27
A1(M) Alconbury–Peterborough	110	367
M1–A1 Link near Leeds	184	613
A50 Stoke–Derby	18	59
A30/A35 Exeter–Bere Regis	65	217
M40 Junctions 1–5	32	106
A419/A417 Swindon–Gloucester	42	140

Sources: RAC and Transport 2000, from Highways Agency figures and *Hansard*.

Table 4. Summary of disposals of British Rail assets.

Activity	*Company*	*Status*
Rail infrastructure (track, signals, stations)	Railtrack	Privatized by share offer in May 1996
Passenger train services	25 train operating companies	20 sold to MBOs, bus companies or French buyers
Freight and parcels	Loadhaul Transrail freight Mainline freight Rail Express Systems (post)	Sold to Winconsin Central Transportation (WCT)
	Freightliner	Sold to MBO
	Railfreight distribution	Sale under negotiation
	Red Star Parcels	Sold to MBO
Rolling stock leasing	Porterbrook Leasing	Sold to MBO, then on to Stagecoach
	Eversholt Leasing	Sold to MBO
	Angel Trains Contracts	Sold to consortium led by Babcock and Nomura
Maintenance and renewals	20 companies	All disposed of by trade sale or MBO
Central services	37 independent companies including BR Telecom	Nearly all sold
Channel Tunnel services	Eurostar Union Railways	Transferred to London & Continental Railways

Sources: Financial Times and *Modern Railways.*

major event was the flotation in May 1996 of Railtrack, owner of the 10,500 mile track network and 2,500 stations, after several months of intense political debate and a generally bad press. Documents were leaked alleging incompetent project management in the company, while public disputes broke out over its disposal of freight depots to supermarket developers and the ownership of advertising revenues from railway sites. In order to fulfil the timetable for flotation, Ministers were persuaded to write off £1 billion in debt. Railtrack was sold for around £1.8 billion, compared to a valuation of 2.6 billion calculated by stockbrokers UBS (*Financial Times*, 13 April 1996) and well below the £3-4 billion originally hoped for.

Meanwhile, rapid progress was made with the award of franchises to companies (TOCs) which run the trains and provide Railtrack with its main source of income, in the form of track access charges. By the end of the year under review, 20 of the 25 franchises available had been awarded, while negotiations with 'preferred bidders' were in progress on the remaining five. The subsidy bill paid to franchise operators is now around £2 billion compared to the £700M paid to BR, but over the life of the concessions (ranging from five to 15 years), subsidies are supposed to fall away. Is this realistic? Some commentators, reading across from the experience of electricity privatization, believe there are substantial savings, especially in staff costs, to be made; others (Walker and Howard, 1997) calculate that a 'near miracle' is needed to achieve the subsidy reduction targets.

The success among bus companies in bidding for rail franchises attracted the attention of the Monopolies & Mergers Commission (MMC), after National Express, the long-distance coach operator, had won the Midland Mainline franchise. For their part, bus companies have made much play with the scope for improving co-ordination of road and rail services in the hands of a single operator and several of them have introduced new feeder services to rail routes. Towards the end of the year, the Franchising Director, Roger Salmon, was finding his task increasingly inimical. Having been criticized by the NAO (1996a) for failing to announce his criteria for service alternations before awarding franchises and for running up a £40M bill for City advisers, he decided to step down in favour of his deputy John O'Brien in November.

Will privatization help investment in rail services as it did in the water industry? The Rail Regulator, John Swift has published a policy document (ORR, 1996) requiring Railtrack to invest in improvements providing it can make a 'fair' return. This is generally understood to be a warning to Railtrack not to concentrate solely on projects bringing high rewards, and followed an earlier ruling that the company should invest up to £3.5 billion in maintenance and renewal of track over the next six years. The Railtrack prospectus prior to flotation referred to a £1.39 billion investment programme over ten years, yet a report to the company from BR's civil engineering design group had mentioned a figure of £10.96 billion needed over the same period to keep up with repairs and renewals.

The investment issue is clouded by worries about safety, and a serious collision near Watford in August 1996 raised concern over Railtrack's priorities. Up till then, rail safety standards had been steadily improving and the number of significant train accidents per million miles run fell from 1.01 in 1975 to 0.5 in 1995. The Watford crash was dwarfed in terms of news impact by a major fire in the Channel Tunnel in later November 1996, which fortunately resulted in no loss of life. Eurotunnel claimed a vindication of its safety procedures, which seem to have worked well, though the damage to the tunnel lining is expected to cost £250M to repair and full services cannot be resumed until well into 1997.

Will privatization help transfer more freight from road to rail? Expansion of the motorway network and the low costs of road haulage have led rail's share of total freight transport to fall from 42% in the 1950s to just 7% today. So far, the new owners of the freight services have stressed their concern to win back business to rail, and the major buyer of BR freight businesses, Wisconsin Central Transportation (WCT) has a good record. It has tripled volumes on the New Zealand network, which it acquired in 1993, and raised volumes by 10-12% annually on its American lines. There is talk of reviving individual wagon-load traffic—abandoned by BR some years ago in favour of moving only block trains of single products like roadstone or containers. Freightliner, sold to a management buy-out team for a mere £5.4M in May (with a £75M grant towards track charges), has raised throughput on its business of transporting containers from ports to inland terminals by 12% in a few months.

There are fresh hopes that new methods, new technology and more aggressive marketing will stem the drift to road; yet the difficulties should not be under-estimated. WCT has bitterly complained about the level of charges levied by Railtrack, and even threatened to construct its own dedicated tracks. Tight conditions for the award of subsidies have been another impediment. An NAO inquiry (1996b) into the freight facilities grant found that the DoT had managed to spend less than half of the £70M allocated. In September, the rail minister, John Watts, responded by announcing that the allowance given to hauliers who switch traffic from motorways to rail would be raised from 5p per mile to 20p and application procedures would be streamlined. Hopes that the Channel Tunnel would act as a significant incentive, by making rail transport quicker and more economic, have so far been disappointed: less than half the forecast 6M tonnes per year of freight has been achieved. The situation may improve after Railfreight Distribution, the BR company responsible for Tunnel freight, is sold, and in readiness for that its entire £500M of assets and commitments were written off in the 1995-96 accounts.

Labour's View

The speed of rail privatization has been far quicker than originally planned, reflecting the Government's determination to capture the proceeds of asset sales and to prevent any future Labour government 'putting the clock back'. Labour would, apparently, 'use its powers to acquire the ownership of Railtrack which is necessary to ensure proper public accountability and a return on investment. We will acquire ownership in the light of available resources, and are examining various means of achieving this objective' (Labour Party, 1996). These carefully chosen words may mean rather little in practice—unless Railtrack proves to be such a financial success that public opinion demands some sort of claw-back. Present indications, based on the company having out-performed the stock exchange average by a remarkable 58% since flotation, make this look increasingly likely.

Labour tackles the strategy question head-on, by aiming to set a framework for national, regional and local government—each to produce its own five-year rolling programmes for transport. These will be tested against six principles:

- Accessibility.
- Economic development.
- Efficiency.
- Environmental sustainability.
- Equity.
- Health and safety.

The strategy will aim to set national transport goals as well as outlining the broad approach for attaining these. Within the strategy, a measure of decentralization will be applied: local government will get 'the range of powers and duties they need to implement transport policies that meet the needs of their own areas'. At regional level, there will be consultation on whether to establish more passenger transport authorities or to encourage more joint authority working. A more planned approach would lead, in Labour's view, to a more integrated public transport network, with simple connections. Three aspects of this integration are suggested: readier access to information on services; easier interchanges (park-and-ride, linking taxis more directly to public transport); and through ticketing and timetabling.

A key part of the Labour proposals is to reduce the need to travel, by 'creating a much stronger framework which integrates transport planning and land use planning at all levels of government'. National planning guidance will encourage new developments in inner cities and in areas well served by public transport, rather than peripheral or green-field sites. Two other proposed measures complement these planning aims: first, Labour would review the national roads programme: 'in all cases, *transport plans will not be driven by accommodating predicted traffic growth* [their emphasis]; and when local areas are required to plan their future traffic management, 'alternative solutions will be preferred to major road schemes'.

Second, Labour intends to shift the balance of motoring costs over time, so that more of the real cost is associated with use. This would mean replacing the flat rate vehicle excise duty with 'a graded system, designed to ensure that more efficient, less polluting cars will pay less'. Similarly, Labour would seek to move towards a system where the largest lorries travelling the furthest pay the most tax. A target of trebling movement of freight by rail would be set (in line with the Royal Commission on Environmental Pollution's recommendation) and shipping policy would seek to promote coastal and short-sea transport.

Many Labour policies lack detail, especially on taxation issues, and it seems surprising that company car taxes (an obvious target for reform) are not, apparently, to be raised. No commitments are given either on setting targets for traffic levels or discouraging car ownership, though this is the first Labour transport policy which has not positively favoured increased car ownership. Although the line taken on public transport is reasonably constructive, the policy towards railways is unclear. *Consensus for Change* says Labour will aim to 'create a new system of mobilizing higher levels of investment and more intensive use of rail' (the same could be said of Conservative policy). The document is regrettably short of ideas on how to reverse the massive subsidy increases associated with privatization or the decline in investment.

Conclusions

The green paper *Transport: the Way Forward* reflects welcome signs of change in official thinking, though it is not yet matched by a review of spending priorities, nor an accompanying strategy for action. It is out of tune with European Commission policies. Much official and parliamentary time went into railway privatization in 1996, as in 1995, leaving most of the difficult transport issues for an incoming Government to face. The rush has led to heavy discounting: apart from Railtrack and the rolling stock companies, each sold for about £1.8 billion, the rest of British Rail has so far raised less than the cost of the privatization process itself—£675M against an estimated £750M+ (Ford, 1997). The National Audit Office has now launched a series of investigations, and has already criticized BR (NAO, 1996c) over the sale of maintenance depots.

The momentous developments in the rail industry raise new questions about competition, on which the Secretary of State puts such emphasis in his objectives. Bus services in Britain are now dominated by three main operators who share 60% of the market, and the same companies are an increasingly powerful force in the railway franchise business. Virtually all rail freight operations are now in the hands of WCT. The ownership of railway maintenance and repair companies is becoming concentrated in fewer and fewer hands. The implications for transport users look problematic: in Winchester for example, Stagecoach dominates all public transport in the area, and another government principle—providing greater choice—looks threatened. The declared aim of creating a more efficient and cost-effective railway still looks a long way off.

Similarly, the prospects for achieving a sustained shift away from ever-increasing car use look dim. Even if public transport were more appealing, a variety of 'push' as well as 'pull' measures would be needed. As Headicar (1995) argues, this is going to take a long time, and it must be locally-driven, within the framework of national policies. Examples of what can be done at local level are readily found (see for example East Midlands Regional Planning Forum, 1995 and Gloucestershire County Council, 1996). From the review of Labour policies, it appears that this point has been taken up and incorporated in the party's planning, but there is a great deal more work to be done before the Opposition has a truly convincing alternative approach to offer. ■

References

Buchan, K. (1996), *For whom the Shadow Tolls—The Effects of Design, Build, Finance and Operate (DBFO) on the A36 Salisbury Bypass* (MTRU/Transport 2000).

Commission of the European Union (1996a), *The Citizen's Network: Fulfilling the Potential of Public Passenger Transport in Europe* (European Commission Green Paper).

Commission of the European Union (1996b), *Towards Fair and Efficient Pricing in Transport* (European Commission Green Paper).

Departments of the Environment and Transport (1994), *Planning Policy Guidance Note 13* (HMSO, London).

Department of Transport (1996a), *Transport: The Government's Expenditure Plans 1996-97 to 1998-99*, Cm 3206 (HMSO, London).

Department of Transport (1996b), *Transport: the Way Forward: The Government's Response to the Transport Debate*, Cm 3234 (HMSO, London).

Department of Transport (1996c), *Lorry Weights: A Consultation Document.*

Department of Transport/Government Office for London (1996), *Transport Strategy for London* (HMSO, London).

East Midlands Regional Planning Forum (1995), *2020: A Vision for Transport in the East Midlands.*

Ford, R. (1997), Family silver goes cheap. In *Modern Railways, 54* (Ian Allan Publishing).

Gloucestershire County Council (1996), *Transport Plan for Gloucestershire 1996–2011.*

Goodwin, P. (1993), *Key Issues in Demand Management* (Paper to Surrey County Council's Workshop on Demand Management).

Headicar, P. (1993), Responding to the environmental challenge. In *Proceedings of the Chartered Institute of Transport, 3*,1.

Labour Party (1996), *Consensus for Change: Labour's Transport Policy for the 21st Century* (London).

London Pride (1995), *Action Programme for London.*

London Transport (1996), *Planning London's Transport—To Win as a World City.*

ORR (1996), *Investment in the Enhancement of the Rail Network.*

National Audit Office (1996a), *The Award of the First Three Passenger Rail Franchises* (HC 701, London).

National Audit Office (1996b), *Department of Transport: Freight Facilities Grants in England* (HC 632, London).

National Audit Office (1996c), *British Rail Maintenance Ltd: Sale of Maintenance Depots* (HC583 London).

Royal Commission on Environmental Pollution (1994), *Eighteenth Report: Transport and the Environment*, Cm 2674 (HMSO, London).
Swedish National Road Administration (1995), *Road Safety Report 1994*.
Walker, C. and Howard, D. (1997), Letters. *Modern Railways*, *54*.

Index